Raspberry Pi®
User Guide

Raspberry Pi® User Guide

4th Edition

Eben Upton and Gareth Halfacree

This edition first published 2016

Registered office

John Wiley & Sons Ltd., The Atrium, Southern Gate, Chichester, West Sussex, PO19 8SQ, United Kingdom

For details of our global editorial offices, for customer services and for information about how to apply for permission to reuse the copyright material in this book please see our website at `www.wiley.com`.

Library of Congress Control Number: 2016946656

Trademarks: Wiley and the Wiley logo are trademarks or registered trademarks of John Wiley & Sons, Inc. and/or its affiliates in the United States and/or other countries, and may not be used without written permission. Raspberry Pi and the Raspberry Pi logo are registered trademarks of the Raspberry Pi Foundation. All other trademarks are the property of their respective owners. John Wiley & Sons, Ltd. is not associated with any product or vendor mentioned in the book.

Google Drive™ is a registered trademark of Google™.

A catalogue record for this book is available from the British Library.

ISBN 978-1-119-26436-1 (Pbk); ISBN 978-1-119-26438-5 (ePDF); ISBN 978-1-119-92437-8 (ePub)

Set in 10 pt. Chaparral Pro by Indianapolis Composition Services

Printed simultaneously in Great Britain and the United States

Publisher's Acknowledgements

Some of the people who helped bring this book to market include the following:

Editorial and Production

VP - Professional Technology Strategy
Barry Pruett

Associate Director–Book Content Management
Martin Tribe

Executive Commissioning Editor
Jody Lefevere

Project Editor
John Sleeva

Technical Editor
Andrew Scheller

Manager of Content Development and Assembly
Mary Beth Wakefield

Editorial Assistant
Matthew Lowe

Marketing

Marketing Manager
Lorna Mein

Associate Marketing Manager
Carrie Sherrill

About the Authors

EBEN UPTON is a founder and trustee of the Raspberry Pi Foundation, and serves as its Executive Director. He is responsible for the overall software and hardware architecture of the Raspberry Pi, and for the Foundation's relationships with its key suppliers and customers. In an earlier life, he founded two successful mobile games and middleware companies, Ideaworks 3d Ltd. and Podfun Ltd., and held the post of Director of Studies for Computer Science at St John's College, Cambridge. He holds a BA, a PhD, and an MBA from the University of Cambridge.

In his day job, Eben works for Broadcom as an ASIC architect and general troublemaker.

GARETH HALFACREE is a freelance technology journalist and the co-author of the *Raspberry Pi User Guide* alongside project co-founder Eben Upton. Formerly a system administrator working in the education sector, Gareth's passion for open source projects has followed him from one career to another, and he can often be seen reviewing, documenting, or even contributing to projects including GNU/Linux, LibreOffice, Fritzing, and Arduino. He is also the creator of the Sleepduino and Burnduino open hardware projects, which extend the capabilities of the Arduino electronics prototyping system. A summary of his current work can be found at `http://freelance.halfacree.co.uk`.

About the Technical Editor

ANDREW SCHELLER is a freelance software developer based in Cambridge in the UK. He has worked on many projects for a variety of clients, including updating the Raspberry Pi NOOBS software to run on the Raspberry Pi 2. Prior to going freelance, he served as a tools programmer for Sony Computer Entertainment, working on a number of titles, including MediEvil Resurrection for the PlayStation Portable and 24: The Game for the PlayStation 2. While there he developed a localisation system which has become adopted as the standard by all Sony game studios worldwide. He spends some of his free time working on open source software, and has been using Linux for more than 20 years. He enjoys walking, cycling, and climbing, and holds a BSc (Hons) in Computer Science from Durham University.

For Liz, who made it all possible.

—Eben

For my father, the enthusiastic past, and my daughters, the exciting future.

—Gareth

Table of Contents

Introduction

"CHILDREN TODAY ARE digital natives", said a man I got talking to at a fireworks party. "I don't understand why you're making this thing. My kids know more about setting up our PC than I do."

I asked him if they could program, to which he replied: "Why would they want to? The computers do all the stuff they need for them already, don't they? Isn't that the point?"

As it happens, plenty of kids today aren't digital natives. We have yet to meet any of these imagined wild digital children, swinging from ropes of twisted-pair cable and chanting war songs in nicely parsed Python. In the Raspberry Pi Foundation's educational outreach work, we do meet a lot of kids whose entire interaction with technology is limited to closed platforms with graphical user interfaces (GUIs) that they use to play movies, do a spot of word-processed homework, and play games. They can browse the web, upload pictures and video, and even design web pages. (They're often better at setting the satellite TV box than Mum or Dad, too.) It's a useful toolset, but it's shockingly incomplete, and in a country where 20 percent of households still don't have a computer in the home, even this toolset is not available to all children.

Despite the most fervent wishes of my new acquaintance at the fireworks party, computers don't program themselves. We need an industry full of skilled engineers to keep technology moving forward, and we need young people to be taking those jobs to fill the pipeline as older engineers retire and leave the industry. But there's much more to teaching a skill like programmatic thinking than breeding a new generation of coders and hardware hackers. Being able to structure your creative thoughts and tasks in complex, non-linear ways is a learned talent, and one that has huge benefits for everyone who acquires it, from historians to designers, lawyers, and chemists.

Programming Is Fun!

It's enormous, rewarding, creative fun. You can create gorgeous intricacies, as well as (much more gorgeous, in my opinion) clever, devastatingly quick, and deceptively simple-looking routes through, under, and over obstacles. You can make stuff that'll have other people looking on jealously, and that'll make you feel wonderfully smug all afternoon. In my day job, where I design the sort of silicon chips that we use in the Raspberry Pi as a processor and work on the low-level software that runs on them, I basically get paid to sit around all day playing. What could be better than equipping people to be able to spend a lifetime doing that?

It's not even as if we're coming from a position where children don't want to get involved in the computer industry. A big kick up the backside came a few years ago, when we were moving quite slowly on the Raspberry Pi project. All the development work on Raspberry Pi was done in the spare evenings and weekends of the Foundation's trustees and volunteers—we're a charity, so the trustees aren't paid by the Foundation, and we all have full-time jobs to pay the bills. This meant that occasionally, motivation was hard to come by when all I wanted to do in the evening was slump in front of the *Arrested Development* boxed set with a glass of wine. One evening, when not slumping, I was talking to a neighbour's nephew about the subjects he was taking for his General Certificate of Secondary Education (GCSE, the British system of public examinations taken in various subjects from the age of about 16), and I asked him what he wanted to do for a living later on.

"I want to write computer games", he said.

"Awesome. What sort of computer do you have at home? I've got some programming books you might be interested in."

"A Wii and an Xbox."

On talking with him a bit more, it became clear that this perfectly smart kid had never done any real programming at all; that there wasn't any machine that he could program in the house; and that his information and communication technology (ICT) classes—where he shared a computer and was taught about web page design, using spreadsheets and word processing—hadn't really equipped him to use a computer even in the barest sense. But computer games were a passion for him (and there's nothing peculiar about wanting to work on something you're passionate about). So that was what he was hoping the GCSE subjects he'd chosen would enable him to do. He certainly had the artistic skills that the games industry looks for, and his maths and science marks weren't bad. But his schooling had skirted around any programming—there were no Computing options on his syllabus, just more of the same ICT classes, with its emphasis on end users rather than programming. And his home interactions with computing meant that he stood a vanishingly small chance of acquiring the skills he needed in order to do what he really wanted to do with his life.

This is the sort of situation I want to see the back of, where potential and enthusiasm is squandered to no purpose. Now, obviously, I'm not monomaniacal enough to imagine that simply making the Raspberry Pi is enough to effect all the changes that are needed. But I do believe that it can act as a catalyst. We've already seen big changes in UK schools, where a revamped Computing curriculum arrived on the syllabus in 2014, and we've seen a massive change in awareness of a gap in our educational and cultural provision for kids just in the four years since the first Raspberry Pi was launched.

Too many of the computing devices a child will interact with daily are so locked down that they can't be used creatively as a tool—even though computing *is* a creative subject. Try using your iPhone to act as the brains of a robot, or getting your PS4 to play a game you've written. Sure, you can program the home PC, but there are significant barriers in doing that which a lot of children don't overcome: the need to download special software, and having the sort of parents who aren't worried about you breaking something that they don't know how to fix. And plenty of kids aren't even aware that doing such a thing as programming the home PC is possible. They think of the PC as a machine with nice clicky icons that give you an easy way to do the things you need to do so you don't need to think much. It comes in a sealed box, which Mum and Dad use to do the banking and which will cost lots of money to replace if something goes wrong!

The Raspberry Pi is cheap enough to buy with a few weeks' pocket money, and you probably already have all the equipment you need to make it work: a TV, an SD card that can come from an old camera, a mobile phone charger, a keyboard, and a mouse. It's not shared with the family; it belongs to the kid; and it's small enough to put in a pocket and take to a friend's house. If something goes wrong, it's no big deal—you just swap out a new SD card and your Raspberry Pi is factory-new again. And all the tools, environments, and learning materials that you need to get started on the long, smooth curve to learning how to program your Raspberry Pi are right there, waiting for you as soon as you turn it on.

A Bit of History

I started work on a tiny, affordable, bare-bones computer in 2006, when I was a Director of Studies in Computer Science at Cambridge University. I'd received a degree at the University Computer Lab as well as studying for a PhD while teaching there, and over that period, I'd noticed a distinct decline in the skillset of the young people who were applying to read Computer Science at the Lab. From a position in the mid-1990s, when 17-year-olds wanting to read Computer Science had come to the University with a grounding in several computer languages, knew a bit about hardware hacking, and often even worked in assembly language, we gradually found ourselves in a position where, by 2005, those kids were arriving having done some HTML—with a bit of PHP and Cascading Style Sheets if you were lucky. They were still fearsomely clever kids with lots of potential, but their experience with computers was entirely different from what we'd been seeing before.

The Computer Science course at Cambridge includes about 60 weeks of lecture and seminar time over three years. If you're using the whole first year to bring students up to speed, it's harder to get them to a position where they can start a PhD or go into industry over the next two years. The best undergraduates—the ones who performed the best at the end of their three-year course—were the ones who weren't just programming when they'd been told to for their weekly assignment or for a class project. They were the ones who were programming in their spare time. So the initial idea behind the Raspberry Pi was a very parochial one with a very tight (and pretty unambitious) focus: I wanted to make a tool to get the small number of applicants to this small university course a kick start. My colleagues and I imagined we'd hand out these devices to schoolkids at open days, and if they came to Cambridge for an interview a few months later, we'd ask what they'd done with the free computer we'd given them. Those who had done something interesting would be the ones that we'd be interested in having in the program. We thought maybe we'd make a few hundred of these devices, or best case, a lifetime production run of a few thousand.

Of course, once work was seriously underway on the project, it became obvious that there was a lot more we could address with a cheap little computer like this. What we started with is a long way indeed from the Raspberry Pi you see today. I began by soldering up the longest piece of breadboard you can buy at Maplin with an Atmel chip at our kitchen table, and the first crude prototypes used cheap microcontroller chips to drive a standard-definition TV set directly. With only 512 K of RAM, and a few MIPS of processing power, these prototypes were very similar in performance to the original 8-bit microcomputers. It was hard to imagine these machines capturing the imaginations of kids used to modern games consoles and iPads.

There had been discussions at the University Computer Lab about the general state of computer education, and when I left the Lab for a non-academic job in the industry, I noticed that I was seeing the same issues in young job applicants as I'd been seeing at the University. So I got together with my colleagues Dr Rob Mullins and Professor Alan Mycroft (two colleagues from the Computer Lab), Jack Lang (who lectures in entrepreneurship at the University), Pete Lomas (a hardware guru), and David Braben (a Cambridge games industry leading light with an invaluable address book), and over beers (and, in Jack's case, cheese and wine), we set up the Raspberry Pi Foundation—a little charity with big ideas.

In my new role as a chip architect at Broadcom, a big semiconductor company, I had access to inexpensive but high-performing hardware produced by the company with the intention of being used in what were then very high-end mobile phones—the sort with the HD video and the 14-megapixel cameras. I was amazed by the difference between the chips you could buy for $10 as a small developer, and what you could buy as a cell-phone manufacturer for roughly the same amount of money: general purpose processing, 3D graphics, video, and memory bundled into a single BGA package the size of a fingernail. These microchips consume very little power, and have big capabilities. They are especially good at multimedia, and were already being used by set-top box companies to play high-definition video. A chip like this seemed the obvious next step for the shape the Raspberry Pi was taking, so I worked on taping out a low-cost variant that had an ARM microprocessor on board and could handle the processing grunt we needed.

Why "Raspberry Pi"?

We get asked a lot where the name "Raspberry Pi" came from. Bits of the name came from different trustees. It's one of the very few successful bits of design by committee I've seen, and to be honest, I hated it at first. (I have since come to love the name, because it works really well—but it took a bit of getting used to since I'd been calling the project the "ABC Micro" in my head for years.) It's "Raspberry" because there's a long tradition of fruit names in computer companies (besides the obvious, there are the old Tangerine and Apricot computers—and we like to think of the Acorn as a fruit as well). "Pi" is a mangling of "Python", which we thought early on in development would be the only programming language available on a much less powerful platform than the Raspberry Pi we ended up with. As it happens, we still recommend Python as our favourite language for learning and development, but there is a world of other language options you can explore on the Raspberry Pi too.

We felt it was important to have a way to get kids enthusiastic about using a Raspberry Pi even if they didn't feel very enthusiastic about programming. In the 1980s, if you wanted to play a computer game, you had to boot up a box that went "bing" and fed you a command prompt. It required typing a little bit of code just to get started, and most users didn't ever go beyond that—but some did, and got beguiled into learning how to program by that little bit of interaction. We realised that the Raspberry Pi could work as a very capable, very tiny, very cheap modern media centre, so we emphasised that capability to suck in the unwary—with the hope that they'd pick up some programming while they're at it.

After about five years' hard grind, we had created a very cute prototype board, about the size of a thumb drive. We included a permanent camera module on top of the board to demonstrate the sort of peripherals that can easily be added (there was no camera when we launched because it brought the price up too much, but we've now made a separate, cheap camera module available for photography projects), and brought it along to a number of meetings with the BBC's R&D department. Those of us who grew up in the UK in the 1980s had learned a lot about 8-bit computing from the BBC Microcomputer and the ecosystem that had grown up around it—with BBC-produced books, magazines and TV programmes—so I'd hoped that they might be interested in developing the Raspberry Pi further. But as it turned out, something has changed since we were kids: various competition laws in the UK and the EU meant that "the Beeb" couldn't become involved in the way we'd hoped. In a last-ditch attempt to get *something* organised with them, we ditched the R&D department idea and David (he of the giant address book) organised a meeting with Rory Cellan-Jones, a senior tech journalist, in May 2011. Rory didn't hold out much hope for partnership with the BBC, but he did ask if he could take a video of the little prototype board with his phone, to put on his blog.

The next morning, Rory's video had gone viral, and I realised that we had accidentally promised the world that we'd make everybody a $25 computer.

While Rory went off to write another blog post on exactly what it is that makes a video go viral, we went off to put our thinking caps on. That original, thumb-drive-sized prototype didn't fit the bill: with the camera included as standard, it was way too expensive to meet the cost model we'd suggested (the $25 figure came from my statement to the BBC that the Raspberry Pi should cost around the same as a text book, and is a splendid demonstration of the fact that I had no idea how much text books cost these days), and the tiny prototype model didn't have enough room around its periphery for all the ports we needed to make it as useable as we wanted it to be. So we spent a year working on engineering the board to lower cost as much as possible while retaining all the features we wanted (engineering cost down is a harder job than you might think), and to get the Raspberry Pi as useable as possible for people who might not be able to afford much in the way of peripherals.

We knew we wanted the Raspberry Pi to be used with TVs at home, just like the ZX Spectrum in the 1980s, saving the user the cost of a monitor. But not everybody has access to an HDMI television, so we added a composite port to make the Raspberry Pi work with an old cathode-ray television instead. Since SD cards are cheap and easy to find, we chose them as our storage medium: the original Model A and Model B used full-size cards, while more recent iterations have moved to the now more common microSD standard. And we went through several iterations of power supply, ending up with a micro USB cable. Recently, micro USB became the standard charger cable for mobile telephones across the EU (and it's becoming the standard everywhere), which means the cables are becoming more and more ubiquitous, and in many cases, people already have them at home.

By the end of 2011, with a projected February release date, it was becoming obvious to us that things were moving faster, and demand was higher, than we were ever going to be able to cope with. The initial launch was always aimed at developers, with the educational launch planned for later in 2012. We had a small number of very dedicated volunteers, but we needed the wider Linux community to help us prepare a software stack and iron out any early-life niggles with the board before releasing into the educational market. We had enough capital in the Foundation to buy the parts for and build 10,000 Raspberry Pis over a period of a month or so, and we thought that the people in the community who would be interested in an early board would come to around that number. Fortunately and unfortunately, we'd been really successful in building a big online community around the device, and interest wasn't limited to the UK, or to the educational market. Ten thousand was looking less and less realistic.

There were 100,000 people on our mailing list wanting a Raspberry Pi—and they all put an order in on day one! Not surprisingly, this brought up a few issues.

Our Community

The Raspberry Pi community is one of the things we're proudest of. We started with a very bare-bones blog at `www.raspberrypi.org` just after Rory's May 2011 video, and put up a forum on the same website shortly after that. That forum now has more than 170,000 members—between them they've contributed nearly a million posts of wit and wisdom about the Raspberry Pi. If there's any question, no matter how abstruse, that you want to ask about the Raspberry Pi or about programming in general, someone there will have the answer (if it's not in this book, you'll find it in the forums).

Part of my job at Raspberry Pi involves giving talks to hacker groups, computing conferences, teachers, programming collectives, and the like, and there's always someone in the audience who has talked to me or to my wife Liz (who runs the community) on the Raspberry Pi website—and some of these people have become good friends of ours. The Raspberry Pi website gets more than one request every single second of the day.

There are now hundreds of fan sites out there. For several years, there was a fan magazine called *The MagPi*, which was produced monthly by community members, with type-in listings, lots of articles, project guides, tutorials, and more. This became so successful that we brought it in-house at the Foundation, which makes it available in print or as a free download from `www.raspberrypi.org/magpi`. Type-in games in magazines and books provided an easy route into programming for me—my earliest programming experience with the BBC Micro was of modifying a type-in helicopter game to add enemies and pick-ups.

We blog something interesting about the device at `www.raspberrypi.org` at least once every day. Come and join in the conversation!

First off, there are the inevitable paper cuts you're going to get boxing up 100,000 little computers and mailing them out—and the fact was that we had absolutely no money to hire people to do this for us. We didn't have a warehouse—we had Jack's garage. There was no way we could raise the money to build 100,000 units at once—we'd envisaged making them in batches of 2,000 every couple of weeks, which, with this level of interest, was going to take so long that the thing would be obsolete before we managed to fulfil all the orders. Clearly, manufacturing and distribution were something we were going to have to give up on and hand over to somebody else who already had the infrastructure and capital to do that, so we got in touch with element14 and RS Components, both UK microelectronics suppliers with worldwide businesses, and contracted with them to do the actual manufacture and distribution side of things worldwide so we could concentrate on development and the Raspberry Pi Foundation's charitable goals.

Demand on the first day was still so large that RS and element14's websites both crashed for most of the day—at one point in the day, element14 were getting seven orders a second, and for a couple of hours on February 29, Google showed more searches were made world-wide for "Raspberry Pi" than were made for "Lady Gaga". We made and sold more than a million Raspberry Pis in the first year of business, making Raspberry Pi the fastest-growing computer company in the world, ever. Things aren't slowing down: we make more than 300,000 Pis every month and have sold more than ten million in a little over four, with no hint of a slowdown. If we'd stuck with our original plans, we'd have made 100 or so of these devices for University open days, and that would have been it.

> **NOTE**   The first production Pis were made in Chinese factories, but in 2012 we managed to repatriate all of the production to the UK. Your Raspberry Pi is now made in South Wales, in an area of the country with a proud manufacturing heritage, but few remaining factories. Amazingly, it costs us less to manufacture in Wales as it did in China, and we're able to do that manufacture without a language or cultural barrier, and with the ability to jump in the car and be on the factory floor in a few hours if necessary.

There is nothing that affects the blood pressure quite like accidentally ending up running a large computer company!

So What Can You Do with the Raspberry Pi?

This book explores a number of things you can do with your Raspberry Pi, from controlling hardware with Python, to using it as a media centre, setting up camera projects, or building games in Scratch. The beauty of the Raspberry Pi is that it's just a very tiny general-purpose computer (which may be a little slower than you're used to for some desktop applications, but much better at some other stuff than a regular PC), so you can do anything you could do on a regular computer with it. In addition, the Raspberry Pi has powerful multimedia and 3D graphics capabilities, so it has the potential to be used as a games platform, and we very much hope to see more people starting to write games for it.

We think physical computing—building systems using sensors, motors, lights, and micro-controllers—is something that gets overlooked in favour of pure software projects in a lot of instances, and it's a shame, because physical computing is *massive fun*. To the extent that there was any children's computing movement when we began this project, it was a physical computing movement. The LOGO turtles that represented physical computing when we were kids are now fighting robots, quadcopters, or parent-sensing bedroom doors, and we love it. However, the lack of General Purpose Input/Output (GPIO) on home PCs is a real handicap for many people getting started with robotics projects. The Raspberry Pi exposes GPIO so you can get to work straight away.

I keep being surprised by ideas the community comes up with which wouldn't have crossed my mind in a thousand years: the Australian school meteor-tracking project; the Boreatton Scouts in the UK and their robot, which is controlled via an electroencephalography headset (the world's first robot controlled by Scouting brain waves); the family who are building a robot vacuum cleaner; Manuel, the talking Christmas moose. And I'm a real space cadet, so reading about the people sending Raspberry Pis into near-earth orbit on rockets and balloons gives me goosebumps.

In the first edition of this book, I said that success for us would be another 1,000 people every year taking up Computer Science at the university level in the UK. That would not only be beneficial for the country, the software and hardware industries, and the economy; but it would be even more beneficial for every one of those 1,000 people, who, I hope, discover that there's a whole world of possibilities and a great deal of fun to be had out there. In the second edition and third editions, I was a little more ambitious, saying that we'd like to see that replicated throughout the developed world. As Raspberry Pi has grown, however, I've become even more ambitious: I want every child, everywhere, to have access to an open, programmable, general-purpose computer, and to have the opportunity to learn to program in the same way that I did on my BBC Microcomputer back in the 1980s. It's a lofty goal, but we've already seen Raspberry Pi labs spring up in the most unlikely places, like a village lab in a part of Cameroon with no electricity network where the Pis run off solar power, generators, and batteries, or a school high in the mountains in Bhutan.

Building a robot when you're a kid can take you to places you never imagined—I know because it happened to me!

—Eben Upton

Part I

The Board

Chapter 1
Meet the Raspberry Pi

YOUR RASPBERRY PI board is a miniature marvel, packing considerable computing power into a footprint no larger than a credit card. It's capable of some amazing feats, but you need to know a few things before you plunge head first into the bramble patch.

If you're eager to get started, skip to the next chapter to find out how to connect your Raspberry Pi to a display, keyboard, and mouse; install an operating system; and jump straight into using the Pi.

A Trip Around the Board

Since its launch as a mere two models, the Raspberry Pi family has expanded considerably. The current range consists of five mainstream models: the Raspberry Pi Model A+, Raspberry Pi Model B+, Raspberry Pi 2, Raspberry Pi 3 (see Figure 1-1), and Raspberry Pi Zero. Aside from the Zero, which is a cut-down model designed specifically for the lowest-possible cost and minimum board footprint, all models share a roughly similar design differing only in features such as the number of USB ports, presence or absence of network ports, and the power of their processor. The range also has a sixth, less-common, member: the Raspberry Pi Compute Module; designed for industrial use in customised carrier boards, the Compute Module runs the same software as its mainstream stable mates, but is otherwise beyond the scope of this book.

If you are the owner of an original-model Raspberry Pi, either the Model B or cut-down Model A, congratulations: you have a collector's item on your hands. The majority of the material in this book is entirely applicable to your boards, though there are some differences, including an inability to use add-ons adhering to the Hardware Attached on Top (HAT) standard, as described in Chapter 16, "Add-On Hardware". If you find yourself needing features missing from your early board, consider retiring it and picking up a Model A+, Model B+, or faster Raspberry Pi 2 or 3; if you're on a budget, look at the cheaper Raspberry Pi Zero.

FIGURE 1-1: The Raspberry Pi 3

In the rough centre of all Raspberry Pi boards is a square *semiconductor*, more commonly known as an integrated circuit or chip. This is the *system-on-chip (SoC) module*, which provides the Pi with its general-purpose processing, graphics rendering, and input/output capabilities. Depending on the model, this may be the original Broadcom BCM2835, the faster quad-core BCM2836, or the more powerful still 64-bit BCM2837. In the case of the Model A+, B+, and Zero, stacked on top of that chip is another semiconductor which provides the Pi with *memory* for temporary storage of data while it's running programs; on the Raspberry Pi 2 and 3, this chip is instead located on the underside of the board. This type of memory is known as *random access memory (RAM)*, because the computer can read from or write to any part of the memory at any time. RAM is *volatile*, meaning that anything stored in the memory is lost when the Pi loses power or is switched off.

Below the SoC are the Pi's video outputs. The wide silver connector is a *High-Definition Multimedia Interface (HDMI)* port, the same type of connector found on media players and many satellite and cable set-top boxes. When connected to a modern TV or monitor, the HDMI port provides high-resolution video and digital audio. A *composite video* port, which is designed for connection to older TVs that don't have an HDMI socket, is provided as part of the black and silver *3.5 mm AV jack* to the right of the HDMI socket. The video quality is lower than is available via HDMI, and only lower-quality analogue audio can be used. You'll need a *3.5 mm AV adapter cable* to use the composite video output, but you can use the analogue audio output with any standard 3.5 mm stereo audio cable.

The Raspberry Pi Zero has a somewhat different layout. In place of a full-size HDMI socket is a *mini-HDMI socket*, which requires a mini-HDMI to HDMI cable or adapter to connect to a TV or monitor. The Pi Zero also lacks the 3.5 mm AV jack of the larger Pi models; there is no analogue audio output by default, and composite video is available only by soldering a cable or RCA jack to the two empty holes on the upper left of the board marked *TV*.

The pins to the top left of the Pi compose the *general-purpose input/output (GPIO) header*, which you can use to connect the Pi to other hardware. The most common use for this port is to connect an *add-on board*. An example, the Sense HAT, is described in Chapter 16. The GPIO port is extremely powerful, but it's fragile. When handling the Pi, always avoid touching these pins, and never connect anything to them while the Pi is switched on.

The plastic and metal connector below the GPIO port is the *Display Serial Interface (DSI)* port, which is used to connect digitally driven flat-panel display systems. These are rarely used because the HDMI port is more flexible, though the official Raspberry Pi touchscreen accessory is one of the few displays to make use of the port. A second plastic and metal connector, found to the right of the HDMI port, is the *Camera Serial Interface (CSI)* port, which provides a high-speed connection to the Raspberry Pi Camera Module. For more details on the CSI port, see Chapter 15, "The Raspberry Pi Camera Module".

The Pi Zero, again, has a different layout: there is no DSI port available on this model of Pi, and a compact CSI port is used in place of the full-size version found on the larger Pi models. This compact CSI port requires the use of an adapter cable or board to connect to the Raspberry Pi Camera Module. Older revisions of the Pi Zero have no CSI port at all and cannot use the Camera Module as a result.

At the very bottom left of the board is the Pi's *power socket*. This is a *micro-USB* socket, the same type found on most modern smartphones and tablets. Connecting a micro-USB cable to a suitable power adapter, detailed in Chapter 2, "Getting Started with the Raspberry Pi", switches the Raspberry Pi on. Unlike a desktop or laptop computer, the Pi doesn't have a power switch and will start immediately when power is connected. For the Raspberry Pi Zero, the power socket is found on the far right of the board rather than the far left.

On the underside of the Raspberry Pi board on the left-hand side is a *micro-SD card slot*. A Secure Digital (SD) memory card provides storage for the operating system, programs, data and other files, and is *non-volatile*. Unlike the volatile RAM, it will retain its information even when power is lost. In Chapter 2, you'll learn how to prepare an SD card for use with the Pi, including installing an operating system in a process known as *flashing*. The Pi Zero has the micro-SD card slot on the top side of the board, rather than the underside.

The right-hand edge of the Pi will have different connectors depending on which model of Raspberry Pi you have; these models are described in more detail in the following pages. The board also includes one or more *light-emitting diodes* which provide visual feedback as to the status of the board: whether it is powered, whether it has a network connection, whether it is actively accessing the micro-SD card, and so forth.

Model A/B

The original Raspberry Pi models launched were known as the Model A and the Model B (see Figure 1-2). Both had the same Broadcom BCM2835 SoC at their heart, but differed in specification: the Model A had 256 MB of RAM, a single USB port, and no networking capabilities; the Model B had either 256 MB or 512 MB of RAM depending on when it was purchased, two USB ports, and a 10/100 wired network port.

FIGURE 1-2: The Raspberry Pi Model B board

These models are immediately recognisable due to the smaller than normal GPIO port, which has only 26 pins compared to a modern Pi's larger 40-pin port. Both models also use full-size SD cards for storage, rather than the compact micro-SD cards of newer models. No longer manufactured, Raspberry Pi Model As and Bs are nevertheless still compatible with the majority of software designed for newer models but cannot use add-on hardware based on the HAT standard, as described in Chapter 16.

If you have a Raspberry Pi Model A or Model B, you can follow most of the material in this book without difficulty; simply pay close attention to sections such as Chapter 14, "The GPIO Port", to ensure that you're not relying on information written with newer models in mind when wiring hardware directly into the Pi.

Model A+/B+

The original Model A and B proved popular, but were quickly replaced with a new board design known as the Plus. Split into the Model A+ and Model B+ (see Figure 1-3), these revisions introduced the now-standard 40-pin GPIO header while also improving various other features; they did not, however, change from the BCM2835 SoC, meaning there is no appreciable difference in performance between the Plus variants and the older non-Plus models.

FIGURE 1-3: The Raspberry Pi Model B+ board

The hardware split between the Model A+ and Model B+ is similar to that of the Model A and Model B: the A+, which has a smaller footprint than the Model A, has either 256 MB or 512 MB of memory depending on when it was purchased, a single USB port, and no network capabilities; the Model B+ has 512 MB of memory, four USB ports, and a 10/100 wired network port.

The Raspberry Pi Model A+ and Model B+ are compatible with all software and devices mentioned in this book, and use the same GPIO layout as the newer-model Pi variants. If you currently own a Model A+ or Model B+, the only reason you may have to upgrade is to improve performance, gain additional memory, or enjoy built-in wireless capabilities.

Raspberry Pi 2

While the Plus and prior boards all used the same BCM2835 SoC, the Raspberry Pi 2 (see Figure 1-4) was the first to feature a brand new processor: the BCM2836 SoC. Featuring four processor cores to the original's lone core, the BCM2836 offers anything between four and eight times the performance of its predecessor—making everything from word processing to compiling code run faster. The board also boasts 1 GB (1024 MB) of RAM, double the maximum previously available, making multitasking and memory-intensive applications smoother and more responsive.

FIGURE 1-4: The Raspberry Pi 2 board

Layout-wise, however, little has changed from the Model B+. The Raspberry Pi 2 features the same 40-pin GPIO header, four USB ports, 10/100 wired network port, and all other ports. If you have a case or add-on device which works with a Model B+, it will also work just fine with the Raspberry Pi 2—but may run considerably faster!

The Raspberry Pi 2 boasts wider software compatibility than its predecessors: as well as Raspbian, the recommended Raspberry Pi operating system, the Pi 2 can run operating systems such as Ubuntu and Windows 10 IoT Core not available for the older models.

Raspberry Pi 3

The latest model of Raspberry Pi to launch, the Raspberry Pi 3 (see Figure 1-5) builds on its predecessors with yet another new processor: the Broadcom BCM2837. The first to feature 64-bit, rather than 32-bit, support, the BCM2837 is significantly faster than the BCM2836 found in the Pi 2, which itself was a major upgrade from the BCM2835 of the original and Plus lineups. The Pi 3 is also the first model to get built-in wireless support, featuring a radio capable of connecting to 2.4 GHz Wi-Fi networks and Bluetooth devices.

As with the Raspberry Pi 2, though, little has changed with the layout: you'll find the same 40-pin GPIO header, four USB ports, 10/100 wired network port, and all other ports as with the previous models. The only wrinkle for compatibility is a minor change in the way the board communicates with certain add-on hardware; if you're unsure whether a device is compatible with the Raspberry Pi 3, contact the manufacturer or vendor before buying to ensure that software has been written with the change in mind.

FIGURE 1-5: The Raspberry Pi 3 board

A major advantage of the Raspberry Pi 3, beyond the improved performance and built-in wireless capabilities, is the 64-bit processor. Although little software exists to take advantage of this at present, a move to 64 bit promises to offer increased software compatibility, security, and performance over the 32-bit code the Raspberry Pi family runs today.

Raspberry Pi Zero

The Raspberry Pi Zero (see Figure 1-6) holds two accolades: it's by far the smallest Raspberry Pi, and it's by far the cheapest. Despite its size—roughly equivalent to a couple of sticks of chewing gum stacked one on top of the other—it loses little: the Pi Zero includes the same BCM2835 SoC and 512 MB of RAM as the Raspberry Pi Model B+, running at a slightly faster speed for improved performance.

Caveats apply to the use of the Pi Zero, however. Even compared to the Model A+, it's cut down: the single micro-USB port and mini-HDMI port both require adapters before they can be connected to standard peripherals; the 3.5 mm AV jack is missing; there's no DSI port, and the CSI port requires an adapter; and the GPIO header, although present, requires pins to be purchased and soldered into place before it can be used.

If you are a Raspberry Pi beginner, the Pi Zero is not the best choice of starter board. When you're more experienced and are looking to add Pi-powered intelligence to embedded projects—especially where size, cost, and power draw are concerns—the Pi Zero should be the first board on your mind.

FIGURE 1-6: The Raspberry Pi Zero board

A Bit of Background

Before heading into Chapter 2, it's a good idea to familiarise yourself with some background details of the Pi and its creation. While the Pi is usable as a general-purpose computer, capable of performing the same tasks as any desktop, laptop, or server—albeit more slowly—it is designed as a *single-board computer* aimed at hobbyists and educational use, and as such differs from a "normal" computer in a couple of important ways.

ARM Versus x86

The processor at the heart of the Raspberry Pi system is a Broadcom BCM283x-series SoC multimedia processor. This means that the vast majority of the system's components, including its central and graphics processing units along with the audio and communications hardware, are built onto that single component at the centre of the board.

It's not just this SoC design that makes the BCM283x family different from the processor found in your desktop or laptop, however. It also uses a different *instruction set architecture (ISA)*, known as ARM.

Developed by Acorn Computers back in the late 1980s, the ARM architecture is a relatively uncommon sight in the desktop world. Where it excels, however, is in mobile devices. The phone in your pocket almost certainly has at least one ARM-based processing core hidden inside. Its combination of a simple *reduced instruction set computing (RISC)* architecture and low power draw make it the perfect choice over desktop chips with high power demands and *complex instruction set computing (CISC)* architectures.

The ARM-based BCM283x family is the secret to the Raspberry Pi's capacity to operate on just the 5V power supply provided via the onboard micro-USB port. It's also the reason why you won't find any metal heat sinks on the device: the chip's low power draw directly translates into very little wasted heat, even during complicated processing tasks.

It does mean, however, that the Raspberry Pi isn't compatible with traditional PC software. The majority of software for desktops and laptops are built with the x86 instruction set architecture in mind, as found in processors from the likes of AMD, Intel, and VIA. As a result, it won't run on the ARM-based Raspberry Pi.

The BCM2835 found in the Model A, Model B, Model A+, Model B+, Pi Zero, and Compute Module uses a generation of ARM's processor design known as *ARM11*, which in turn is designed around a version of the instruction set architecture known as ARMv6. The BCM2836 found in the Raspberry Pi 2 uses the newer ARMv7 instruction set architecture, giving it higher performance and compatibility with a broader array of operating systems. The BCM2837 found in the Raspberry Pi 3, finally, uses the 64-bit ARMv8 architecture, boosting performance still further and opening the door to supporting native 64-bit code in the future.

It is true that most software you'd find on a desktop or laptop computer is written with x86 rather than ARM in mind, but that's not to say you're going to be restricted in your choices. As you'll discover later in the book, plenty of software is available even for the older ARMv6 instruction set, and as the Raspberry Pi's popularity continues to grow, availability will only increase. In this book, you'll also learn how to create your own software for the Pi, even if you don't have experience with programming.

Windows Versus Linux

Another important difference between the Raspberry Pi and your desktop or laptop, other than the size and price, is the operating system—the software that enables you to control the computer.

The majority of desktop and laptop computers available today run one of two operating systems: Microsoft Windows or Apple OS X. Both platforms are *closed source*, created in a secretive environment using proprietary techniques.

These operating systems are known as closed source because of the nature of their *source code*, the computer-language recipe that tells the system what to do. In closed source software, this recipe is a closely guarded secret. Users are able to obtain the finished software but never to see how it's made.

The Raspberry Pi, by contrast, is designed primarily to run an operating system called *GNU/ Linux*—hereafter referred to simply as Linux. Unlike Windows or OS X, Linux is *open source*, so you can download the source code for the entire operating system and make whatever changes you desire. Nothing is hidden, and all changes are made in full view of the public. This open source development ethos has allowed Linux to be altered quickly to run on the Raspberry Pi. At the time of writing, several versions of Linux—known as *distributions*— have been ported to the Raspberry Pi, including Raspbian and Arch Linux. For the newer models, additional operating systems are available—even a variant of Windows 10 designed for embedded computing projects, a rare example of a closed source operating system being made available on the Raspberry Pi.

The different Linux distributions cater to different needs, but they all have something in common: they're all open source. They're also all, by and large, compatible with each other— software written on a Debian system will usually operate perfectly well on Arch Linux, and vice versa.

Linux isn't exclusive to the Raspberry Pi. Hundreds of different distributions are available for desktops, laptops, and even mobile devices. Even Google's popular Android platform is developed on top of a Linux core. If you find that you enjoy using Linux on the Raspberry Pi, you might want to consider adding it to other computing devices you use as well. It will happily coexist with your current operating system, allowing you to enjoy the benefits of both while giving you a familiar environment when your Pi is unavailable.

As with the difference between ARM and x86, there's a key point to make about the practical difference between Windows and OS X and Linux: software written specifically for Windows or OS X won't run on Linux. Thankfully, there are plenty of compatible alternatives for the overwhelming majority of common software products. Better still, the majority are free to use and as open source as the operating system itself, and can even be installed on both Windows and OS X to provide a familiar experience across all three platforms.

Chapter 2

Getting Started with the Raspberry Pi

NOW THAT YOU have a basic understanding of how the Raspberry Pi differs from other computing devices, it's time to get started. If you've just received your Pi, take it out of its protective antistatic bag and place it on a flat, nonconductive surface before continuing with this chapter.

To use your Pi, you'll need some extra peripherals. A display will allow you to see what you're doing, and a keyboard and mouse will be your input devices. In this chapter, you find out how to connect these to the Pi, along with a network connection in the case of the Model B, Model B+, Pi 2, and Pi 3. You also learn how to download and install an operating system for the Pi.

Your Mileage May Vary

The information and instructions in this book give you all you need to get your Raspberry Pi up and running and to make the most of its capabilities. Be aware that some of the software for the Raspberry Pi is evolving so quickly that what you see on your screen may differ slightly from some of the images in the book.

Connecting a Display

Before you can start using your Raspberry Pi, you need to connect a display. The Pi supports three different video outputs: composite video, HDMI video, and DSI video. Composite video and HDMI video are readily accessible to the end user, as described in this section, whereas DSI video requires some specialised hardware as found in the Raspberry Pi Touch Screen Display (see Chapter 16, "Add-On Hardware").

Composite Video

Composite video, previously available via the yellow-and-silver port at the top of older Pi models known as an *RCA phono connector*, is available from the *3.5 mm AV jack* at the bottom of most boards (see Figure 2-1). Composite video is designed for connecting the Raspberry Pi to older display devices. As the name suggests, the connector creates a composite of the colours found within an image—red, green, and blue—and sends it down a single wire to the display device, typically an old cathode-ray tube (CRT) TV.

FIGURE 2-1: The multipurpose AV jack on a Raspberry Pi 3

When no other display device is available, a composite video connection will get you started with the Pi. The quality isn't great, however. Composite video connections are significantly more prone to interference, lack clarity, and run at a limited *resolution*, meaning that you can fit fewer icons and lines of text on the screen simultaneously.

To use the composite video output, you need an *AV adapter cable*. These cables, available at a very low cost from any electronics outlet, split the output from the jack into three RCA jacks: a yellow jack provides the composite video connection, while red and white jacks provide the two channels of stereo audio output. Simply plug the adapter cable into the AV jack, and then connect RCA cables between the adapter cable's jacks and those of your TV or other display device.

The Raspberry Pi Zero does not have a 3.5 mm AV jack; instead, a composite video cable can be soldered to the two holes on the top of the board marked TV. Note, however, that the signal from the Pi Zero does not include analogue audio, unlike the AV jack of the larger Pi models.

HDMI Video

A better quality picture can be obtained using the *High-Definition Multimedia Interface (HDMI)* connector, found on the bottom of the Pi (see Figure 2-2). Unlike the analogue composite connection, the HDMI port provides a high-speed digital connection for pixel-perfect pictures on both computer monitors and high-definition TV sets. Using the HDMI port, a Pi can display images at the Full HD 1920 x 1080 resolution of most modern HDTV sets. At this resolution, significantly more detail is available on the screen.

FIGURE 2-2: The silver HDMI connector for high-definition video output

If you're hoping to use the Pi with an existing computer monitor, you might find that your display doesn't have an HDMI input. That's not a disaster: the digital signals present on the HDMI cable map to a common computer monitor standard called *Digital Video Interconnect (DVI)*. By purchasing an HDMI-to-DVI cable, you'll be able to connect the Pi's HDMI port to a monitor with DVI-D connectivity.

If your monitor has a VGA input—a D-shaped connector with 15 pins, typically coloured silver and blue—the Raspberry Pi can't connect to it directly. To use this type of monitor, you must purchase what is known as an *adapter dongle*. Look for models that convert HDMI to VGA and specifically mention Raspberry Pi compatibility when making a purchase; then simply connect the HDMI end to the Pi and your VGA monitor cable to the other end of the dongle.

The Raspberry Pi Zero is unique among the Pi family in having a *mini-HDMI* connector rather than the more common full-size connector. To use the HDMI output on a Pi Zero, purchase a mini-HDMI to HDMI adapter or mini-HDMI to HDMI cable. Make sure any adapter or cable you buy is specifically for a mini-HDMI port; the smaller micro-HDMI adapters won't fit.

DSI Video

The final video output on the Pi is above the micro-Secure Digital (micro-SD) card slot on the top of the printed circuit board—it's a small ribbon connector protected by a layer of plastic. This is for a video standard known as *Display Serial Interface (DSI)*, which is used in the flat-panel displays of tablets and smartphones. The most common use of the DSI port on the Raspberry Pi is to connect to the Raspberry Pi touchscreen display as described in Chapter 16.

The Raspberry Pi Zero does not include a DSI connector, and cannot be used with DSI-only displays such as the Raspberry Pi touchscreen display.

Connecting Audio

If you're using the Raspberry Pi's HDMI port, audio is simple. When properly configured, the HDMI port carries both the video signal and a digital audio signal. This means that you can connect a single cable to your display device to enjoy both sound and pictures.

Assuming you're connecting the Pi to a standard HDMI display, there's very little to do at this point; it's enough simply to connect the cable.

If you're using the Pi with a DVI-D monitor via an adapter or cable, audio is not included. This highlights the main difference between HDMI and DVI: HDMI can carry audio signals, but DVI cannot and is instead used exclusively for video signals.

For those with DVI-D monitors, or those using the composite video output, the multipurpose 3.5 mm AV jack is located at the bottom of the board (refer to Figure 2-1). This is the same connector used for headphones and microphones on consumer audio equipment, and it's wired in exactly the same way bar an extra connection for composite video output. If you want, you can simply connect a pair of headphones to this port for quick access to audio. If you're looking for something more permanent, you can either use standard PC speakers that have a 3.5 mm connector or buy some adapter cables.

Headphones can be connected directly to the Raspberry Pi, but you might find the volume **TIP** a little lacking. If possible, connect a pair of powered speakers instead. The internal amplifier will help boost the signal to a more audible level, and many powered speakers also provide a physical volume control.

If you are connecting the Pi to an amplifier or stereo system, you'll either need a 3.5 mm to RCA phono cable or a 3.5 mm to 3.5 mm cable, depending on what spare connections you have on your system. Both cable types are readily and cheaply available at consumer electronics shops, or you can purchase them even more cheaply from online retailers such as Amazon.

Connecting a Keyboard and Mouse

Now that you've got your Raspberry Pi's output devices sorted, it's time to think about input. At a bare minimum, you need a keyboard, and for the majority of users a mouse or trackball is a necessity, too.

First, some bad news: if you've got a keyboard and mouse with a PS/2 connector—a round plug with a horseshoe-shaped array of pins—you have to go out and buy a replacement. The old PS/2 connection has been superseded, and the Pi expects your peripherals to be connected over the *Universal Serial Bus (USB)*. An alternative is to buy a *USB to PS/2 adapter*, although be aware that some particularly old keyboards may not operate correctly through such an adapter.

Depending on which model of Raspberry Pi you purchased, you'll have either one, two, or four USB ports available on the right side of the Pi (see Figure 2-3). If you're using a Model B, B+, Pi 2, or Pi 3, you can connect the keyboard and mouse directly to these ports. If you're using a Model A or A+, you must purchase an *external USB hub* to connect two USB devices simultaneously, use a keyboard with built-in pointer or trackpad, or use a wireless keyboard and mouse with unified USB receiver.

The Raspberry Pi Zero has no full-size USB ports. Instead, it uses a micro-USB port, the same type of port used for connecting the power cable. Both these ports are found at the bottom right of the board: the power input is on the right, labelled PWR IN; the USB port is on the left and is labelled USB. To connect full-size USB devices to this port, you need a *micro-USB to USB adapter*, also known as a *USB On-The-Go (OTG) adapter*. This converts the micro-USB port to a full-size equivalent, after which it can be treated just as the single USB port on a Model A or A+.

A USB hub is a good investment for any Pi user. Even if you have a Model B, B+, Pi 2, or Pi 3, you can quickly fill your USB ports when adding additional devices such as an external optical drive, storage device, or joystick. Make sure you buy a powered USB hub. Passive models are cheaper and smaller but lack the ability to run current-hungry devices like CD drives and external hard drives. A powered USB hub can also provide more current to devices than can the Pi's own USB ports—a device which fails to work properly when connected directly to the Pi may work fine when connected via a high-quality powered hub.

FIGURE 2-3: The Raspberry Pi 3's USB ports

> **TIP** If you want to reduce the number of power sockets in use, connect the Raspberry Pi's USB power lead to your powered USB hub. This way, the Pi can draw its power directly from the hub, rather than needing its own dedicated power socket and mains adapter. This works only on hubs with a power supply capable of providing at least 1A to the Pi's USB port—more than will be available on cheaper hub models—along with whatever power is required by other peripherals. The Raspberry Pi 3 draws more power than its predecessors, so this trick is not guaranteed to work.

Connecting the keyboard and mouse is as simple as plugging them into the USB ports, either directly, through a USB hub, or using a USB OTG adapter in the case of the Raspberry Pi Zero. It doesn't matter which USB port you connect a device to; all ports are connected to the Raspberry Pi's processor in the same way.

The Raspberry Pi 3 offers an alternative method of connecting a keyboard and mouse: a wireless Bluetooth connection. This provides freedom from cables cluttering up your desk and frees up the USB ports for other devices. Before you can configure a Bluetooth keyboard and mouse, though, you need a wired USB keyboard and mouse. Connect these now and, when your operating system is installed and running, see the section titled "Connecting Bluetooth Devices" at the end of this chapter. Models without Bluetooth support can use the same devices via a USB Bluetooth dongle, if required.

A Note on Storage

As you've probably noticed, the Raspberry Pi doesn't have a traditional hard drive. Instead, it uses a *Micro Secure Digital (micro-SD) memory card*, a solid-state storage system typically used in digital cameras, tablets, and smartphones. Almost any SD card will work with the Raspberry Pi, but because it holds the entire operating system, you need a card with at least 8 GB to store all the required files.

SD cards with the operating system preloaded are available from the official Raspberry Pi Store as well as at numerous other sites on the Internet. If you've purchased one of these preloaded SD cards or received it in a bundle with your Pi, you can simply plug it into the micro-SD card slot.

Installing NOOBS on an SD Card

The Raspberry Pi Foundation supplies a software tool for the Pi known as *New Out-Of-Box Software*, or *NOOBS*. The purpose of this tool is to make it as easy as possible to start using the Pi. It comes preinstalled on micro-SD cards bundled with Raspberry Pi boards; it is also available separately as a free download. This tool provides a selection of different operating systems for installation on the Pi, along with tools for changing software and hardware configurations.

If you purchased a micro-SD card with NOOBS already installed on it, you don't need to do anything at this stage. If not, download the latest version of the NOOBS software from the Raspberry Pi Foundation at www.raspberrypi.org/downloads. Note that this is a large file and can take considerable time to download; if you are on an Internet connection capped 1 GB a month or less, you will not be able to download the file. In this case, invest in a micro-SD card with NOOBS preloaded from any Raspberry Pi-carrying retailer.

To install NOOBS on a blank micro-SD card, you need a micro-SD card with at least 8 GB capacity to give you space to install additional software as you use the Pi. You also need an existing computer with a micro-SD card reader, either built in, as it is in some models of laptops, or as an add-on device, or a full-size SD card reader and a micro-SD adapter shell. To begin, insert the micro-SD card into the card reader. If you used your micro-SD card previously with another device, such as a digital camera or games console, follow the link on the Raspberry Pi NOOBS setup guide to the SD Card Association's formatting tool and use this tool to *format* the SD card and prepare it for the installation. If the card is new, you can safely skip this step.

The NOOBS software is provided as a *Zip archive*. This is a file format where the data is *compressed*, enabling the data to take up less space and download more quickly. Double-clicking the file should be enough to open it on most operating systems; if not, download an archive utility like 7-Zip (www.7-zip.org) and try again.

After you open the file, use your archive software's *extract* or *copy* function to transfer the files from within the archive to your micro-SD card (see Figure 2-4). This can take some time to complete, thanks to the number and size of the files involved. Be patient, and when the extraction has finished and the activity light—if applicable—turns off, use your operating system's Eject option before removing the micro-SD card and then insert the card into the Pi's micro-SD card slot.

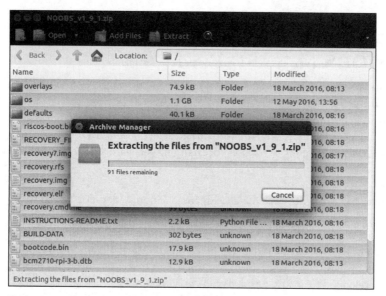

FIGURE 2-4: Extracting NOOBS to the SD card

Connecting External Storage

While the Raspberry Pi uses a micro-SD card for its main storage device—known as a boot device—you may find that you run into space limitations quite quickly. Although large micro-SD cards holding up to 256 GB of data are available, they are often prohibitively expensive.

Thankfully, there are devices that provide additional hard drive storage to any computer when connected via a USB cable. Known as *USB mass storage (UMS) devices*, these devices can be physical hard drives, solid-state drives (SSDs), or even portable pocket-sized flash drives (see Figure 2-5).

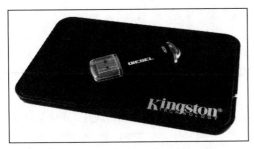

FIGURE 2-5: Two USB mass storage devices: a pen drive and an external hard drive

The majority of USM devices can be read by the Pi, whether or not they have existing content. For the Pi to access these devices, their drives must be mounted—a process you learn about in Chapter 3, "Linux System Administration". For now, it's enough to connect the drives to the Pi.

Connecting the Network

While the majority of these setup instructions are equally applicable to all models of Raspberry Pi, networking is a special exception. To keep the component count—and therefore the cost—as low as possible, the Model A, Model A+, and Pi Zero don't feature onboard networking. Fortunately, that doesn't mean you can't network these models, only that you need some additional equipment to do so.

Networking the Model A, A+, or Pi Zero

To give the Model A, A+, or Pi Zero the same networking capabilities as its full-size counterparts, you need a *USB-connected Ethernet adapter* or *Wi-Fi dongle*. This connects to a free USB port on the Raspberry Pi or a connected hub and provides a wired Ethernet connection with an RJ-45 connector or radio for connection to a wireless Wi-Fi network.

You can purchase a 10/100 USB Ethernet adapter—with the numbers referring to its two-speed mode, 10 MB and 100 MB—from online retailers for very little money. When buying an Ethernet adapter, be sure to check that Linux is listed as a supported operating system. A few models work only with Microsoft Windows and are not compatible with the Raspberry Pi.

Don't be tempted to go for a gigabit-class adapter, which may be referred to as a 10/100/1000 USB Ethernet adapter. Standard USB ports, as used on the Raspberry Pi, can't cope with the speed of a gigabit Ethernet connection, and you'll see no benefit from the more expensive adapter.

Wired Networking

To get your Raspberry Pi on the network, you need to connect an *RJ-45 Ethernet patch cable* between the Pi and a switch, router, or hub. If you don't have a router or hub, you can get your desktop or laptop talking to the Pi by connecting the two directly together with a patch cable.

Usually, connecting two network clients together in this way requires a special cable, known as a *crossover cable*. In a crossover cable, the receive and transmit pairs are swapped so that the two devices are prevented from talking over each other—a task usually handled by a network switch or hub.

The Raspberry Pi is smarter than that, however. The RJ-45 port on the side of the Pi (see Figure 2-6) includes a feature known as *auto-MDI*, which allows it to reconfigure itself automatically. As a result, you can use any RJ-45 cable—crossover or not—to connect the Pi to the network, and it will adjust its configuration accordingly.

TIP If you do connect the Pi directly to a PC or laptop, you won't be able to connect out onto the Internet by default. To do so, you must configure your PC to *bridge* the wired Ethernet port and another (typically wireless) connection. Doing so is beyond the scope of this book, but if you are completely unable to connect the Pi to the Internet in any other way, you can try searching your operating system's help file for "bridge network" for guidance.

FIGURE 2-6: The Raspberry Pi 3's Ethernet port

With a cable connected, the Pi will automatically receive the details it needs to access the Internet when it loads its operating system through the *Dynamic Host Configuration Protocol (DHCP)*. This assigns the Pi an *Internet Protocol (IP)* address on your network and tells it the gateway it needs to use to access the Internet (typically the IP address of your router or modem).

For some networks, no DHCP server provides the Pi with an IP address. When connected to such a network, the Pi must be configured manually (see Chapter 5, "Network Configuration", for more on this topic).

Wireless Networking

The Raspberry Pi 3 is at the time of writing the only model in the range which comes with integrated Wi-Fi network support, but—as with adding wired Ethernet—it's possible to add Wi-Fi support to any Pi using a USB wireless adapter (see Figure 2-7).

FIGURE 2-7: A Pi Zero with Wi-Fi dongle (right) and mini-HDMI to HDMI adapter (left)

Using such a device, the Pi can connect to a wide range of wireless networks, including those running on the latest 802.11ac high-speed standard. Before purchasing a USB wireless adapter, check the following:

- Be sure that Linux is listed as a supported operating system. Some wireless adapters are provided with drivers for Windows and OS X only, making them incompatible with the Raspberry Pi. You can find a list of Wi-Fi adapters known to work with the Raspberry Pi on the following website: `http://elinux.org/RPi_USB_Wi-Fi_Adapters`.

- Be sure that your Wi-Fi network type is supported by the USB wireless adapter. The network type is listed in the specifications as a number followed by a letter. If your network type is 802.11a, for example, an 802.11g wireless adapter won't work.

- Check the frequencies supported by the card. Some wireless network standards, like 802.11a, support more than one frequency. If a USB wireless adapter is designed to work exclusively on a 2.4 GHz network, as with the adapter built into the Raspberry Pi 3, it won't connect to a 5 GHz network.

- Check the encryption type used by your wireless network. Most modern USB wireless adapters support all forms of encryption, but if you're buying a secondhand or older model, you may find it won't connect to your network. Common encryption types include the outdated WEP and the more modern WPA and WPA2.

Configuration of the wireless connection is done within Linux, so for now it's enough simply to connect the adapter to the Pi (ideally through a powered USB hub). You find out how to configure the connection in Chapter 5.

Connecting Power

The Raspberry Pi is powered by the small *micro-USB connector* found on the lower-left side of the circuit board (lower-right for the Raspberry Pi Zero). This connector is the same as is found on the majority of smartphones and many tablet devices.

Many chargers designed for smartphones will work with the Raspberry Pi, but not all. The Pi is more power hungry than most micro-USB devices; for example, the Pi 3 can require anything up to 2 A of current to operate. Some chargers can only supply up to 500 mA, causing intermittent problems in the Pi's operation (see Chapter 4, "Troubleshooting").

Connecting the Pi to the USB port on a desktop or laptop computer is possible, but not recommended. As with weaker chargers, the USB ports on a computer can't provide the power required for the Pi to work properly. Connect the micro-USB power supply only when you are ready to start using the Pi. With no power button on the device, it will start working the instant power is connected.

To safely turn off the Raspberry Pi, issue a shutdown command at the console or terminal by typing the following:

```
sudo shutdown -h now
```

For more information on using the terminal, see Chapter 3.

If you have prepared or purchased your micro-SD card with the NOOBS tool, as described earlier in this chapter, the Pi will load this tool and wait for your instructions; if not, powering the Pi on with a blank SD card will result in a blank screen. In this case, switch off the power and remove the SD card before following the manual installation instructions described in the following section.

Installing the Operating System

If you purchased your Raspberry Pi with a bundled micro-SD card featuring a preloaded operating system or followed the instructions for installing NOOBS earlier in this chapter, you can simply insert the card into the SD card slot on the Pi before connecting power. If you bought the Pi by itself, you need to install an operating system on the micro-SD card before the Pi is ready to use.

Installing Using NOOBS

If you installed NOOBS on your SD card or purchased a micro-SD card with NOOBS preinstalled, a menu appears when you first power on the Raspberry Pi (see Figure 2-8). This menu provides a list of operating systems suitable for the Pi, any one (or more) of which can be installed. You can also choose to change the interface language by clicking the arrow next to Language at the bottom of the screen, and you can choose a different keyboard layout using the arrow next to Keyboard.

If this is your first time running NOOBS on that micro-SD card, a delay will occur while the micro-SD card's first *partition* is resized to make room for your chosen operating system; do not unplug the Pi's power while this is in progress; otherwise, you will risk damaging your SD card.

If you see only a blank screen but the Pi's ACT and PWR lights are on, you may need to choose a different *display mode*. Press 1 on the keyboard for standard HDMI mode, 2 for a "safe" mode with a lower resolution, 3 if you are using the composite port in a PAL region, or 4 if you are using the composite port in an NTSC region. If you're not sure which is suitable, try all the options until you find one that works for you. The chosen display mode will also be passed automatically to the installed operating system. **TIP**

Using the keyboard or mouse, browse through the list of operating systems and click the box to the left of its logo to mark it for installation. Note that you can install multiple operating systems if your micro-SD card is large enough: simply click two or more operating systems in the list. For beginners, we recommend the Raspbian operating system. The remainder of this book is written with Raspbian in mind, but much of what you'll learn is applicable to almost any Linux-based operating system on both the Pi and other devices.

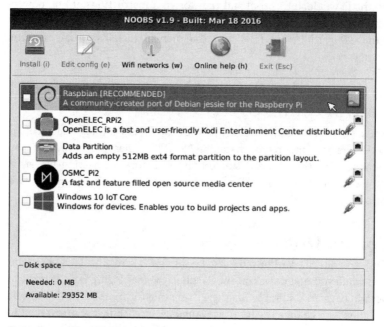

FIGURE 2-8: The NOOBS operating system menu

To begin the installation process, click the Install icon at the top left of the menu and, when asked, confirm that the micro-SD card can be overwritten. As with installing NOOBS itself, this process can take a long time to complete; be patient, watch the progress bar and slide-show (see Figure 2-9), and don't remove the power cable or SD card from the Pi until the process finishes. When the operating system is installed, click OK to reboot and load the operating system you selected.

If you installed more than one operating system, NOOBS will bring up a menu asking which one to boot. If you don't make a choice after 10 seconds, the last operating system chosen boots automatically. If you have not booted at least one operating system from the card before, the system will halt until you choose which operating system to load.

For more information on using NOOBS after the operating system is installed, to either install a different operating system or to change the Pi's various settings, see Chapter 7, "Advanced Raspberry Pi Configuration".

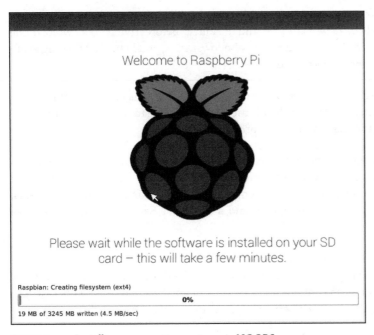

FIGURE 2-9: Installing an operating system via NOOBS

Installing Manually

Installing an operating system manually is a more complicated procedure than using the NOOBS tool, but doing so is sometimes preferable. By installing the software manually—a process known as *flashing*—you can choose to install operating systems that aren't available through NOOBS or newer versions that the tool doesn't yet have available.

First, you must decide which Linux distribution or other operating system you want to use with your Raspberry Pi. Each has its advantages and disadvantages. Don't worry if you change your mind later and want to try a different version: you can flash an SD card again with a new operating system at any point and, if you choose to, you can have multiple cards each with a different operating system installed.

The most up-to-date list of Linux releases compatible with the Pi is available at the Raspberry Pi website: `www.raspberrypi.org/downloads`.

The Foundation provides *BitTorrent* links for each distribution. These are small files that you can use with BitTorrent software to download files from other users. Using these links is an efficient and fast way to distribute large files, and it keeps the Foundation's download servers from becoming overloaded.

To use a BitTorrent link, you need a compatible *client* installed. If you don't already have a BitTorrent client installed, download one and install it before trying to download the Raspberry Pi Linux distribution. One client for Windows, OS X, and Linux is μTorrent, available at www.utorrent.com/downloads.

Which distribution you choose to download is up to you. Instructions in the rest of the book are based on the Raspberry Pi Raspbian distribution, a good choice for beginners. Where possible, instructions for other distributions are provided as well.

Linux distributions for the Raspberry Pi are provided as a single *image file*, compressed to make it faster to download. Once you've downloaded the Zip archive for the distribution you selected, you must decompress it somewhere on your system. In most operating systems, you can simply double-click the file to open it and then choose Extract or Unzip to retrieve the contents.

After you decompress the archive, you may find that there are two separate files. The file ending in .sha1 is a *hash*, which can be used to verify that the download wasn't corrupted in transit. The file ending in .img contains an exact copy of an SD card set up by the distribution's creators in a way that the Raspberry Pi understands. This is the file that needs to be flashed to the SD card.

> **WARNING** In the following instructions, you use a software utility called dd. Used incorrectly, dd will happily write the image to your main hard drive, erasing your operating system and all your stored data. Make sure you read the instructions in each section thoroughly and note the device address of your SD card carefully. Read twice, write once!

Flashing from Linux

If your current PC is running a variant of Linux already, you can use the dd command to write the contents of the image file out to the SD card. This is a text-interface program operated from the command prompt, known as a *terminal* in Linux parlance. Follow these steps to flash the SD card:

1. Open a terminal from your distribution's applications menu.

2. Plug your blank SD card into a card reader connected to the PC.

3. Type **sudo fdisk -l** to see a list of disks. Find the SD card by its size, and note the device address—/dev/sd$X$, where X is a letter identifying the storage device. Some systems with integrated SD card readers may use the alternative format /dev/mmcblk$X$—if this is the case, remember to change the target in the following instructions accordingly.

4. Use the cd command to change to the directory with the .img file you extracted from the Zip archive.

5. Type **sudo dd if=imagefilename.img of=/dev/sdX bs=2M** to write the file imagefilename.img to the SD card connected to the device address in Step 3. Replace imagefilename.img with the actual name of the file extracted from the Zip archive. This step takes a while, so be patient! During flashing, nothing will be shown on the screen until the process is fully complete (see Figure 2-10).

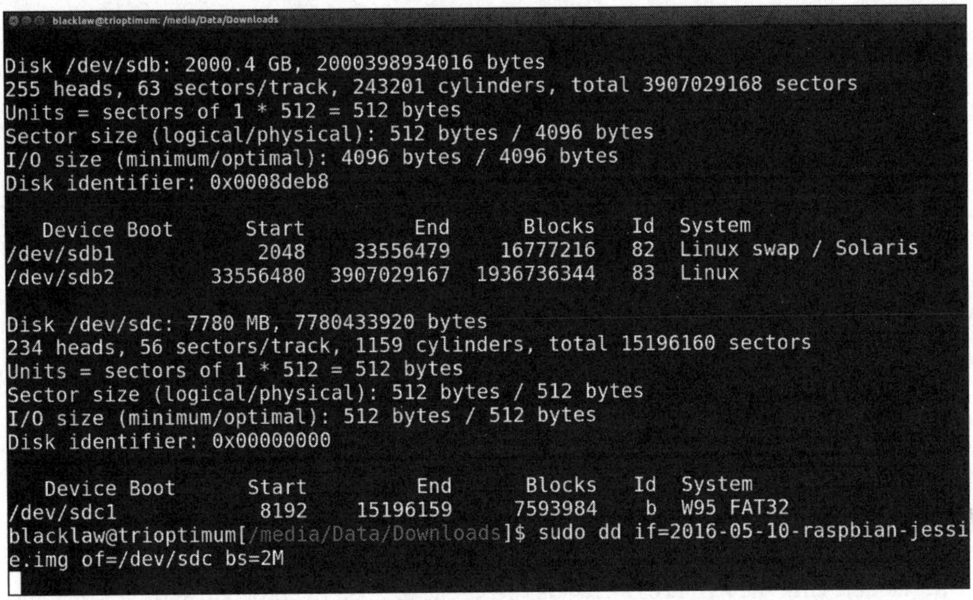

```
blacklaw@trioptimum: /media/Data/Downloads
Disk /dev/sdb: 2000.4 GB, 2000398934016 bytes
255 heads, 63 sectors/track, 243201 cylinders, total 3907029168 sectors
Units = sectors of 1 * 512 = 512 bytes
Sector size (logical/physical): 512 bytes / 4096 bytes
I/O size (minimum/optimal): 4096 bytes / 4096 bytes
Disk identifier: 0x0008deb8

   Device Boot      Start         End      Blocks   Id  System
/dev/sdb1            2048    33556479    16777216   82  Linux swap / Solaris
/dev/sdb2        33556480  3907029167  1936736344   83  Linux

Disk /dev/sdc: 7780 MB, 7780433920 bytes
234 heads, 56 sectors/track, 1159 cylinders, total 15196160 sectors
Units = sectors of 1 * 512 = 512 bytes
Sector size (logical/physical): 512 bytes / 512 bytes
I/O size (minimum/optimal): 512 bytes / 512 bytes
Disk identifier: 0x00000000

   Device Boot      Start         End      Blocks   Id  System
/dev/sdc1            8192    15196159     7593984    b  W95 FAT32
blacklaw@trioptimum[/media/Data/Downloads]$ sudo dd if=2016-05-10-raspbian-jessi
e.img of=/dev/sdc bs=2M
```

FIGURE 2-10: Flashing the SD card using the dd command in Linux

Flashing from OS X

If your current computer is a Mac running Apple OS X, you'll be pleased to hear that things are just as simple as with Linux. Thanks to a similar ancestry, OS X and Linux both contain the dd utility, which you can use to flash the system image to your blank SD card as follows:

1. Select Utilities from the Application menu and then click the Terminal application.

2. Plug your blank SD card into a card reader connected to the Mac.

3. Type **diskutil list** to see a list of disks. Find the SD card by its size, and note the device address (/dev/diskX, where X is a letter identifying the storage device).

4. If the SD card has been automatically mounted and appears on the desktop, type **diskutil unmountdisk /dev/diskX** to unmount it before proceeding.

5. Use the cd command to change to the directory with the .img file you extracted from the Zip archive.

6. Type **dd if=imagefilename.img of=/dev/diskX bs=2m** to write the file image-filename.img to the SD card connected to the device address from Step 3. Replace imagefilename.img with the actual name of the file extracted from the Zip archive. This step takes a while, so be patient!

Flashing from Windows

If your current PC is running Windows, things are slightly trickier than with Linux or OS X. Windows does not have a utility like dd, so some third-party software is required to get the image file flashed onto the SD card. Although it's possible to install a Windows-compatible version of dd, there is an easier way: the Image Writer for Windows. Designed specifically for creating USB or SD card images of Linux distributions, Image Writer for Windows features a simple graphical user interface that makes creating a Raspberry Pi SD card straightforward.

You can find the latest version of Image Writer for Windows at this website: https://sourceforge.net/projects/win32diskimager. Follow these steps to download, install and use the Image Writer for Windows software to prepare the SD card for the Pi:

1. Click the green Download button to download the Image Writer for Windows Zip file and extract it to a folder on your computer.

2. Plug your blank SD card into a card reader connected to the PC.

3. Double-click the Win32DiskImager.exe file to open the program and click the blue folder icon to open a file browse dialogue box.

4. Browse to the imagefilename.img file you extracted from the distribution archive, replacing imagefilename.img with the actual name of the file extracted from the Zip archive; then click the Open button.

5. Select the drive letter corresponding to the SD card from the Device drop-down dialogue box. If you're unsure about which drive letter to choose, open My Computer or Windows Explorer to check.

6. Click the Write button to flash the image file to the SD card. This process takes a while, so be patient!

No matter which operating system you're writing from, it's important to ensure that you leave **WARNING**
the SD card connected until the image is completely written. If you don't, you might find that
Pi doesn't *boot* when the SD card is connected. If this happens, start the process again.

When the image is flashed onto the SD card, remove it from the computer and insert it into
the Raspberry Pi's SD card slot, located underneath the circuit board. The SD card should be
inserted with the metal contacts facing towards the board and pushed fully home to ensure
a good connection.

Connecting Bluetooth Devices

The Raspberry Pi 3, in addition to having integrated Wi-Fi networking, includes a Bluetooth
radio compatible with Bluetooth keyboards, mice, trackballs, and trackpads. Typically sold for
use with tablet computers, these wireless input devices free up the Pi's USB ports and clear
your desk of cables, at the cost of slight input lag—the time between pressing a key and having
it take effect—and the need to replace or charge batteries every now and again.

Although the Pi 3 is the only model of Raspberry Pi which supports Bluetooth devices
natively, the same functionality can be added to any model of Raspberry Pi by connecting a
USB Bluetooth dongle to a free USB port. As with purchasing Wi-Fi dongles, check to make
sure that drivers for your chosen dongle are available for Linux and that the device has been
confirmed to work with the Raspberry Pi.

To connect a Bluetooth device, you need to use an existing USB keyboard and mouse to
navigate the menus. If you're using an operating system other than Raspbian, follow
the instructions included with your operating system; if you're using Raspbian, follow the
instructions below.

Switch your Bluetooth device on and activate *pairing mode*. This typically involves holding
down a button or key, and will be described in your device's documentation. With the device
in pairing mode, click the Bluetooth icon on the Raspbian taskbar—near the clock at the
right edge of the screen—followed by Add Device. This will launch the Add New Device menu
(see Figure 2-11). Find your chosen device in the list, and then click Pair. The Pi will then
launch the pairing procedure, which differs from device to device; simply follow the onscreen
instructions to pair the two devices together.

As well as keyboards and other input devices, you can connect Bluetooth headphones and
speakers to the Pi. Follow the pairing process, and then click the speaker icon in the taskbar
followed by your paired Bluetooth audio device to change the output device. Note that, at the
time of writing, not all software on the Raspberry Pi supports Bluetooth audio output.

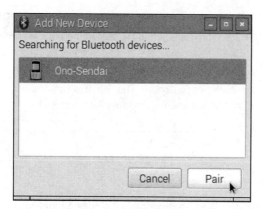

FIGURE 2-11: Pairing a Raspberry Pi 3 to a Bluetooth device

Chapter 3
Linux System Administration

THE MAJORITY OF modern Linux distributions are user friendly, with a *graphical user interface (GUI)* that provides an easy way to perform common tasks. It is, however, quite different to both Windows and OS X, so to get the most out of your Raspberry Pi, you first need a quick primer on using the operating system.

Linux: An Overview

As briefly explained in Chapter 1, "Meet the Raspberry Pi", Linux is an open source project that was originally founded to produce a *kernel* that was free for anyone to use. The kernel is the heart of an operating system, and it handles the communication between the user and the hardware.

Although it rightly refers only to the kernel, the term *Linux* is often used to refer to a collection of different open source projects from a variety of companies. These collections come together to form different *flavours* of Linux known as *distributions*.

The original version of Linux was combined with a collection of tools created by a group called *GNU*. The resulting system, known as *GNU/Linux*, was basic but powerful. Unlike many mainstream operating systems of the era, it offered facilities such as multiple user accounts in which several users share a single computer. Rival closed source operating systems have taken this system on board, with both Windows and OS X now supporting multiple user accounts on the same system. It's also still present in Linux and provides security and protection for the operating system.

In Linux, you spend most of your time running a *restricted* user account. This doesn't mean you're limited in what you can do; instead, it prevents you from accidentally doing something that will break the software on your Raspberry Pi. It also prevents *viruses* and other *malware* from infecting the system by locking down access to critical system files and directories.

Before you can get started, it's worth familiarising yourself with some of the terms and concepts used in the world of Linux, as defined in Table 3.1. Even if you're experienced with other operating systems, it's a good idea to review this table before booting your Pi for the first time.

Table 3.1   The Quick Linux Glossary

Term/Concept	Definition
Bash	The most popular *shell* choice, used in the majority of Linux distributions.
Bootloader	Software responsible for loading the Linux kernel. The most common is GRUB.
Console	A version of the terminal that is always available, and the first thing you see on the Pi.
Desktop environment	Software to make the GUI look pretty. GNOME and KDE are popular desktop environments.
Directory	The Linux term for what Windows calls *folders* where files are stored.
Distribution	A particular version of Linux. Pidora, Arch, and Raspbian are distributions.
Executable	A file that can be run as a program. Linux files must be marked executable in order to run.
EXT2/3/4	The EXTended file system, the most common file system used in Linux.
File system	The way a hard drive or other storage device is formatted so that it's ready for file storage.
GNOME	One of the most common Linux desktop environments.
GNU	A free software project, which provides many of the tools used in Linux distributions.
GRUB	The GRand Unified Bootloader, created by GNU and used to load the Linux kernel.
GUI	A graphical user interface, in which the user operates the computer via a mouse or touch.
KDE	Another extremely popular Linux desktop environment.

Term/Concept	Definition
Linux	Properly, the kernel used by GNU/Linux. Popularly, an open source operating system.
Live CD	A Linux distribution provided as a CD or DVD which doesn't require installation.
Package	A collection of files required to run an application, typically handled by the package manager.
Package manager	A tool for keeping track of and installing new software.
Partition	A section of a hard drive that is ready to have a file system applied to it for storage.
root	The main user account in Linux, equivalent to the Windows `administrator` account. Also called the *superuser*.
Shell	A text-based command prompt, loaded in a terminal.
sudo	A program that allows restricted users to run a command as the `root` user.
Superuser	See *root*.
Terminal	A text-based command prompt in which the user interacts with a *shell* program.
X11	The X Window system, a package that provides a GUI.

The Terminal and the GUI

As in OS X and Windows, there are typically two main ways to achieve a given goal in Linux: through the GUI and through the command line (known in Linux parlance as the *console* or the *terminal*).

The appearance of various Linux distributions can be quite different, depending on the desktop environment in use. In this book, the recommended Raspbian distribution is used, but most of the commands you will be learning are entered at the *terminal* and are typically the same across all distributions.

Where other distributions differ, you will be given alternative methods of achieving the same goals.

Linux Basics

Although hundreds of different Linux distributions are available, they all share a common set of tools known as *commands*. These tools, which are operated via the terminal, are analogous to similar tools on Windows and OS X. To get started, you need to understand the following commands:

- **ls**—Short for *listing*, ls provides a list of the contents of the current directory. Alternatively, it can be called with the directory to be listed as an argument. As an example, typing ls /home provides a list of the contents of /home, regardless of your current directory. The Windows equivalent is dir.

- **cd**—An initialism of *change directory*, cd allows you to navigate your way through the file system. Typing cd alone puts you back in your home directory. Typing the command along with the name of the directory you want to move to, by contrast, switches to that directory. Note that directories can be absolute or relative: cd boot moves you to the directory called boot under your current directory, but cd /boot moves you straight to the /boot directory wherever you are.

- **mv**—The *move* command has two purposes in Linux: it allows a file to be moved from one directory to another, and it also allows files to be renamed. The latter feature may seem out of place, but in Linux terms, the file is being moved from one name to another. The command is called mv *oldfile newfile*.

- **rm**—Short for *remove*, rm deletes files. All files—or list of files—provided after the command name are deleted. The Windows equivalent is del, and the two share the common requirement that care is taken to ensure that the right file is deleted.

- **rmdir**—By itself, rm cannot usually remove directories. As a result, rmdir is provided to delete directories once rm deletes their files.

- **mkdir**—The opposite of rmdir, the mkdir command creates new directories. For example, typing mkdir myfolder at the terminal creates a new directory called myfolder under the current directory. As with cd, directories provided to the command can be relative or absolute.

Introducing Raspbian

Raspbian is the name given to a customised variant of the popular Debian Linux distribution. Debian is one of the longest-running Linux distributions and concentrates on stability, high compatibility, and excellent performance even on modest hardware—making it a great partner for the Raspberry Pi. Raspbian takes Debian as its base, or *parent distribution*, and adds custom tools and software to make using the Raspberry Pi as easy as possible.

To keep the download size to a minimum, the Raspberry Pi image for Raspbian includes only a subset of the software you'd find on a regular desktop version. It includes tools for browsing the web, programming in Python, and using the Pi with a GUI. You can quickly install additional software using the distribution's package manager, *apt*. Raspbian includes a desktop environment known as the *Lightweight X11 Desktop Environment (LXDE)*. Designed to offer an attractive user interface using the *X Window System* software, LXDE provides a familiar point-and-click interface that is immediately convenient if you've used Windows, OS X, or other GUI-based operating systems in the past.

To use Raspbian, you must enter a username and password. The default username is *pi*, and the default password is *raspberry*; you will learn how to change these later in this chapter.

Although the Raspbian GUI loads by default, you can disable it with a menu option. If your Raspbian installation boots to a text-based screen—known as the *console*—then log in, type **startx**, and then press Enter. To return to the console, while leaving the GUI running in the background, hold down Ctrl+Alt, and then press F1 before releasing all keys. **TIP**

If you're using the recommended Raspbian distribution, you have plenty of preinstalled software to get started. While hardly an exhaustive example of the software available for the Pi, which numbers in the thousands of *packages*, it's a good introduction to precisely what the system can do.

The software provided with the Raspbian distribution is split into themed categories. To view these categories, left-click the Menu button found on the top left of the screen as part of the *taskbar* (see Figure 3-1). The following lists describe the software packages, grouped by category.

The Raspbian operating system is under constant development, with software being added to and removed from the default list on a regular basis. While the following listing is correct at the time of writing, don't be surprised to find the software on your installation differing somewhat. **WARNING**

Programming

- **BlueJ Java IDE**—A powerful *integrated development environment (IDE)* written specifically for the Java programming language.

- **Geany Programmer's Editor**—A cross between a simple text editor and a fully-featured IDE, Geany is a popular choice for writing programs in a variety of languages.

- **Greenfoot Java IDE**—A visual IDE for the Java programming language, designed specifically for younger users and beginners to programming in general.

FIGURE 3-1: The Raspbian desktop

- **Mathematica**—A powerful computational software program based on symbolic mathematics and developed by Stephen Wolfram. All Raspbian installations are granted a free license to use this usually pricey package.

- **Node-RED**—A browser-based flow editor for the Node.JS framework, designed to make it easy to build relatively complex hardware and software projects.

- **Python 2 (IDLE)** —An IDE written specifically for Python. You learn more about using IDLE to write your own Python programs in Chapter 11, "An Introduction to Python".

- **Python 3 (IDLE)**—Clicking this entry loads IDLE configured to use the newer Python 3 programming language, rather than the default Python 2.7 language. Both are largely compatible with each other, but some programs may require features of Python 3.

- **Scratch**—A graphical programming language aimed at young children. You find out more about Scratch and its capabilities in Chapter 10, "An Introduction to Scratch".

- **Sonic Pi**—A programming environment designed to teach core concepts through the creation of music, designed specifically for the Key Stage 3 Computer Science curriculum in the UK but of interest internationally.

- **Wolfram**—A language developed by the creator of Mathematica and designed for the processing of knowledge. Although it can take some time to master, Wolfram is extremely powerful.

Office

- **LibreOffice Base**—Part of the LibreOffice productivity suite described in Chapter 9, "The Pi as a Productivity Machine", LibreOffice Base is a database package equivalent to Microsoft Access.

- **LibreOffice Calc**—A spreadsheet application equivalent to Microsoft Excel.

- **LibreOffice Draw**—A vector illustration application, equivalent to Microsoft Visio.

- **LibreOffice Impress**—A slideshow application, equivalent to Microsoft PowerPoint.

- **LibreOffice Math**—A mathematical formulae editor, equivalent to Microsoft Equation Editor.

- **LibreOffice Writer**—A word processing application, equivalent to Microsoft Word.

Internet

- **Claws Mail**—A powerful email client, equivalent to Microsoft Outlook.

- **Epiphany Web Browser**—A web browser, equivalent to Microsoft Edge or Internet Explorer.

- **Raspberry Pi Resources**—A shortcut to online resources to help you get the most from your Raspberry Pi and Raspbian.

- **The MagPi**—A shortcut to the home page of The MagPi, the official Raspberry Pi Magazine. Published monthly, every issue of the magazine is free to download as a PDF document.

Games

- **Minecraft Pi**—An educational version of Mojang's popular Minecraft, described in full in Chapter 12, "Minecraft Pi Edition".

- **Python Games**—A selection of simple games written in the Python programming language, available both to play and to experiment with to assist with learning the language.

Accessories

- **Archiver**—If you need to create or extract compressed files, such as Zip archives, this is the tool for the job.

- **Calculator**—An open source scientific calculator, offering a variety of functions for both quick and complex sums.

- **File Manager**—The file manager provides a graphical browser for files stored on the Pi or any connected storage device.

- **Image Viewer**—Allows you to view images, such as those from a digital camera or on a connected storage device.

- **PDF Viewer**—Opens Portable Document Format (PDF) files, such as free copies of The MagPi Magazine.

- **SD Card Copier**—Create a backup copy of your current micro-SD card using this tool, a blank card, and a USB micro-SD card reader.

- **Task Manager**—View the applications you currently have open, the resources they are using, and if any are misbehaving *kill* them to close them down.

- **Terminal**—This terminal package allows you to use the Linux command line in a window without leaving the GUI.

- **Text Editor**—This is a simple text editor, which is useful for making quick notes or writing simple programs.

Help

- **Debian Reference**—A detailed guide for the Debian Linux distribution and how programmers can contribute to its development.

- **Raspberry Pi Help**—A shortcut to resources designed to assist you when you run into trouble with your Raspberry Pi.

Finding Help

Linux is designed to be as user friendly as possible for new users, even at the terminal command prompt. Although you discover the most common ways to use each command in this chapter, not every option is covered; to do so would require a much larger book.

If you find yourself stuck, or if you want to learn more about any of the tools that are discussed in the following pages, you need to learn about this command: man.

Each Linux application comes with a help file known as a *man page*—short for "manual page". It provides background on the software as well as details on what its options do and how to use them.

To access the man page for a given tool, just type **man** followed by the command name. To see the man page for ls, a tool for listing the contents of directories, just type **man ls**. Alternatively, try the links from the Help menu to see if your question is answered there.

Preferences

- **Add/Remove Software**—A tool for installing new software or uninstalling existing software, demonstrated later in this chapter under the heading "Installing and Uninstalling Software".

- **Appearance Settings**—A toolkit for adjusting the appearance of the GUI, including the style and colour of windows.

- **Audio Device Settings**—A tool for changing which audio device your system is currently configured to use, allowing you to change between analogue, HDMI, and Bluetooth audio outputs.

- **Main Menu Editor**—A tool for editing these menu entries directly, allowing you to add shortcuts for applications or websites which do not install their own by default or to edit any existing shortcut.

- **Mouse and Keyboard Settings**—A tool for adjusting input devices. If your keyboard is typing the wrong characters for certain keys, or your mouse is too sensitive, you can alter the settings here.

- **Raspberry Pi Configuration**—Loads a graphical utility for modifying many of the Pi's hardware and software settings, described in full in Chapter 6, "The Raspberry Pi Configuration Tool".

About Raspbian's Parent, Debian

Raspbian is based on one of the original Linux distributions, Debian. Named after its creator and his girlfriend—Ian and Deb—Debian is a popular distribution in its own right. Raspbian is a *fork* of Debian, a version adapted by the community for a particular task. It isn't alone. Ubuntu Linux, from Canonical, is also based on Debian, while Linux Mint, one of the most popular distributions for desktops and laptops, is based in turn on Ubuntu.

This process of forking and forking again is unique to open source software. With a closed source package, like Microsoft Windows, it's not possible to customise it to your individual requirements. This is one of the biggest strengths of open source software, and is brilliantly demonstrated by the ease with which Raspbian was tailored to the requirements of the Raspberry Pi.

Alternatives to Raspbian

Raspbian is the recommended Linux distribution for the Raspberry Pi, but there are alternatives. The most popular are available from the Raspberry Pi Foundation's Downloads page at `www.raspberrypi.org/downloads`, and most can be installed easily using NOOBS, as described in Chapter 2, "Getting Started with the Raspberry Pi".

Next to Raspbian, the most common distributions installed are LibreELEC and OSMC, which both turn the Pi into a dedicated home theatre system as demonstrated in Chapter 8, "The Pi as a Home Theatre PC". The next most popular is Pidora, a distribution based on the Fedora Linux project, which, in turn, has Red Hat as its parent distribution. Another alternative, Arch Linux is designed for those already familiar with Linux; unlike the others in the list, it doesn't include a GUI by default.

One of the available operating systems is not a variant of Linux at all: RISC OS. Originally produced by Acorn Computers in the late 1980s for its Archimedes range of personal computers—which, like the Raspberry Pi, were based on an ARM processor—RISC OS is a fast, easy-to-use operating system with a clean-looking GUI. While the breakup of Acorn in 1998 saw the popularity of RISC OS decline, the platform still has its fans, and they were quick to add support for the Raspberry Pi.

Running RISC OS on the Raspberry Pi results in an environment that is significantly more responsive than any of the other operating systems offered, thanks to its origins as a platform designed specifically for the ARM instruction set architecture. Sadly, that speed comes at a cost: RISC OS runs only applications that are written specifically for RISC OS, which are far fewer in number than those written for Linux.

NOOBS is smart enough to show you only operating systems which are supported by your model of Pi. Operating systems which require the BCM2836 processor or above, such as Windows 10 IoT Core, will not appear when running NOOBS on the BCM2835-based Model A, Model B, Model A+, Model B+, or Raspberry Pi Zero, for example.

Using External Storage Devices

The Pi's micro-SD card, which stores all the various Pi files and directories, isn't very big. The largest available micro-SD card at the time of writing has 256 GB, which is tiny compared to the 10,000 GB (10 TB) available with the largest full-size desktop hard drives.

If you're using your Pi to play back video files (see Chapter 8), you'll likely need more storage than you can get from an SD card. As you learned in Chapter 2, it's possible to connect USB mass storage (UMS) devices to the Pi to gain access to more storage space.

Before these external devices are accessible, however, the operating system needs to know about them. In Linux, this process is known as *mounting*. If you're running a version of Linux with a desktop environment loaded, this process is automatic. Simply connect the device to a free USB port on the Pi or a USB hub, and the device and its contents will immediately be accessible (see Figure 3-2).

FIGURE 3-2: Raspbian automatically mounting a USB mass storage device

From the console, things are only slightly more difficult. To make a device accessible to Linux when the desktop environment isn't loaded, follow these steps:

Note that a ↵ symbol means the command was split over multiple lines because of the size of the book's pages. Enter the command as a single line, continuing to type for each line that ends in a ↵ and pressing Enter only at the very end of the command.

1. Connect the USB storage device to the Pi, either directly or through a connected USB hub.

2. Type **sudo fdisk -l** to get a list of drives connected to the Pi and find the USB storage device by size. Note the device name: /dev/sdXN, where X is the drive letter and N is the partition number. If it is the only device connected to the Pi, this will be /dev/sda1.

3. Before the USB storage device is accessible, Linux needs a mount point for it. Create this by typing **sudo mkdir /media/externaldrive**.

4. Currently, the directory is accessible only to the root user. To make it accessible to all users, type the following as a single line:

```
sudo chgrp -R users /media/externaldrive && ↵
sudo chmod -R g+w /media/externaldrive
```

5. Type the following command to mount the USB storage device to gain access to the device and its contents:

```
sudo mount /dev/sdXN /media/externaldrive -o=rw
```

Creating a New User Account

Unlike many desktop operating systems, which were originally designed for use by individuals, Linux is at heart a social operating system designed to accommodate numerous users. By default, Raspbian is configured with two user accounts: *pi*, which is the normal user account, and *root*, which is a superuser account with additional permissions.

> **TIP** Don't be tempted to log in as *root* all the time. Using a nonprivileged user account, you're protected against accidentally wrecking your operating system and from the ravages of viruses and other malware downloaded from the Internet.

While it's certainly possible for you to use the *pi* account, you may prefer to create your own dedicated user account. Further accounts can also be created for friends or family members who might want to use the Pi.

Creating a new account on the Pi is straightforward and is roughly the same on all distributions, except for the username and password used to log in to the Pi initially. Just follow these steps:

1. Log in to the Pi using the existing user account (username *pi* and password *raspberry* if you're using the recommended Raspbian distribution).

2. Type the following as a single line with no spaces after any of the commas:

   ```
   sudo useradd -m -G
      adm,dialout,cdrom,sudo,audio,video,plugdev,games,users,↵
   input,netdev,gpio,i2c,spi username
   ```

   This creates a new, empty user account.

3. To set a password on the new account, type **sudo passwd username** followed by the new password when prompted.

Here's what just happened: the command `sudo` tells the operating system that the command you're typing should be run as if you were logged in as the *root* account. The `useradd` command says you want to create a new user account. The `-m` section—known as a *flag* or an *option*—tells the `useradd` program to create a home directory where the new user can store his or her files. The big list following the `-G` flag is the list of groups of which the user should be a member.

File System Layout

The content of the SD card is known as its *file system* and is split into multiple sections, each with a particular purpose. Although to use the Raspberry Pi it's not necessary for you to understand what each section does, that background knowledge can be helpful should anything go wrong.

Users and Groups

In Linux, each user has three main attributes: a *user ID (UID)*, a *group ID (GID)*, and a list of supplementary group memberships. A user can be a member of as many groups as he or she pleases, although only one of these can be the user's primary group. This is usually a self-named group matching the username.

Group membership is important. Users can be granted direct access to files and devices on the system, but it's more common for a user to receive access to these via group membership. The group `audio`, for example, grants all members the ability to access the Pi's sound playback hardware. Without that membership, the user won't be listening to any music.

To see a user's group memberships, type **groups username** at the terminal. If you use this on the default user *pi*, you'll see the list of groups any new member should join to make use of the Pi. This is where the information used in Step 2 of the preceding procedure was found.

Logical Layout

The way Linux deals with drives, files, folders, and devices differs somewhat from other operating systems. Instead of having multiple drives labelled with a letter, everything appears as a branch beneath what is known as the *root file system*.

If you log in to the Pi and type **ls /**, you'll see various directories displayed (see Figure 3-3). Some of these are areas of the SD card for storing files, while others are *virtual directories* for accessing different portions of the operating system or hardware.

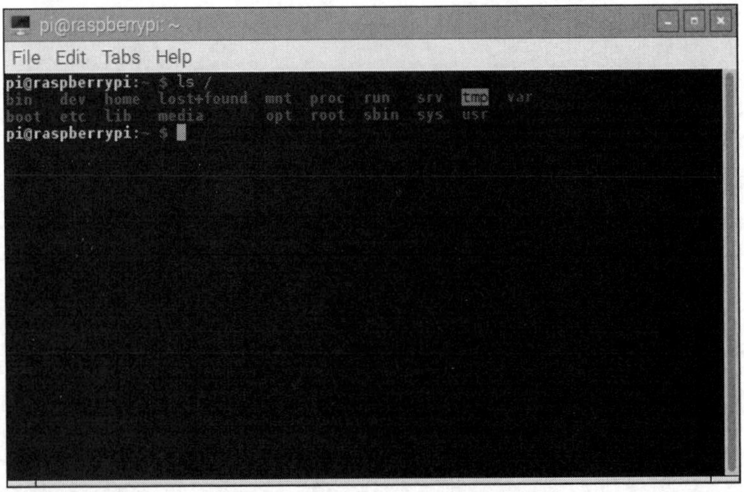

FIGURE 3-3: A directory listing for the Pi's root file system

The directories visible on the default Raspbian distribution are as follows:

- **boot**—This contains the Linux kernel and other packages needed to start the Pi.
- **bin**—Operating system-related binary files, such as those required to run the GUI, are stored here.
- **dev**—This is a virtual directory, which doesn't actually exist on the SD card. All the devices connected to the system—including storage devices and the sound card—can be accessed from here.
- **etc**—This stores miscellaneous configuration files, including the list of users and their encrypted passwords.
- **home**—All users get a subdirectory beneath this directory to store all their personal files.
- **lib**—This is a storage space for *libraries*, which are shared bits of code required by numerous different applications.
- **lost+found**—This is a special directory where *file fragments* are stored if the system crashes.
- **media**—This is a special directory for removable storage devices, such as USB memory sticks or external CD drives.
- **mnt**—This folder is used to manually *mount* storage devices, such as external hard drives.
- **opt**—This stores optional software that is not part of the operating system. If you install new software to your Pi, it will usually go here or in usr.
- **proc**—This is another virtual directory, containing information about running programs, which are known in Linux as *processes*.
- **run**—A special directory used by various *daemons*, processes which run in the background.
- **root**—Although most user's files are kept in a subdirectory of home, the root (superuser) account's files are kept here.
- **sbin**—This stores special binary files, primarily used by the root (superuser) account for system maintenance.
- **srv**—A directory used to store data served by the operating system. This is empty in Raspbian.
- **sys**—This is a virtual directory storing system information used by the Linux kernel.
- **tmp**—Temporary files are stored here automatically.
- **usr**—This directory provides storage for user-accessible programs.
- **var**—This is a directory which programs use to store changing values or *variables*.

Physical Layout

Although the preceding list is how the file system appears to the Linux operating system, it's not how it's laid out on the SD card. For the default Raspbian distribution, as installed from the official image, the SD card is organised into two main sections, known as *partitions* because they split the device into different areas in much the same way as the chapters of this book help to organise its contents.

The first partition on the disk is a small (approximately 75 MB) partition formatted as FAT32, the same partition format used by Microsoft Windows for removable drives. This is *mounted*, or made accessible, by Linux in the /boot directory and contains all the files required to configure the Raspberry Pi and to load Linux.

The second partition is far larger and formatted as EXT4, a native Linux file system designed for high-speed access and data safety. This partition contains the main chunk of the distribution. All the programs, the desktop, the users' files, and any software that you install yourself are stored here. This takes up the bulk of the SD card.

Installing and Uninstalling Software

The default software installed with the Raspbian distribution is enough to get you started, but chances are you're going to want to customise your Pi according to your own requirements. Installing software from the Internet requires the Raspberry Pi to have an active network connection, either wired or using an optional Wi-Fi wireless adapter.

Managing Software Graphically

The easiest way to install new software within Raspbian is to use the Add/Remove Software utility, found in the Preferences menu (see Figure 3-4). This maintains a list of all the software available from the Raspbian *repositories*, any of which can be installed in no more than a couple of clicks of the mouse. Using the Add/Remove Software utility does, however, require an active internet connection; if you are using a Pi Zero, Model A, or Model A+, you need a USB network dongle before you can install extra software this way.

Software in the Raspbian repositories is split into categories, ranging from games to system software. Clicking a category from the list on the left shows the software from that category in the main window region to the right, which you can scroll through using the keyboard or mouse. Clicking a piece of software provides more information about that software, ranging from a description to the size of the download. The search box to the upper left of the window can be used to find software across any category, based on its title or words appearing in its description.

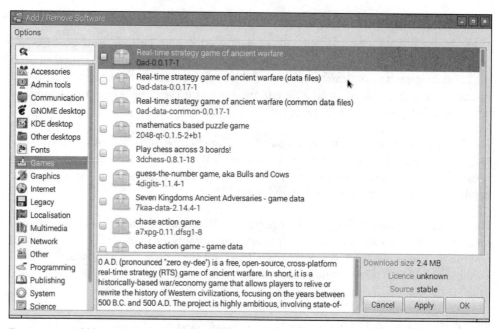

FIGURE 3-4: Add/Remove Software, main window

To install any of the listed software, simply place a tick in the box to the left of its name with a click of the mouse. You can select multiple packages at the same time; if any of your packages require other packages to be installed—such as a game needing its data files to operate—these will be selected for you automatically.

When you have chosen the software you want to install, click the Apply button in the bottom right of the window. You are then prompted for your password (see Figure 3-5). This confirms that you want to install the software, and also elevates your user account to *root privileges*, which allows you to make changes to the software configuration. When your software is installed, click OK to close the window.

Uninstalling software is as easy as installing it: simply click on the ticked box next to the name of the software you want to remove, then click the Apply button to have it removed. Be aware, however, that it's entirely possible to remove software you actually need this way; always double-check the name of the software you're uninstalling before clicking Apply!

Managing Software at the Command Line

If you're running your Pi without the GUI, you can access the same software packages using a tool called `apt`, which is a powerful *package manager*. When you're adding or removing software in the GUI, you're actually using `apt`—but at one remove.

Other Distributions

Raspbian, as with most Debian-based distributions, uses a tool called apt as the package manager. It's not the only tool out there, and other distributions make different choices. Arch Linux, for example, uses the yum tool.

Pacman is no more difficult to use than apt, but its syntax (the way it expects you to phrase instructions to install new software or remove existing software) is different. For instructions on how to use pacman instead of apt, type **man pacman** at the Arch Linux terminal.

Other distributions may use the yum package manager. If you're trying a distribution that uses yum, simply type **man yum** at the terminal for instructions.

FIGURE 3-5: Authenticating a software installation instruction

A package manager's job is to keep track of all the software installed on the system. It doesn't just install new software; it also keeps tabs on what is currently installed, allows old software to be removed, and installs updates as they become available.

Package management is one of the areas where Linux differs greatly from operating systems like Windows or OS X. Although it's possible to manually download new software to install, it's far more common to use the built-in package management tools instead.

Before trying to install new software or upgrade existing software, you need to make sure the apt *cache* is up-to-date. To do this, simply type the command **sudo apt-get update**.   **TIP**

Finding the Software You Want

The first step to installing a new piece of software is to find out what it's called. The easiest way to do so is to search the *cache* of available software packages. This cache is a list of all the software available to install via apt, stored on Internet servers known as *repositories*.

The apt software includes a utility for managing this cache, called apt-cache. Using this software, it's possible to run a search on all the available software packages for a particular word or phrase.

For example, to find a game to play, you can type the following command:

```
apt-cache search game
```

That tells apt-cache to search its list of available software for anything that has the word "game" in its title or description. For common search terms, you can end up with quite a list (see Figure 3-6), so try to be as specific as you can.

TIP If your search term brings up too many different packages to see on a single screen display, you can tell Linux that you want it to pause on each screenful by *piping* the output of apt-cache through a tool called less. Simply change the command to apt-cache search game | less and use the cursor keys to scroll through the list. Press the letter Q on the keyboard to exit.

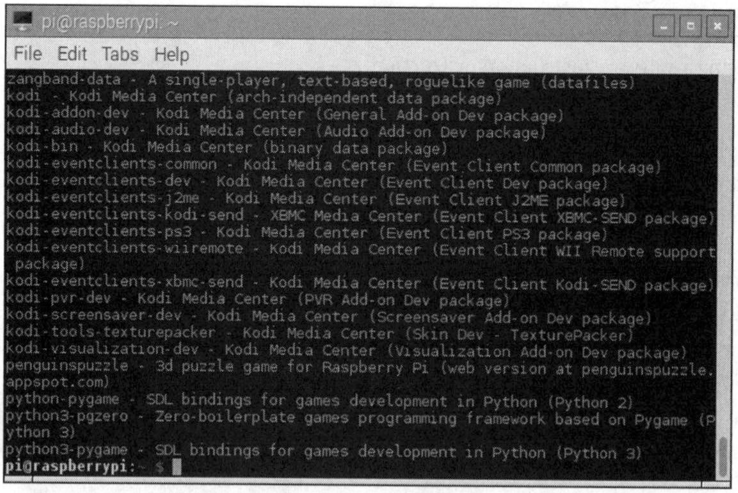

FIGURE 3-6: The last few results for an apt-cache "game" search

Installing Software

Once you know the name of the package you want to install, switch to the `apt-get` command to install it. Installing software is a privilege afforded only to the *root* user, as it affects all users of the Raspberry Pi. As a result, the commands will need to be prefaced with `sudo` to tell the operating system that it should be run as the *root* user.

For example, to install the package `nethack-console` (a console-based randomly generated role-playing game), you simply use the `install` command with `apt-get` as follows:

```
sudo apt-get install nethack-console
```

Some packages rely on other packages in order to operate. A programming language may depend on a compiler, a game engine on graphics files, or an audio player on codecs for playing back different formats. These are known in Linux terms as *dependencies*.

Dependencies are one of the biggest reasons for using a package manager like `apt` rather than installing software manually. If a package depends on other packages, `apt` will automatically find them (see Figure 3-7) and prepare them for installation. If this happens, you'll be shown a prompt asking whether you want to continue. If you do, type the letter **Y** and press Enter.

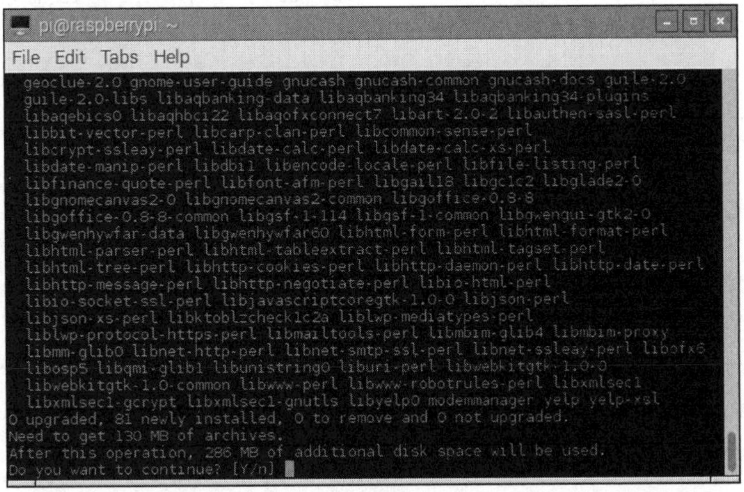

FIGURE 3-7: Apt listing the dependencies for the gnucash package

Uninstalling Software

If you decide you no longer want a piece of software, `apt-get` also includes a `remove` command that cleanly uninstalls the package along with any dependencies that are no longer required. When you're using a smaller SD card with the Pi, your ability to try out software and quickly remove it is very useful.

To remove `nethack-console`, simply open the terminal and type the following command:

```
sudo apt-get remove nethack-console
```

The `remove` command has a more powerful brother in the form of the `purge` command. Like `remove`, the `purge` command gets rid of software you no longer require. Where `remove` leaves the software's configuration files intact, however, `purge` removes everything. If you've got yourself into a mess customising a particular package and it no longer works, `purge` is the command to use. For example, to purge `nethack-console`, you just type this:

```
sudo apt-get purge nethack-console
```

Upgrading Software

In addition to installing and uninstalling packages, `apt` can be used to keep them up-to-date. Upgrading a package through `apt` ensures that you've received the latest updates, bug fixes, and security patches.

Before trying to upgrade a package, make sure the `apt` cache is as fresh as possible by running an update:

```
sudo apt-get update
```

When upgrading software, you have two choices: you can upgrade everything on the system simultaneously or upgrade individual programs. If you just want to keep your entire distribution updated, the former is achieved by typing the following:

```
sudo apt-get upgrade
```

To upgrade an individual package, simply tell `apt` to install it again. For example, to install a `nethack-console` upgrade, you type this:

```
sudo apt-get install nethack-console
```

If the package is already installed, apt will treat it as an in-place upgrade. If you're already running the latest version available, apt will simply tell you it cannot upgrade the software and then exit.

For more information on package management with apt—in particular, how certain packages can be "kept back" and excluded from upgrades—type **man apt** at the terminal.

TIP

Shutting the Pi Down Safely

Although the Pi doesn't have a power switch like a traditional computer, that doesn't mean you can simply pull the power cable out when you're finished. Even when it doesn't appear to be doing anything, the Pi is often reading from or writing to the SD card, and if it loses power while this is happening, the contents of the card can become *corrupt* and unreadable.

To shut down using the terminal, type the following command:

```
sudo shutdown -h now
```

If you are in Raspbian's graphical desktop, click the Menu at the upper-left of the screen and click the Shutdown option to load a menu with Shutdown, Reboot, and Log Out options. Click the Shutdown option to shut the Pi down safely.

The Pi will close all open applications, prompting you to save any open files if you haven't done so already and shut itself down, at which point the screen will go black and the ACT light will switch off. Once the light is off, it's safe to remove the micro-USB cable or switch the Pi off manually.

When you want to switch the Pi back on, or if you accidentally shut down the Pi without meaning to, simply reconnect the power and it will start to boot automatically.

Chapter 4
Troubleshooting

SOMETIMES THINGS DON'T go entirely smoothly. The more complex the device, the more complex the problems that can occur—and the Pi is an extremely complex device indeed.

Thankfully, many of the most common problems are straightforward to diagnose and fix. In this chapter, you look at some of the most common reasons for the Pi to misbehave and how to fix them.

Keyboard and Mouse Diagnostics

Perhaps the most common problem that users experience with the Raspberry Pi is when the keyboard repeats certain characters. For example, if the command `startx` appears onscreen as `stttttttttttartxxxxxxxxxxxxx`, it will, understandably, fail to work when the Enter key is pressed.

There are typically two reasons why a USB keyboard fails to operate correctly when connected to the Raspberry Pi: It's drawing too much power, or its internal chipset is conflicting with the USB circuitry on the Pi.

Check the documentation for your keyboard or the label on its underside to see if it has a power rating given in *milliamps (mA)*. This is how much power the keyboard attempts to draw from the USB port when it's in use. The Pi's USB ports are not able to provide as much power as those of a full-size laptop or desktop computer. This can be a problem for keyboards that have built-in LED lighting, which require far more power to operate than a standard keyboard.

If you find that your USB keyboard may be drawing too much power, try connecting it to a powered USB hub instead of directly to the Pi. Doing so allows the keyboard to draw its power from the hub's power supply unit, instead of from the Pi itself. Alternatively, swap the keyboard out for a model with lower power demands. The repeating-letter problem may also be traced to an inadequate power supply for the Pi, which is addressed in the next section, "Power Diagnostics".

The issue of compatibility, sadly, is harder to diagnose. The overwhelming majority of keyboards work just fine with the Pi, but a few exhibit strange symptoms. These range from intermittent response to the repeating-letter syndrome, or even crashes that prevent the Pi from operating. Sometimes, these issues don't appear until other USB devices are connected to the Pi. If your keyboard was working fine until another USB device, in particular a USB wireless adapter, was connected, you might have an issue of incompatibility, or your particular USB dongle may be drawing too much power.

If possible, try swapping out the keyboard for another model. If the new keyboard works, your old one might be incompatible with the Pi. For a list of compatible keyboards, visit the eLinux wiki at `http://elinux.org/Rpi_USB_Keyboards`, but be aware this list is user-generated and is far from exhaustive.

The same advice on checking compatibility in advance applies to problems with the mouse. The majority of USB mice and trackballs work fine, but some exhibit incompatibility with the Pi's USB circuitry. This usually results in symptoms like a jerky or unresponsive mouse pointer, but it can sometimes lead to the Pi failing to load or crashing at random intervals. If you're looking to buy a new mouse, a list of models known to work with the Pi is available at the eLinux wiki site at `http://elinux.org/RPi_USB_Mouse_devices`.

Power Diagnostics

Many problems with the Raspberry Pi can be traced to an inadequate power supply. While the low-power Model A draws a maximum of 500 mA, the high-performance Raspberry Pi 3 can draw up to 1,200 mA (1.2 A), a figure which increases the more accessories are added. Not all USB power adapters are designed to offer this much power, even if their labelling claims otherwise.

TIP   The formal USB standard states that devices should draw no more than 500 mA, with even that level of power available only to the device following a process called *negotiation*. The Pi doesn't negotiate for power, which can cause problems when trying to power the Pi from a PC's USB port. While lower-power models such as the Raspberry Pi Zero may work, higher-power models like the Raspberry Pi 2 and 3 should never be powered from a PC's USB port.

If you're having intermittent problems with your Pi—particularly if it works until you connect something to a USB port or start a processor-intensive operation like playing video—the chances are that the power supply in use is inadequate. The power LED of the Raspberry Pi acts as an in-built voltage test, letting you know if the power supply you're using is below the standard required for stable operation. If the power LED is flashing or unlit, your power supply is providing less than 4.65 V—well below the 5 V USB standard—and should be replaced.

Another warning sign for inadequate power is the appearance of a square of rainbow colours in the top right of the display. If your power is borderline, you might see this square appear and disappear as you change the amount of power the system is drawing by running something that uses the graphics processor, for example, or by connecting hardware to the GPIO header.

If you want to get a better idea of the power your Pi is receiving, the easiest way is to buy a *USB power meter*. A simple form of *multimeter*, a USB power meter is designed to sit in-between your USB power supply and the Raspberry Pi and measure the voltage and amperage.

There are contact points on the Raspberry Pi you can use with a traditional multimeter's probes **WARNING** to take a reading of the voltage from your power supply, but you should not use these because there is too great a risk of accidentally shorting a probe to nearby pins.

A USB cable suitable for use with your USB power meter should be connected to the USB power meter's input, and a micro-USB cable should be connected from its output to the Raspberry Pi. When connected to power, the USB power meter starts reading out statistics about the quality of the power from the power supply. These statistics include the voltage, typically labelled with a V for volts on the display, and the current, labelled with an A for amps (see Figure 4-1).

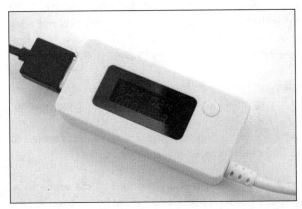

FIGURE 4-1: A USB power meter, reading the power flowing into a Raspberry Pi 2

The voltage reading on the USB power meter should be somewhere between 4.65 V and 5.2 V. If it's lower than 4.65 V, this indicates that the Pi is not being provided with enough power. Try swapping the USB adapter for a different model, and check that the label says it can supply 700 mA or more for lower-powered Raspberry Pis including the Model A and Pi Zero, 1.8 A or more for the A+, B+, and Raspberry Pi 2, and 2.5 A or more for the Raspberry PI 3. Beware of cheap power supplies and thin micro-USB cables: They sometimes have inaccurate labelling and fail to supply the promised current. Genuine branded power supplies such as the official Raspberry Pi model rarely have this problem, but cheap unbranded devices—often sold as *compatible adapters*—should be avoided.

The current reading can be used to determine how close you are to the upper limit of your power supply's output. If the readout says "0.62 A", for example, this means you are currently drawing 620 mA (milliamps, thousandths of an amp), which is above the rated output of a 500 mA power supply but safely below that of a 1 A or greater power supply. A Raspberry Pi in normal operation should draw less than 500 mA, but this figure can increase if you connect additional hardware such as Wi-Fi dongles, onboard displays, or wireless keyboards and mice. A USB power meter is the easiest and safest way to keep track of the current being used.

Display Diagnostics

Although the Pi is designed to work with almost any HDMI, DVI, or composite video display device, it simply might not work as expected when you plug it in. For example, you could find that your picture is shifted to the side or not fully displayed, or is only visible as a postage-stamp-sized cutout in the middle of the screen or in black and white—or even missing entirely.

First, check the type of device to which the Pi is connected. This is especially important when you're using the composite connection to plug the Pi into a TV. Different countries use different standards for TV video, meaning that a Pi configured for one country may not work in another. This is the usual explanation for a Pi showing black-and-white video. You find out how to adjust this setting in Chapter 7, "Advanced Raspberry Pi Configuration".

When you use the HDMI output, the display type is usually automatically detected. If you're using an HDMI to DVI or VGA adapter to plug the Pi into a computer monitor, this occasionally goes awry. Common symptoms include snow-like static, missing picture portions, or no display at all. To fix the problem, note the resolution and refresh rate of your connected display, and then jump to Chapter 7 to find out how to set these manually.

Another issue is a too-large or too-small image, either missing portions at the edge of the screen or sitting in the middle of a large black border. This issue is caused by a setting known as *overscan*, which is used when the Pi is connected to TVs to avoid displaying on portions of the display that may be hidden under a bezel/surround. As with other display-related settings, you learn how to adjust—or even completely disable—overscan in Chapter 7.

Boot Diagnostics

The most common cause for a Pi to fail to boot is a problem with the SD (or microSD) card. Unlike a desktop or laptop computer, the Pi relies on files stored on the SD card for everything. If the Pi can't talk to the card, the Pi won't display anything on the screen or show any signs of life at all.

If your Pi's PWR (power) light glows when you connect the micro-USB power supply but nothing else happens and the ACT (activity) light isn't flickering to indicate data access, you more than likely have an SD card problem. First, ensure that the card works when you connect it to a PC and that it shows the partitions and files expected of a well-flashed card. (For more details, see Chapter 3, "Linux System Administration", particularly the section titled "File System Layout".)

If the card works on a PC but not on the Pi, it may be a compatibility problem. Some SD cards don't operate correctly when connected to the Pi's onboard SD card interface. You can find a list of cards known to be compatible with the Pi on the eLinux wiki at `http://elinux. org/RPi_SD_cards`.

Sadly, if you have an incompatible card, you will probably need to replace it with a different card in order for the Pi to work. As the Pi's software base is developed, however, work is being carried out to ensure that a wider range of cards operates correctly with the Pi. Before giving up on it completely, check to see if an updated version of your chosen Linux distribution is available. (See Chapter 1, "Meet the Raspberry Pi", for more information about distributions.)

If you've been changing the speed of your Raspberry Pi by overclocking (see Chapter 6, "The Raspberry Pi Configuration Tool"), it might not boot correctly. To temporarily disable the overclock and run the Pi at its default speed, hold down the Shift key as the boot messages appear on-screen.

Network Diagnostics

The most useful tool for diagnosing network problems is `ifconfig`. If you're using a wireless network connection, jump to Chapter 5, "Network Configuration", for information on a similar tool for those devices. Otherwise, read on.

Designed to provide information on connected network ports, ifconfig is a powerful tool for controlling and configuring the Pi's network ports. For its most basic usage, simply type the tool's name in the terminal:

```
ifconfig
```

Called in this manner, ifconfig provides information on all the network ports it can find (see Figure 4-2). For the standard Raspberry Pi Model B, Model B+, and Raspberry Pi 2, there are two ports: the physical Ethernet port on the right side of the board, and a virtual *loopback* interface that allows programs on the Pi to talk to each other. The Raspberry Pi 3, meanwhile, has a third port representing the built-in wireless network adapter.

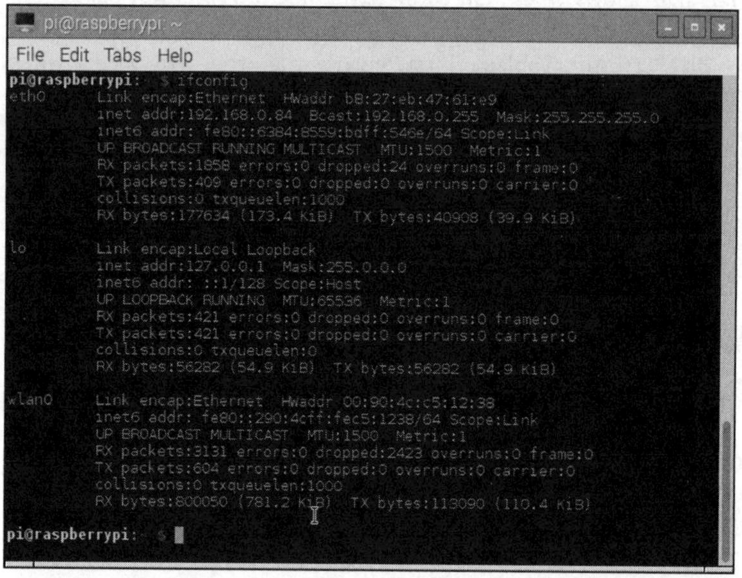

FIGURE 4-2: The output of ifconfig on a Raspberry Pi 3

The output of ifconfig is split into the following sections:

- **Link encap**—The type of *encapsulation* used by the network, which on the Model B will either read Ethernet for the physical network port (usually named eth0) or Local Loopback for the virtual loopback adaptor (usually named lo).

- **Hwaddr**—The *Media Access Control (MAC) address* of the network interface, written in hexadecimal. This is unique for every device on the network, and each Pi has its own MAC address, which is set at the factory.

- **inet addr**—The *Internet Protocol (IP) address* of the network interface. This is how you find the Pi on the network if you're using it to run a network-accessible service, such as a web server or file server.

- **Bcast**—The *broadcast address* for the network to which the Pi is connected. Any traffic sent to this address will be received by every device on the network.

- **Mask**—The *network mask*, which controls the maximum size of the network to which the Pi is connected. For most home users, this will read 255.255.255.0.

- **MTU**—The *maximum transmission unit* size, which is how big a single packet of data can be before the system needs to split it into multiple packets.

- **RX**—This section provides feedback on the received network traffic, including the number of errors and dropped packets recorded. If you start to see errors appearing in this section, something is wrong with the network.

- **TX**—This provides the same information as the RX section, but for transmitted packets. Again, any errors recorded here indicate a problem with the network.

- **Collisions**—If two systems on the network try to talk at the same time, you get a *collision*, which requires them to retransmit their packets. Small numbers of collisions aren't a problem, but a large number here indicates a network issue.

- **txqueuelen**—The length of the *transmission queue*, which will usually be set to 1000 and rarely needs changing.

- **RX bytes, TX bytes**—A summary of the amount of traffic the network interface has passed.

If you're having problems with the network on the Pi, first try to disable, and then re-enable the network interface. The easiest way to do so is with two tools called `ifup` and `ifdown`.

If the network is up but not working correctly—for example, if `ifconfig` doesn't list anything in the `inet addr` section—start by disabling the network port. From the terminal, type the following command:

```
sudo ifdown eth0
```

Once the network is disabled, make sure that the cable is inserted tightly at both ends and that whatever network device the Pi is connected to (hub, switch, or router) is powered on and working. Then bring the interface back up again with the following command:

```
sudo ifup eth0
```

You can test the networking by using the `sudo ping` command, which sends data to a remote computer and waits for a response. If everything's working, you should see a similar response as shown in Figure 4-3. If not, you might need to manually configure your network settings, which you can learn how to do in Chapter 5, "Network Configuration".

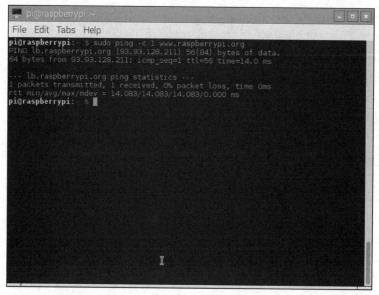

FIGURE 4-3: The result of a successful test of the network, using the `sudo ping` command

Chapter 5
Network Configuration

FOR MOST USERS, configuring the Raspberry Pi's network is as easy as plugging a cable into the Ethernet port on a Model B, B+, Pi 2, or Pi 3—or a USB Ethernet adapter, in the case of the Model A, A+, or Pi Zero. For others, however, the network requires manual configuration.

If you know that your network doesn't have a *Dynamic Host Configuration Protocol (DHCP)* server—a system that tells the Pi and other devices on the network how they should connect—or if you want to use a USB wireless adapter with the Pi, read on.

Wired Networking

In some instances, for the Pi's network to operate correctly, you may need to configure it manually. Normally, the network in a home, school, or office has a DHCP server that tells the Pi and other devices on the network how they should connect. Some networks don't have a DHCP server, however, and need to be set up manually.

If you just want your Raspberry Pi to have an IP address that doesn't change, known as a **NOTE** *static IP*, configuring it directly on the Pi is the wrong approach. Instead, consult your router or other DHCP server's manual for instructions on how to make static IP reservations; a static IP address prevents the Pi from clashing with another device on the network.

Connecting to a Wired Network via the GUI

The easiest way to manually configure networking on the Pi is through the graphical user interface (GUI). The Raspbian desktop is already configured for networking support: find the network icon on the system tray, which looks like two computers linked together with a cable, and right-click it. Left-click WiFi Networks (dhcpcdui) Settings—even though you're configuring a wired network, as this is simply the name of the configuration tool—and the configuration window will appear (see Figure 5-1).

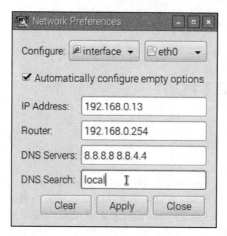

FIGURE 5-1: The Raspbian network configuration window

This configuration window provides multiple options. You do not need to fill out all of these to activate wired networking. Instead, just fill in as many as you can using the following guide:

- **IP Address**—The static IP address you want to assign to the Raspberry Pi. This is a required setting, and cannot be left blank.

- **Router**—The IP address of your network router or other network gateway. If this is left blank, your Pi will only be able to connect to other devices on your local network and not out onto the Internet.

- **DNS Servers**—The IP addresses of one or more *domain name system servers*, used to translate friendly domain names into the IP address of the server. If you don't know your ISP's DNS server addresses, and you're not running any local DNS servers, enter 8.8.8.8 and 8.8.8.4 separated by a space to use Google's public DNS servers.

- **DNS Search**—The search suffix that should be applied to DNS searches for local names. For most home networks this is either "local" or "home"; if you're not sure, you can safely leave this blank.

With the entries filled in, click the Apply button. If you receive an error message, double-check your entries; a common mistake is to use anything other than a single space to separate multiple DNS server addresses. If no error appears, you can skip ahead to the section "Testing Your Connectivity".

Connecting to a Wired Network via the Console

As an alternative to the graphical method, you can configure your network connectivity using the console. Either launch a terminal window from the Menu button or use the Raspbian console, and enter the following command:

```
sudo nano /etc/dhcpcd.conf
```

This launches the powerful but user-friendly nano text editor with root (superuser) permissions, and tells it to open the file dhcpcd.conf located in the /etc directory for editing (see Figure 5-2). This file is a configuration file—hence the .conf file extension—for the *dynamic host configuration protocol client daemon (DHCPCD)*. This file controls how the Raspberry Pi gets its network information: by default it's configured to query a DHCP server on the network for dynamic configuration information, but it can also be edited to input manual configuration information.

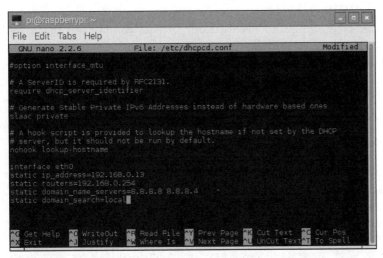

FIGURE 5-2: Editing the /etc/dhcpcd.conf file in nano

Scroll to the bottom of the file, and add your manual configuration in using the following example as a guide and replacing the example entries with the data for your own network:

```
interface eth0
static ip_address=192.168.0.13
static routers=192.168.0.254
static domain_name_servers=8.8.8.8 8.8.4.4
static domain_search=local
```

If your Raspberry Pi has more than one network adapter—such as the Raspberry Pi 3 with its built-in wired and wireless network adapters, or an older Pi model with a USB network adapter attached—you can configure each adapter in turn by repeating the configuration options under a new `interface` line.

When you have finished configuring your network settings, write the file using Ctrl+O, and then close the text editor using Ctrl+X. Restart the Pi's network stack using the following command:

```
sudo service networking restart
```

If you were connected to the Pi via Secure Shell (SSH) and you have changed its IP address, this will disconnect you. Wait a few moments for the Pi to bring its network back up, and then reconnect using the new IP address you have configured.

Testing Your Connectivity

When you have finished configuring your new network settings, you can test them. The easiest way to do this is to launch the web browser and attempt to visit a website; if the site appears, your network connection is working fine.

You can also test your network connectivity from the command line. If you are not already at the console, open a terminal window and type the following command:

```
sudo ping -c 1 www.raspberrypi.org
```

This sends a single packet to the Raspberry Pi website's server and waits for a response. After a second or so, you should see a response back from the server confirming that your message was received (see Figure 5-3).

If you receive an error message, there is something wrong with your configuration. The message "network is unreachable" suggests that you have not configured your router address correctly; the message "unknown host" suggests that you have not configured your DNS server addresses correctly. Double-check all settings, comparing them if possible to a system on the same network which is operating correctly, to find and fix the mistake—after double-checking that your network cable is plugged in at both ends, of course!

Wireless Networking

The Raspberry Pi 3 includes an onboard wireless networking radio, capable of connecting to 802.11b/g/n-standard networks on the 2.4 GHz frequency. Wireless networking can also be added to any other model of Pi using a low-cost USB Wi-Fi adapter; before purchasing one, make sure that the manufacturer confirms it is compatible with Linux in general and the Raspberry Pi specifically, as some adapters only support specific operating systems such as Microsoft Windows.

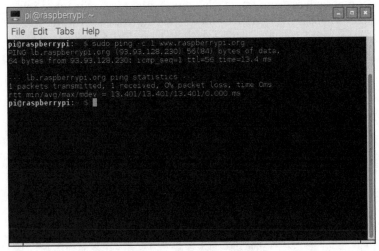

FIGURE 5-3: Testing network connectivity with ping

USB Wi-Fi adapters are very power hungry. If you connect one designed for use with a desktop computer directly to the Pi's USB port, it might not work. Instead, connect a powered USB hub to the Pi, and then insert the Wi-Fi adapter into that.   **TIP**

Before you start to set up the wireless interface, you need to know the *service set identifier (SSID)*—also known as the *network name*—of the wireless router to which you want to connect, along with the type of encryption in use and the password required. You also need to know what type of wireless network it is. A USB adapter designed for 802.11a Wi-Fi may not connect to an 802.11g network, and vice versa. In the case of the Raspberry Pi 3's onboard wireless adapter, you can use it exclusively with 2.4 GHz networks; it will not connect to 5 GHz networks.

Connecting to a Wireless Network via the GUI

The simplest way to connect to a wireless network from the Raspberry Pi is to use the graphical tool built in to Raspbian. This provides a graphical user interface for software that would otherwise require the use of the terminal. Begin by left-clicking on the network icon in the system tray near the clock; depending on what devices you have connected to your Pi, it will either appear as a series of increasingly-sized stacked semicircles designed to mimic radio waves or as a pair of computers.

Left-clicking the network icon will bring up a list of nearby wireless networks, along with one or more icons (see Figure 5-4). A radio tower icon with a small shield in front of it indicates that the network is protected via encryption and will require a key in the form of a password or passphrase to access; a series of stacked semicircles to the right of each network SSID indicates the strength of that network connection. Networks with an access point or router physically closer to yours will appear stronger; networks farther away will appear weaker. If a network has only the bottom of the icon highlighted, it might be too weak to sustain a stable connection.

FIGURE 5-4: Viewing nearby wireless networks on a Raspberry Pi 3

Find the entry for your network in the list, and left-click it. If your network is unencrypted—not the best idea, as it allows anybody within range to use your network without your permission—the Pi will immediately connect to the network. If it is encrypted—whether it's encrypted by the older, insecure *Wired Equivalent Privacy (WEP)* standard or the newer *Wireless Protected Access (WPA)* or WPA2 standard—a dialogue will pop up requesting the network key (see Figure 5-5).

The network key, also known as a *pre-shared key (PSK)*, is a secret shared between all devices with access to the network. If you're connecting to a wireless router provided by your Internet service provider (ISP), you'll usually find the network key written on the underside of the router or on a card provided with it. Otherwise, ask whoever is in charge of the network for the key. Make sure to enter it carefully: network keys are case sensitive, which means that you need to type it exactly as it is written in order to successfully connect.

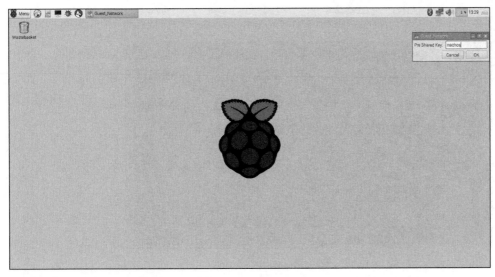

FIGURE 5-5: Entering a wireless network key

When you're happy you've entered the network key correctly, click OK. If you receive an error message, double-check your network key and that you're trying to connect to the right network: in built-up areas, there can be dozens of networks within range, and many ISPs have generic SSIDs which are difficult to tell apart.

To test your connection, see the "Testing Your Connectivity" section earlier in this chapter.

Connecting to a Wireless Network via the Console

If you are running your Pi without a graphical user interface, you can also connect to wireless networks at the terminal or console. First, check that the wireless adapter is working as it should by using the iwlist command to scan for nearby wireless access points. This list will probably be larger than a single screen, so pipe the command's output through less to pause after each screenful, like this:

```
sudo iwlist scan | less
```

This command returns a list of all the wireless networks reachable from the Pi, together with their details (see Figure 5-6). If you receive an error message at this point—in particular, one that claims the network or interface is down—and are using a USB wireless adapter, it's possible the adapter isn't receiving enough power. Reconnect the adapter through a powered USB hub; if it still doesn't work, it may not be compatible with the Raspberry Pi.

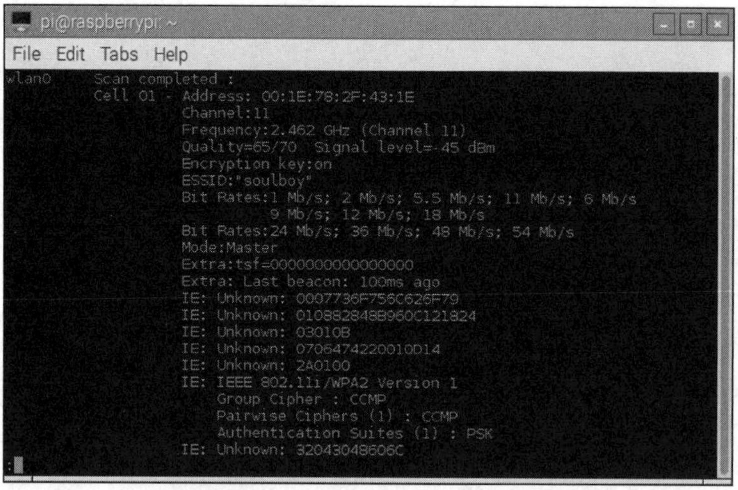

FIGURE 5-6: Scanning for wireless networks with `iwlist`

You can check the current status of the network using the `iwconfig` command. Like `ifconfig`, the `iwconfig` command enables you to check the status of a network interface and issue configuration commands. Unlike `ifconfig`, however, `iwconfig` is specifically designed for wireless networks and includes specific features for this. Type the command name at the terminal as follows:

```
iwconfig
```

The output of `iwconfig`, as shown in Figure 5-7, is split into the following sections:

- **Interface Name**—Each device has its own interface name, as with wired networks. If the interface is a wireless connection, additional details will be shown. The default name for a Pi's wireless connection is `wlan0`.

- **Standard**—The IEEE 802.11 wireless standards have a variety of different types, distinguished by a letter suffix. This section lists the standards supported by the USB wireless adapter. For the example adapter, this reads `IEEE 802.11bgn` for the network types it can address.

- **ESSID**—The SSID of the network to which the adapter is connected. If the adapter is not currently connected to a network, this will read `off/any`.

- **Mode**—The mode that the adapter is currently operating in, which will be one of the following:

  - **Managed**—A standard wireless network, with clients connecting to access points. This mode is used for almost all home and business networks.

- **Ad-Hoc**—A device-to-device wireless network, with no access points.

- **Monitor**—A special mode in which the card listens for all traffic whether or not it is the addressee. This mode is typically used in network troubleshooting for capturing wireless network traffic.

- **Repeater**—A special mode that forces a wireless card to forward traffic on to other network clients, to boost signal strength.

- **Secondary**—A subset of the Repeater mode, which forces the wireless card to act as a backup repeater.

- **Access Point**—The address of the access point to which the wireless adapter is currently connected. If the adapter isn't connected to a wireless access point, this will read Not-Associated.

- **Tx-Power**—The transmission power of the wireless adapter. The number displayed here indicates the strength of the signal that the adapter is sending: the higher the number, the stronger the signal.

- **Retry**—The current setting for the wireless adapter's transmission retry, used on congested networks. This does not normally need changing, and some cards won't allow it to be changed.

- **RTS**—The adapter's current setting for *Ready To Send* and *Clear To Send (RTS/CTS)* handshaking, used on busy networks to prevent collisions. This is normally set by the access point on connection.

- **Fragment**—The maximum fragment size, used on busy networks to split packets up into multiple fragments. This is normally set by the access point on connection.

- **Power Management**—The current status of the adapter's power management functionality, which reduces the device's power demands when the wireless network is idle. This has little effect on the Pi, but is typically enabled for battery-powered devices like a laptop.

The configuration of wireless networks on the Pi is handled using a tool called wpasupplicant. Using wpasupplicant, you can connect the Pi to almost any wireless network—regardless of whether it's protected by WPA or its newer replacement, WPA2—in both *Advanced Encryption Standard (AES)* and *Temporal Key Integrity Protocol (TKIP)* modes. Despite its name, wpasupplicant also allows connection to wireless networks using the older *Wired Equivalent Privacy (WEP)* encryption standard.

Open the wpasupplicant configuration file by typing the following command:

```
sudo nano /etc/wpa_supplicant/wpa_supplicant.conf
```

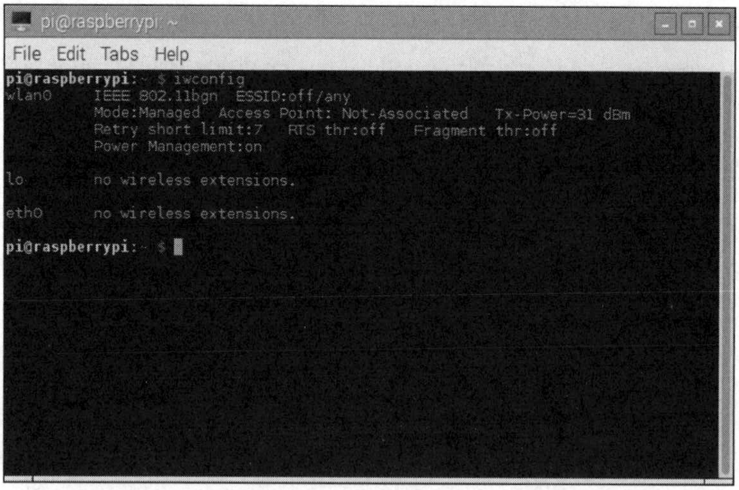

FIGURE 5-7: The output of `iwconfig` when not connected to a wireless network

Enter the following two lines, which, again, are the same for any wireless network type. Replace *Your_SSID* with the SSID for the wireless network to which you want to connect and then finish the file with the lines that match your network's encryption type:

```
network={
[Tab] ssid="Your_SSID"
```

At this point in the configuration file, the details required differ depending on the type of wireless network you are configuring. The following subsections provide instructions for completing the configuration for unencrypted, WEP and WPA networks.

No Encryption

If your wireless network has no encryption in place, finish the `wpa_supplicant.conf` file as follows:

```
[Tab] key_mgmt=NONE
}
```

Save the file with Ctrl+O and then exit nano with Ctrl+X.

WEP Encryption

If your wireless network uses WEP encryption, finish the `wpa_supplicant.conf` file as follows:

```
[Tab] key_mgmt=NONE
[Tab] wep_key0="Your_WEP_Key"
}
```

Replace *Your_WEP_Key* with the ASCII key for your wireless network's WEP encryption. Save the file with Ctrl+O and then exit nano with Ctrl+X.

WEP encryption is extremely unsecure. Readily available software can break the encryption on a WEP-protected network in just a few minutes, allowing a third party to use your network. If you're still running WEP, consider switching to WPA or WPA2 for better security.

WPA/WPA2 Encryption

If your wireless network uses WPA or WPA2 encryption, finish the wpa_supplicant. conf file as follows:

```
[Tab] key_mgmt=WPA-PSK
[Tab] psk="Your_WPA_Key"
}
```

Replace *Your_WPA_Key* with the pass phrase for your wireless network's encryption. Figure 5-8 shows an example configuration for a wireless network with the SSID "Guest_ Network" and the WPA pass phrase "nachos". Save the file with Ctrl+O and then exit nano with Ctrl+X.

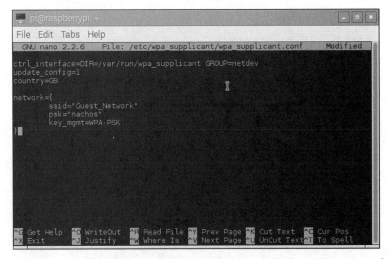

FIGURE 5-8: Editing the wpa_supplicant.conf file for a WPA-protected network

Connecting to the Wireless Network

The Pi's wireless networking is now configured and will begin the next time the Pi is restarted. To start the wireless network without rebooting, type the following:

```
sudo ifup wlan0
```

To make sure that the network is operational, unplug the Pi's Ethernet cable (if attached) and type the following:

```
sudo ping -c 1 www.raspberrypi.org
```

TIP   If you start having problems with your Pi following the installation of a USB wireless adapter, it could be due to a conflict with other USB devices. Some adapter models are known to cause problems with certain USB keyboards. For an up-to-date list of adapters that are known to be good, as well as those that are known to cause conflicts, visit www.element14. com/community/docs/DOC-44703/1/raspberry-pi-wifi-adapter-testing or the eLinux wiki at http://elinux.org/RPi_USB_Wi-Fi_Adapters.

Chapter **6**
The Raspberry Pi Configuration Tool

THE RASPBERRY PI is designed to be as controllable as possible, through the editing of configuration files found in the /boot and /etc directories on the SD card. For beginners, these files can seem dauntingly complex—although, with a little time, they soon give up their secrets—but without them, some of the more advanced features of the Pi are unavailable.

The Raspberry Pi Configuration tool is designed to solve this problem. Offering access to the majority of common configuration tasks through a simple menu-based interface, the Raspberry Pi Configuration tool makes it easy for newcomers to adjust system performance, change the memory split, alter overscan settings, or simply change the keyboard layout.

At the time of writing, the Raspberry Pi Configuration tool is exclusive to the Raspbian Linux distribution. Work is in progress to bring the tool's functionality to other operating systems, but for now it is recommended that beginners stick with the well-supported Raspbian distribution to take advantage of this most useful of configuration tools.

Although the Raspberry Pi Configuration tool is designed to be safe, some settings—in particular, the overclock option—can leave your Raspberry Pi unable to boot. Make sure you read each section in this chapter carefully before you use the tool to make any changes to your Raspberry Pi.

WARNING

Running the Tool

There are two ways to run the Raspberry Pi Configuration Tool: from the desktop, or from the console. If you are running your Pi with the desktop enabled, the former is the easiest: Simply click on the Menu button at the top-left of the screen, scroll down to Preferences, and then click on Raspberry Pi Configuration from the pop-out menu that appears.

If you are running your Pi without the desktop enabled, an alternative is to run the console-based version of the tool by typing the following command:

```
sudo raspi-config
```

You navigate the text-based menu of `raspi-config` using the cursor keys: The up- and down-arrow keys move the red selection band through the available options, and the left- and right-arrow keys move between the option list and the Select and Finish buttons below it.

Use the Enter key to activate an option when it is highlighted by the red band. The default action is always Select; so if you've highlighted an option in the menu, there's no need to press the right-arrow key to choose Select before pressing Enter.

Any option from the desktop version of the Raspberry Pi Configuration tool is also available in the console-based version; the remainder of this chapter focuses on using the desktop version.

> **TIP** When you make changes in either version of the Raspberry Pi Configuration tool, you are prompted to reboot to make those changes active. You can choose to reboot immediately or dismiss the notification to exit the application without rebooting, but the changes will not be activated until the next time you reboot the Raspberry Pi.

The System Tab

The Raspberry Pi Configuration tool's window is split into four *tabs*: System, Interfaces, Performance, and Localisation. The default tab is System (see Figure 6-1), which provides a variety of utilities for configuring the Raspbian operating system to your requirements. You can navigate the window using the mouse: click on any button to execute that command, click on text boxes to change their contents, or click on toggles to switch settings on and off.

The System menu is split into eight subsections, described below.

Filesystem

The first option, Expand Filesystem (under the Filesystem section), offers the capability to increase the Raspbian filesystem to take up the full space available on the SD card. If you have installed Raspbian via NOOBS, this step has already been done for you and can safely be ignored.

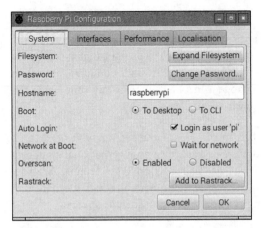

FIGURE 6-1: The Raspberry Pi Configuration tool in desktop interface mode, showing the System tab

To run the filesystem expansion, click the Expand Filesystem button. This is required only if you have manually installed Raspbian on your microSD card; if you are using the NOOBS installer, the filesystem will already have been expanded to its maximum size. Once the initial resize finishes, you must reboot the Pi to finish resizing the filesystem.

When the Pi reboots, it performs the remainder of the filesystem expansion. On larger or slower cards, this can take a little time. It's important that the Pi not be disturbed during this process, because if the power is lost, the Pi's filesystem can be corrupted. If this happens, you will lose all the files stored on the Pi's SD card and will have to reinstall your operating system from scratch. The card itself, however, will not be damaged.

Password

By default, Raspbian includes a single non-root user account named *pi*. This account is used for the day-to-day operation of the Pi, and comes with the default password *raspberry*. Although this is fine for private use, if you have your Pi on a publicly accessible network—including a Wi-Fi hotspot or other Internet connection—it's a good idea to change at least the password, if not also the username, to improve security, especially given that Raspbian runs a Secure Shell (SSH) server by default to allow remote logins from the local network.

It is possible to change the password manually using the `passwd` command (see Chapter 3, "Linux System Administration", for details), but beginners might find it easier to change the password using the Raspberry Pi Configuration tool. Click Change Password (under the Password section) to enter a new password for the current user, but make sure you don't forget it; otherwise, you'll find it difficult to log back in!

Hostname

A system's *hostname* is the name it uses to identify itself on the network. When you use the console or terminal on the Pi, you see the hostname as part of the prompt that accepts your command. Hostnames should be unique, which can cause a problem if you have more than one Raspberry Pi on your network. You can change a Pi's hostname at any time using the Hostname section of the Raspberry Pi Configuration tool.

When typing a new hostname into the text box in the Hostname section, you need to be aware of the rules of a hostname. Because hostnames adhere to an international standard, one of a group of standards known as a *Request For Comments* or *RFC*, certain characters aren't allowed—a hostname should contain only letters and numbers, although it can include hyphens so long as they aren't at the beginning or end, and cannot include spaces.

You can opt for a descriptive hostname, such as living-room-pi, or name your devices based on a theme, such as bladerunner for science fiction films. You can confirm your change with the OK button, but the new hostname won't come into effect until you reboot the Pi.

Boot

Normally, Raspbian loads into the graphical user interface known as the desktop. It does so to ensure that the Pi is ready to use as quickly as possible. Many common uses of the Pi—including using it as a web server or for recording video or still images with the Raspberry Pi Camera Module—work fine at the text-based console, however, without the need to load the desktop graphical user interface, speeding the time taken to load the Pi and reducing the amount of memory wasted on software you're not actively using.

You have two options in the Boot section: To Desktop, and to CLI. Clicking on the round radio button next to To Desktop will have the Pi automatically boot into the graphical user interface; clicking on the radio button next to To CLI will have the Pi remain at the console until the desktop is manually loaded with the `startx` command.

Auto Login

By default, Raspbian automatically logs you in as the user pi when the system is powered on. This makes the Pi ready for use faster, as you don't need to log in; it also introduces a potential security concern if you use your Pi in a shared environment.

Clicking in the box marked Login as user pi to remove the check mark means that you'll have to type the username and password in every time you turn the Pi on or reboot it. This is best used in combination with the option to change the user's password: It doesn't take a master spy to try logging in to a Raspberry Pi with the default user name pi and password raspberry!

Network at Boot

To make the Pi ready for use as quickly as possible, Raspbian doesn't wait for a network connection to come up before continuing the boot process. Normally, this is fine; if you're using your Pi to provide certain network services, though, it can cause issues with applications that load at startup and expect a network connection that hasn't yet been made ready.

To solve this issue, simply click the box Wait for network to add a check mark. Be aware, though, that this will delay the boot process if a network isn't available.

Overscan

Many TV sets feature *overscan*, which means the visible picture area is slightly smaller than the transmitted picture. In broadcast TV, this is often used to hide additional data such as time code information, but in computing, it can result in the edges of the display becoming hidden. By contrast, using a TV signal with a modern monitor can reveal the previously hidden edges with their additional data.

You may need to adjust the overscan for one of two reasons: The image from your Pi is surrounded by black bars, in which case the overscan needs to be reduced or disabled altogether; or the image from your Pi extends beyond the visible edges of your screen, in which case the overscan needs to be increased. The latter is most common when using the Pi's composite video output (see Chapter 2, "Getting Started with the Raspberry Pi") with an older TV set.

From the desktop version of the Raspberry Pi Configuration tool, it's only possible to enable or disable overscan. You can do this by clicking on the radio button next to either option in the Overscan section, clicking OK to apply, and then rebooting the Pi. To control the size of the overscan to maximise the visible screen area on an old TV, see Chapter 7, "Advanced Raspberry Pi Configuration".

Rastrack

Rastrack is an interactive map of Raspberry Pi created by Ryan Walmsley. It is designed to help enthusiasts in close proximity to find each other and to show areas of the world that have a large concentration of Raspberry Pi users. The service is voluntary and is not connected with the Raspberry Pi Foundation.

To appear on the Rastrack map, a Raspberry Pi must be registered. This is an optional process, and if you have any concerns about privacy, you can skip it without losing any features or functionality. If you want your Pi to appear on the map, however, click the Add to Rastrack button in the Rastrack section of the Raspberry Pi Configuration tool.

Confirm you have read the message that appears, and then enter your name—or a nickname—in the Username field. Enter an email address in the Email Address field, and finally click OK to add your Raspberry Pi to the map. You don't need to give your location; instead, the software uses your Internet connection to place your Pi on the map. It does not give your exact location at street level, but it does show others roughly where in the world you and your Pi are located. To see the map, visit `http://rastrack.co.uk` in your web browser.

The Interfaces Tab

The next tab in the Raspberry Pi Configuration tool, labelled Interfaces, allows you to enable or disable various ancillary interfaces of the system-on-chip processor that powers the Pi (see Figure 6-2). This is typically required if you're adding new hardware to the Pi, particularly through the CSI or GPIO ports; usually, the documentation that comes with your new hardware will tell you if enabling a default-off interface is required. You can toggle any interface by clicking on the Enabled or Disabled radio button next to its name, but the change will not take place until you reboot the Pi.

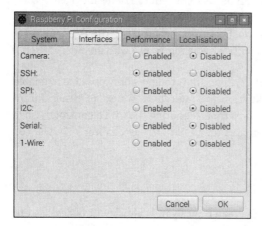

FIGURE 6-2: The Raspberry Pi Configuration tool Interfaces tab

 Disabling an interface that is currently active will mean that any hardware that relies on that interface will stop working the next time you reboot the Pi. To fix this, simply go back into the Raspberry Pi Configuration tool, click the Interfaces tab, re-enable the interface, and click OK before rebooting the Pi.

Camera

Enable this interface only if you have a Raspberry Pi Camera Module (see Chapter 15, "The Raspberry Pi Camera Module") attached to your system. If you remove the Camera Module from your Raspberry Pi, you can disable it again using the same section of the Raspberry Pi Configuration tool. Although, strictly speaking, this step isn't required—having the Raspberry Pi configured for a camera that isn't connected will do no harm—it can help to keep things tidy.

SSH

The *Secure Shell (SSH)* provides a way to use the Pi's terminal over a network, creating an encrypted connection between the Pi and any other computer capable of running an SSH *client*. This can even be used to control a Pi that does not have a monitor or keyboard attached—known as a *headless* system—or to transfer files to and from the Pi's storage.

By default, the SSH server on the Raspberry Pi is enabled. If you know you aren't going to use SSH, you can disable it here to save a small amount of memory and reduce the chance of your system being attacked on a shared network. If you do keep the SSH server enabled, be sure to change your password from the System tab to keep your Pi secure!

SPI

The *serial peripheral interface (SPI)* is a communications standard used by the Pi to control or otherwise communicate with external hardware over the GPIO port (see Chapter 14, "The GPIO Port") Many add-on boards for the Raspberry Pi require SPI support; check the documentation included with your hardware to see if you need to enable SPI support manually through the Raspberry Pi Configuration tool or whether the vendor has an installation script that will do it for you automatically.

I²C

The *inter-integrated circuit (I²C)* interface is similar to SPI, in that it is used to control or communicate with external hardware via the GPIO port. Add-on boards that don't use SPI typically use I²C instead. As with SPI, check the documentation included with your hardware to see if you need to enable I²C support manually through the Raspberry Pi Configuration tool or whether the vendor has an installation script that will do it for you automatically.

Serial

By default, the Raspberry Pi uses the serial connection on the GPIO header to provide a terminal into which you can log in and control the Pi without a monitor attached. Some add-on boards use this serial connection for other purposes, such as driving an external display, in which case the serial interface needs to be disabled. Before disabling it here, however, check the documentation for your hardware; some boards need the interface disabled completely, but others require you to make changes to its configuration instead.

1-Wire

The *1-Wire* interface is yet another alternative to I²C and SPI, offering connectivity to and communication with sensors and other external hardware. Typically, 1-Wire is used to connect simple sensors—such as devices for reading the temperature or humidity of the environment—to the Raspberry Pi, and is rarely used by add-on boards. If you're using 1-Wire devices with the Pi's GPIO port, make sure to enable the feature here.

Performance

The Performance tab of the Raspberry Pi Configuration tool provides settings to increase the computational power of the Pi by *overclocking* its processor or increasing the *GPU memory* (see Figure 6-3). This can help eke out a little more power from your Pi, but comes with risks.

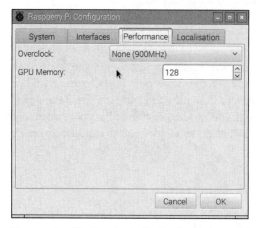

FIGURE 6-3: The Raspberry Pi Configuration tool Performance tab

Overclock

Overclocking refers to the process of running a device at a speed higher than its manufacturers intended. The Raspberry Pi's system-on-chip processor can be run above its default speed to boost the performance of the system. Such performance comes at a price, however, in that the chip will run hotter than before, will draw more power, and may suffer from a shorter lifespan than a Pi running at its default speed.

Although it's possible to alter the performance of the processor manually (see Chapter 7, "Advanced Raspberry Pi Configuration"), the safest way is to use the Raspberry Pi Configuration tool. This limits you to a selection of preconfigured overclock settings that are known to be safe for use with most Raspberry Pis. The particular settings that appear will depend on the model of Raspberry Pi you are using; the newer models have a faster default speed than the older models, and therefore have correspondingly fewer options available.

While the overclock settings available to the Raspberry Pi Configuration tool are reasonably safe and will not affect your warranty, not all Raspberry Pis can reach the top speeds. If you find your Pi is unstable—particularly if you are experiencing corruption of files on the SD card—drop down to the setting below the one you're currently using or return the Pi to its default speed.

WARNING

To overclock your Raspberry Pi, click the drop-down box in the Overclock section and choose a setting. The default speed for your model of Raspberry Pi is listed with the label None. Higher speeds carry labels describing how severe an overclock you are attempting.

If you want to try overclocking your Pi, click on one of the higher-speed options in the drop-down list. Depending on the model, these may include Modest, Medium, High, and Turbo settings. Almost all Raspberry Pi models should be able to use the Modest setting, which simply increases the processor's clock speed a minor amount. Many will also be able to use Medium, which increases the voltage applied to the processor to reach higher speeds and also increases the memory speed.

The remaining two settings might not work on all Raspberry Pi models. The system-on-chip processor at the heart of a Raspberry Pi is a complex circuit that differs in its ability to be overclocked from unit to unit—even two Pis from the same batch. If you want to use the Turbo mode, make sure to first back up all your important files stored on the Pi. If you do start to have problems, drop down to the High setting or lower, and your Pi should return to normal.

All changes made in the Performance section only take effect the next time the Pi reboots. If you select a speed higher than the Pi can tolerate, it might not boot correctly. If you find your Pi loads to a black screen or constantly restarts itself without prompting you to log in, you have chosen a speed that is too high. Hold down the Shift key as the Pi loads up; this temporarily bypasses the overclocking setting, loading the Pi at its default speed. Once the Pi is booted, release the Shift key and log in. Then load the Raspberry Pi Configuration tool and enter the Overclock section to choose a more conservative setting.

GPU Memory

Depending on your Raspberry Pi model, you will have 256 MB, 512 MB, or 1 GB of memory available to the system. This memory is split between the system-on-chip's general-purpose processor, known as the *central processing unit (CPU)*, and the graphics processor, known as the *graphics processing unit (GPU)*. By default, 128 MB of memory is reserved for the GPU on most models or 64 MB on models with 256 MB of memory; the remainder is given over to the CPU.

If you're not using the graphics processor, such as when the Pi is used as a web server with no display connected, you can reduce the amount of memory reserved for the GPU by using the GPU Memory section in the Raspberry Pi Configuration tool. Click in the text box next to GPU Memory, and then enter a new value. The minimum you should give to the GPU to ensure proper operation is 16 MB, which you enter simply as the number 16. If you have a Raspberry Pi model with 512 MB or 1 GB of memory, you can increase the split as high as 448 MB for 512 MB models or 880 MB for 1 GB models, which might improve performance when you're using the GPU to render complex 3D scenes in games.

You can choose other values, but you should restrict this to doubling the value at each step. For example, 16 MB can be increased to 32 MB, 32 MB to 64 MB, 64 MB to 128 MB, and so on. Choosing an uneven value, such as 17 MB, will not harm the Pi, but might result in a different value being used than the one selected.

As with the Overclock option, your Raspberry Pi will not use the new setting until the next time it is rebooted.

Localisation

The Localisation tab provides a way for users in countries other than the UK to configure the Pi for their needs (see Figure 6-4). By default, Raspbian sets itself to use UK English language settings, UTC time zone settings, and keyboard layout. Users in other countries will find that certain keys on their keyboards don't type the right characters, particularly those using non-QWERTY keyboard layouts such as AZERTY or QWERTZ.

Locale

Clicking the Set Locale button in the Locale section provides a list of all the languages, countries, and character sets available to the Pi. The list is extensive and includes most common languages.

FIGURE 6-4: The Raspberry Pi Configuration tool Localisation tab

Language

Each language in the drop-down box is named in a particular way. The letters at the beginning are the language code used by the operating system, and the name in brackets is a friendly name representing the language. Scroll through the list with your mouse, and then click on the language you want the Pi to use as its default.

Country

The language setting is independent to the country setting; it's possible to choose a language like Gaelic with a country where it is rarely spoken, such as Botswana. Use the mouse to choose the country in which you reside, and then click on your selection to have the operating system tailor certain settings, such as the way currency is displayed.

Character Set

Each language on a computer has one or more *character sets* associated with it. This is the list of possible letters, numbers, and symbols that can be displayed in that language. Most languages have more than one option here, but the majority of users will need to select only one: UTF-8, which specifies the Unicode Transformation Format 8-bit encoding—the most common and compatible encoding standard.

Confirm your selections in these submenus with the OK button on the Locale window, and then apply them from the main Raspberry Pi Configuration window by clicking on its OK button. As with most settings, the new locale takes full effect only when you reboot the Pi.

TIP   Changing the locale of the system won't translate *all* applications into your native language. Where a translation is available, it is used; otherwise, English text displays as the default. Changing the locale also has no effect on command names: echo is still called echo, for example, regardless of your locale.

Timezone

The system clock of the Raspberry Pi is set to Universal Time by default. If you live in a different time zone, your Pi will display the wrong time. Clicking the Set Timezone button pops up a secondary window with two further options: Area and Location.

Area

The Area drop-down box lists geographic areas such as the Atlantic, the US, and Europe. Use the cursor keys to select your local area, and then press Enter. The list also includes some nongeographic options, offering the ability to directly set time zones such as EST, CET, and GMT; these are more readily viewable by selecting the generic Etc option here and choosing a time zone from the Location drop-down. Scroll through the list with your mouse, and click to make a selection.

Location

With a general geographic area selected, click on the Location drop-down to bring up a list of cities local to that area. If your particular city isn't listed, look for larger nearby cities and choose one of these. If the Etc option has been selected in the Area drop-down box, the Location section instead shows a list of time zones that you can manually select. When doing so, however, the system cannot automatically adjust the system clock for local daylight savings time changes.

Keyboard

The Keyboard section controls one of the most important options in the internationalisation menu: It allows you to alter the layout of your keyboard. By default, the Pi is configured to expect a British English keyboard in the standard QWERTY layout. If you use a different keyboard layout, such as a QWERTZ, AZERTY, Dvorak, or US layout, click the Set Keyboard button to pop up a new window where you can make and test your selection (see Figure 6-5).

Country

In the Country section of the Keyboard Layout window, click either the country in which you reside or the country in which the layout of your keyboard represents the primary language.

FIGURE 6-5: The Raspberry Pi Configuration tool Keyboard Layout window

Variant

With a country selected, look through the list of variants to the right of the window and select the one that most closely matches the layout of your keyboard. If you're not sure, click on the closest and try typing in the box labelled "Type here to test your keyboard". If you find that what you're typing doesn't match what's appearing, especially with symbol keys such as the single- and double-quote keys, choose a different variant from the list until you get a match.

Apply your changes with the OK button on the Keyboard Layout window, and then again by clicking OK on the main Raspberry Pi Configuration tool window.

WiFi Country

Wi-Fi radios are permitted to transmit on particular frequencies, which are split into smaller *channels*. The channels available to use are regulated by communications authorities and vary from country to country. Click the Set WiFi Country button and choose your country from the drop-down dialogue that appears.

Note that choosing a country other than your own is likely to be in violation of radio licensing laws and could result in the Wi-Fi radio transmitting on an unlicensed frequency. So make sure to change the setting before taking your Raspberry Pi on holiday!

Chapter 7

Advanced Raspberry Pi Configuration

OWING TO ITS origins in embedded computing, the BCM2835 chip at the heart of the Raspberry Pi doesn't have anything like a PC's *Basic Input/Output System (BIOS)* menu where various low-level system settings can be configured. Instead, it relies on text files containing configuration strings that are loaded by the chip when the power is switched on.

Before taking a look at the various options available in these files—config.txt and cmdline.txt—a word of warning: changing some of these settings from their defaults can result in a Pi that doesn't boot until the files are reverted, in the best case, and that can physically damage the system, in the worst case. These potentially dangerous settings are highlighted with warnings in this chapter.

If you're using the Raspbian distribution, the easiest way to change the majority of settings is to use the raspi-config utility (refer to Chapter 6, "The Raspberry Pi Configuration Tool"). These instructions are provided for those on other distributions or those who would prefer to do things manually.

Editing Configuration Files via NOOBS

If you edited your configuration files in such a way that your operating system no longer boots, the easiest way to restore them is to use the NOOBS software (refer to Chapter 2, "Getting Started with the Raspberry Pi"). If you installed your operating system via NOOBS, you can use the tool to edit the configuration files; if you installed your operating system manually, you must remove the SD card and use a second computer to edit the files.

To load NOOBS after you used it to install your operating system, hold down the Shift key as you apply power to the Pi. Doing so bypasses loading of the operating system and instead boots into NOOBS, but with a new option: the Edit Config button at the top of the menu (see Figure 7-1).

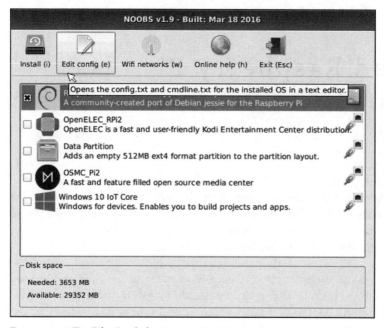

FIGURE 7-1: The Edit Config button in NOOBS

Clicking the Edit Config button (or pressing the E key), after choosing an installed operating system from the list, loads a text editor window with the two configuration files—`config.txt` and `cmdline.txt`—preloaded (see Figure 7-2). You can make changes as described in this chapter in the text editor with your keyboard and mouse and then click OK at the bottom right to save your changes to the SD card. When you finish making changes, click Exit on the main window to boot the Pi with its new settings.

> **TIP** If you have a Raspberry Pi that is connected to the Internet, you can also click the Online Help button or press the H key on the keyboard to load a web browser that will take you to the Raspberry Pi Help pages. This is an invaluable resource if your Pi isn't working properly, allowing you to find help or post a question to get your Pi computing back on track.

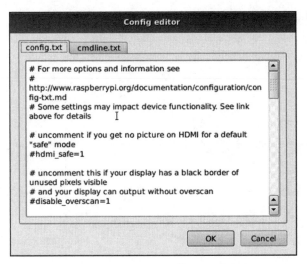

FIGURE 7-2: Editing configuration files in NOOBS

Hardware Settings: config.txt

The Pi's hardware is controlled by settings contained in a file called `config.txt`, which is located in the `/boot` directory (see Figure 7-3). This file tells the Pi how to set up its various inputs and outputs, and at what speed the BCM283x chip and its connected memory module should run.

If you're having problems with graphics output, such as the image not filling the screen or spilling over the edge, `config.txt` is where you can fix it. Normally, the file contains comments on its usage with no active settings or, on some distributions, simply not present; this just means that the Pi will operate using its preset defaults. If you want to make changes and the file isn't there, just create a new text file called `config.txt` and fill in the settings you want to change.

The `config.txt` file can control almost all aspects of the Pi's hardware. The file is read only when the system first starts up. Any changes made while the Pi is running won't take effect until the system is restarted or switched off and back on again. In the event that you don't want the changes, simply deleting the file from the `/boot` directory should be enough to restore the defaults once more. If the Pi won't boot with your new settings, remove the SD card and delete `config.txt` from the `boot` partition on another PC and then reinsert the card into the Pi and try again.

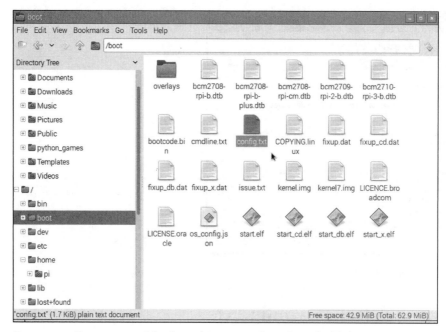

FIGURE 7-3: The contents of the /boot directory, with config.txt highlighted

Modifying the Display

Usually, the Raspberry Pi will detect the type of display that's connected and alter its settings accordingly. Sometimes, however, this automatic detection doesn't work. This is often the case when a Raspberry Pi from one country is connected to an older TV from another country. If you connect your Pi to your TV and don't see anything, you may need to override these defaults.

You can use various settings in the `config.txt` file to improve or alter the video output. These settings, and their possible values, are described in the following list:

WARNING   Manually adjusting the High-Definition Multimedia Interface (HDMI) or composite video output settings can leave your Pi unable to communicate with your monitor. It's usually best to use the automatically detected settings, unless you're unable to see a picture in the first place.

- **overscan_left**—This setting moves the picture inward a set number of pixels to compensate for a TV's *overscan*. If the text on the Pi is disappearing off the edge of the screen, adjusting the overscan will fix it. Values should be given as the number of pixels to skip.

- **overscan_right**—This setting does the same job as overscan_left, but on the right side of the screen.

- **overscan_top**—Again, this setting ignores a certain number of pixels, but this time on the top of the screen.

- **overscan_bottom**—This setting can be used to skip a number of pixels from the bottom of the display. Typically, the values for all the overscan_ settings are the same, creating a regular border around the display.

- **disable_overscan**—If you use a monitor or TV via HDMI, you may find that your image has a black border around it. To get rid of this border, you can disable any default overscan settings by setting this value to 1.

- **framebuffer_width**—This value is measured in pixels, and adjusting it will change the width of the console. If text appears too small on your screen, try changing this value to a value lower than the default width of the connected display.

- **framebuffer_height**—This setting affects the size of the console in the same way as framebuffer_width, but vertically rather than horizontally.

- **framebuffer_depth**—Controls the colour depth of the console in bits per pixel. The default is 16 bits per pixel, which gives 65,536 colours. Other values are valid, including 8 bits per pixel (256 colours), 24 bits per pixel (around 16.7 million colours), and 32 bits per pixel (around 1 billion colours), but may cause graphical corruption.

- **framebuffer_ignore_alpha**—Set to 1, this value disables the *alpha channel*, which controls transparency in the console. Disabling the alpha channel is not normally required, but it may correct graphical corruption caused when setting framebuffer_depth to 32 bits per pixel.

- **sdtv_mode**—This value affects the analogue composite video output of the Pi, adjusting it to operate in various countries. By default, the Pi uses the North American version of the NTSC video standard; users in other countries may need to change this value to get a picture on an analogue TV. Possible values are

  - **0**—NTSC, the North American video standard

  - **1**—NTSC-J, the Japanese video standard

  - **2**—PAL, the video standard for the UK and other countries

  - **3**—PAL-M, the Brazilian video standard

- **sdtv_aspect**—Controls the aspect ratio of the analogue composite output. If the picture looks stretched or squished, alter this value to correspond to your TV's aspect ratio. Possible values are

- **1**—4:3 aspect ratio, common on older sets

- **2**—14:9 aspect ratio, common for smaller widescreen TVs

- **3**—16:9 aspect ratio, common for modern widescreen TVs

- **hdmi_mode**—In addition to setting the video mode for the analogue composite output, it's also possible to override automatic resolution detection on the HDMI port. Doing so proves handy if you want to run your Pi at a lower resolution than the display's native resolution so as to make things more readable from a distance. Appendix C, "HDMI Display Modes", lists the possible values for this setting.

- **hdmi_drive**—It's also possible to alter the voltage output by the HDMI port. This is important when you're using an HDMI to DVI adapter because HDMI and DVI voltages differ slightly. If you find that your picture is snowy or blown out with too bright an image, try altering this setting. Possible values are

  - **1**—DVI output voltages. In this mode, no audio is included on the HDMI cable.

  - **2**—HDMI output voltages. In this mode, audio is included on the HDMI cable.

- **hdmi_force_hotplug**—Forces the Raspberry Pi to use the HDMI port, even if it doesn't detect a connected display. A value of 0 allows the Pi to attempt to detect the display, while a value of 1 forces the Pi to use HDMI regardless.

- **hdmi_group**—Sets the HDMI group mode to CEA or DMT. You should change this setting according to the display type you're trying to connect before using hdmi_mode to control the output resolution and frequency. The two possible values are

  - **1**—Sets the HDMI group to that defined by the Consumer Electronics Association of America (CEA). Use this setting when the Pi is connected to a high-definition television (HDTV) over HDMI and use the first settings list from Appendix C.

  - **2**—Sets the HDMI group to that defined by the Video Electronics Standards Association (VESA) in the Display Monitor Timings (DMT) specification. Use this setting when the Pi is connected to a computer monitor over DVI and use the second settings list from Appendix C.

- **hdmi_safe**—Forces the Pi to use a preset collection of HDMI settings designed to provide maximum compatibility with displays connected to the HDMI port. Setting this to a value of 1 is equivalent to setting hdmi_force_hotpug=1, config_hdmi_boost=4, hdmi_group=1, hdmi_mode=1, and disable_overscan=0.

- **config_hdmi_boost**—Some monitors require more power on the HDMI output to operate. If your picture looks snowy, try increasing this value in stages from 1 (for short cables) to 7 (for long cables).

Each option in config.txt should be on its own line, with the option name followed by an equals sign (=) and then the required value. For example, to tell the Pi to use a PAL-format analogue TV with a 4:3 aspect ratio and a 20-pixel overscan on all sides, enter the following lines in config.txt:

```
sdtv_mode=2
sdtv_aspect=1
overscan_left=20
overscan_right=20
overscan_top=20
overscan_bottom=20
```

To tell the Pi to use a DVI display through the HDMI port in the 720p60 format with no overscan at all, use the following values instead:

```
hdmi_group=1
hdmi_mode=4
hdmi_drive=1
disable_overscan=1
```

For the changes to take effect, you must restart the Pi. If you find that your changes disabled the Pi's video output on your monitor, insert the SD card into another computer and either modify the config.txt file with new settings or delete it altogether to restore the defaults.

Boot Options

You can also use the config.txt file to control how Linux is loaded on the Raspberry Pi. Although the most common method for controlling the loading of the Linux kernel is to use a separate file called cmdline.txt (which you learn about later in this chapter), it is possible to use just config.txt. The following options control the boot process:

- **disable_commandline_tags**—This tells the start.elf module that loads first during the Pi's boot process to skip filling in memory locations past 0x100 before loading the Linux kernel. This option should not be changed, as doing so can cause Linux to load incorrectly and crash.

- **cmdline**—The name of a text file containing the command-line parameters to be passed to the Linux kernel. This can be used in place of the cmdline.txt file, which is usually found in the /boot directory.

- **kernel**—The name of the kernel file to be loaded.

- **ramfsfile**—The name of the initial RAM file system (RAMFS) to be loaded. This should rarely be modified, unless you've built a new initial file system with which to experiment.

- **init_uart_baud**—The speed of the serial console in bits per second. The default is 115200, but lower values may improve the connection if the Pi is used with an older hardware serial terminal.

- **enable_uart**—By default, the Raspberry Pi 3 does not have an active serial console. To enable it, place a 1 after this option; your Pi 3 will behave like any early model with regards to the serial console.

Overclocking the Raspberry Pi

The `config.txt` file not only controls the graphics outputs of the Pi's BCM283x processor but also enables you to control the chip in other ways. In particular, it allows you to alter the speed at which the chip runs, increasing its performance at the expense of the part's lifespan—a process known as *overclocking*.

WARNING   Adjusting any of the settings listed in this section can result in damage to your Pi. In particular, changing settings corresponding to memory, GPU, or CPU voltages will set a fuse in the chip, which invalidates the Raspberry Pi's warranty even if the setting is returned to normal before any damage is done. Damage caused when using these settings will not be put right by the Raspberry Pi Foundation or by the retailer from whom you purchased your Pi. If in doubt, *don't alter these settings*: the performance gains through overclocking are rarely worth the risk to the Pi.

The BCM2835 multimedia processor at the heart of the Pi is a system-on-chip (SoC) design split into two main parts: the graphics processor (GPU) and the central processor (CPU). Simply put, the CPU handles all the day-to-day processing tasks, and the GPU handles drawing things on the screen, in both 2D and 3D.

Using `config.txt`, you can overclock one or both parts of the BCM2835. You can also increase the speed at which the memory module—located on top of the chip in a package-on-package (PoP) mounting format—operates.

Boosting the operating frequency of these components results in a small increase in the Pi's performance. An increase to the GPU's clock frequency means that 3D graphics (such as game graphics) will render at a faster pace and that video will be decoded quicker for smoother playback; and increasing the CPU's clock frequency will boost overall performance of the device, as will increasing the memory's frequency.

The reason the Pi isn't provided with higher operating speeds in the first place is related to the chip's lifespan. The BCM2835 is rated by its manufacturer, Broadcom, to operate at a speed of 700 MHz to 1,000 MHz depending on its revision, while the newer BCM2836 and BCM2837 chips run at higher speeds. Increasing the speed above these officially rated levels may work, but it will also have a deleterious effect on the lifespan of the chip. Unlike a desktop processor, SoC designs rarely have much headroom for overclocking.

Overclocking Settings

If you're willing to take the risk of breaking the Pi—a process known as *bricking* in embedded device circles—for the sake of a small performance gain, there are settings in `config.txt` that can help. The following settings control performance of the Pi's SoC:

- **arm_freq**—Sets the core clock frequency of the CPU portion of the BCM2835, for a boost in general-purpose performance. The default speed is model-dependent.

- **gpu_freq**—Sets the clock frequency of the GPU portion of the BCM2835, for a boost in graphics performance across all operations. The default speed is 250 MHz. Additionally, you can adjust individual portions of the GPU's hardware using the following options:

  - **core_freq**—Sets the core clock frequency of the GPU, leaving the other frequencies alone, to improve overall GPU performance. The default speed is model-dependent.

  - **h264_freq**—Sets the clock frequency of the GPU's hardware video decoder to improve playback of H.264 video data. The default speed is model-dependent.

  - **isp_freq**—Sets the clock frequency of the image sensor pipeline, for improving the capture rate of connected video hardware (such as a camera). The default speed is model-dependent.

  - **v3d_freq**—Sets the clock frequency of the GPU's 3D rendering hardware, for a boost in visualisation and gaming performance. The default speed is model-dependent.

- **sdram_freq**—Sets the clock speed of the random access memory (RAM) chip on the Pi, to give the entire system a small increase in performance. The default speed is model-dependent.

- **init_uart_clock**—Sets the default clock speed of the *Universal Asynchronous Receiver/ Transmitter (UART)*, used to control the serial console. The default is 3000000, which sets a speed of 3 MHz. Altering this option is likely to have little effect beyond corrupting the output of the serial console.

- **init_emmc_clock**—Sets the default clock speed of the SD card controller. The default is 80000000, which sets a speed of 80 MHz. Increasing this value can result in faster reading and writing from the SD card, but can also lead to data corruption.

As an example, to overclock the CPU of a Raspberry Pi Model B+ to 800 MHz, the GPU to 280 MHz, and the RAM to 420 MHz, enter the following options into `config.txt`, one per line:

```
arm_freq=800
gpu_freq=280
sdram_freq=420
```

As with adjusting the display configuration, any changes made regarding overclocking won't take effect until the Pi is restarted. To return the settings to normal, you can either delete the entire `config.txt` file or—if you're using it to control the display settings as well—simply delete the lines that deal with overclocking, and then restart the Pi.

If you have overclocked your Pi and it no longer boots, either place the SD card into another computer to edit the configuration and then try again or hold down the Shift key while the Pi boots to temporarily disable your new settings and run the Pi at its normal clock speed. If you want to disable any option in `config.txt` without deleting the line, place a # (hash) character at the beginning of the line to comment it out.

Overvoltage Settings

If you're overclocking your Pi, you will eventually hit a brick wall past which the device won't go. The precise point at which the Pi won't reliably overclock depends on the individual device because of natural variations in the chip introduced during the manufacturing stage. For some users, this limit may be as low as 800 MHz; others may find that they can push their Pi as high as 1 GHz (1000 MHz) without issue.

If you want to eke a little more performance out of your Pi, there is a way to potentially boost this upper limit: a process known as *overvoltage* or *overvolting*. The Pi's BCM283x SoC processor and the associated memory module usually run at 1.2 V. It's possible, although potentially inadvisable, to override this default and force the components to run at higher or lower voltages. Boosting the voltage means boosting the signal within the chip, making it more likely to hit higher speeds; it also means that the chip runs hotter, reducing its lifespan dramatically compared to overclocking alone.

WARNING Setting any of the voltage options in `config.txt` causes a fuse within the BCM2835 to trip in a way that cannot be reset. It's a foolproof way to tell if someone has been attempting to overclock the chip outside its rated specifications, and *renders your warranty null and void*— even if the cause of failure is unrelated to overclocking. If you return a Pi for replacement under warranty and the fuse is tripped, *it will not be replaced*. Do not attempt to overvolt a Pi that you cannot afford to replace yourself.

Unlike the previously described settings, which are provided in `config.txt` as absolute values, the voltage adjustment is carried out using values relative to the Pi's stock 1.2 V setting. For each whole number above zero, the voltage is increased by 0.025 V from stock. For each whole number below zero, the voltage is decreased by 0.025 V from stock.

The voltage adjustment settings have upper and lower limits of 8 and –16, equivalent to 0.2 V above stock voltage or 1.4 V absolute and 0.4 V below stock voltage or 0.8 V absolute. The voltage must be adjusted in whole numbers, and it cannot be adjusted below 0.8 V (–16) or above 1.4 V (8).

The following settings are accessible from `config.txt`:

- **over_voltage**—Adjusts the BCM2835's core voltage. Values are given as a whole number (an integer) corresponding to 0.025 V above or below the default value (0), with a lower limit of –16 and an upper limit of 8.

- **over_voltage_sdram**—Adjusts the voltage given to the memory chip on the Pi. As with `over_voltage`, values are given as a whole number corresponding to 0.025 V above or below the stock (0), with a lower limit of –16 and an upper limit of 8. Additionally, you can adjust voltages for individual memory components using the following options:

  - **over_voltage_sdram_c**—Adjusts the voltage given to the memory controller. Acceptable values are the same as with `over_voltage_sdram`.

  - **over_voltage_sdram_i**—Adjusts the voltage given to the memory's input/output (I/O) system. Acceptable values are the same as with `over_voltage_sdram`.

  - **over_voltage_sdram_p**—Adjusts the voltage given to the memory's physical layer (PHY) components. Acceptable values are the same as with `over_voltage_sdram`.

As an example, the following lines entered into `config.txt` give the BCM2835 a small boost of 0.05 V to 1.25 V and the memory chip a bigger boost of 0.1 V to 1.3 V:

```
over_voltage=2
over_voltage_sdram=4
```

As with other settings, deleting the lines from `config.txt` or deleting the file itself will return things to normal. Unlike the other settings in this section, however, the evidence remains in the form of a blown fuse in the BCM2835, rendering the Pi's warranty null and void even after the default settings are restored.

Disabling L2 Cache

The Pi's BCM283x SoC processor has 128K of *Layer 2 cache memory* onboard. Although this memory is small, it's extremely fast. It's used to temporarily store—or *cache*—data and instructions between the slower main memory and the processor itself to improve performance.

Because of the BCM283x's origins as a multimedia processor targeted at set-top boxes, this L2 cache is designed to be used by the GPU portion of the chip alone. Unlike a traditional processor, the CPU doesn't have a L2 cache of its own.

Using `config.txt`, you can tell the BCM283x to allow or disallow its CPU portion access to the L2 cache memory. In some cases, doing so can improve performance. In other cases, it can harm performance because of the physical location of the cache being a relatively long distance from the CPU section of the chip and closer to the GPU.

Use of the L2 cache memory also requires a Linux distribution that was compiled with the cache memory in mind. Raspbian is one such distribution, and it comes with the L2 cache enabled for improved performance. It should be left this way, and disabled only if it causes problems with alternative operating systems.

To switch the L2 cache off for CPU access, simply add the following line to the `config.txt` file:

```
disable_l2cache=1
```

As with all `config.txt` settings, you must reboot the system before the change will take place. To enable the CPU's access to the cache memory, replace the 1 with a 0.

Enabling Test Mode

This final option in `config.txt`, test mode, is one most Pi users won't need to touch, but we include it here for completeness. Used during production of the Raspberry Pi at the factory, test mode—combined with special hardware used to electrically check the board—allows the factory staff to make sure the Pi is operating as it should.

> **WARNING**   Enabling test mode won't do any permanent damage, but the Pi won't boot into its operating system until the mode is disabled again and the power to the Pi is switched off and back on.

If you're curious to see what the Pi looks like to factory staff, you can enable test mode by entering the following option into the `config.txt` file:

```
test_mode=1
```

As with other `config.txt` settings, test mode won't be enabled until the Pi is restarted. Test mode can be disabled again by removing the line in `config.txt`, deleting the file altogether or replacing the 1 with a 0.

Memory Partitioning

Although the Raspberry Pi has either a 256 MB, 512 MB, or 1 GB memory chip, that memory can be apportioned to the hardware in a variety of ways. The BCM283x SoC design is split into two main sections: the general-purpose CPU and the graphics-oriented GPU. Both of these sections require memory to operate, meaning that the memory on the Raspberry Pi needs to be shared between the two.

The typical split is chosen by the maintainers of the Linux distribution installed on the Pi. Some choose to provide 128 MB to the GPU, ensuring that the graphics hardware can perform to its fullest potential. Others, to improve general-purpose performance, allow the CPU to have a larger share.

Previously, the memory split was controlled by using different versions of a firmware file called `start.elf`, where different files were used to supply different amounts of memory to the CPU. These files have now been replaced by a single line in `config.txt`, which can be edited to control the memory split.

Applications that do heavy graphics work, such as 3D games and high-definition video playback software, typically need 128 MB of memory for the GPU. Reducing this amount of memory can result in a dramatic drop in performance. The Raspberry Pi Camera Module is unable to record video with less than 128 MB of graphics memory. **WARNING**

You can change the memory split by editing `config.txt` as with other hardware settings and editing or inserting the line marked `gpu_mem`. This line tells the Pi how much of the total memory should be given to the GPU, with the remainder going to the CPU.

You can set the value to 16 MB as a minimum or to 192 MB as a maximum for models with 256 MB of memory, 448 MB for models with 512 MB, and 944 MB for models with 1 GB. The setting should be adjusted in 16 MB increments and written without the MB suffix—giving possible values of 16, 32, 48, 64, 80, 96, 112, 128, and so on up to the model-dependent maximum. To give the GPU the minimum 16 MB of memory, for example, edit the line as follows:

```
gpu_mem=16
```

Software Settings: cmdline.txt

In addition to `config.txt`, which controls various features of the Pi's hardware, there's another important text file in the `/boot` directory: `cmdline.txt` (see Figure 7-4). This file contains what is known as the *kernel command line*—options passed to the Linux kernel as the Pi boots.

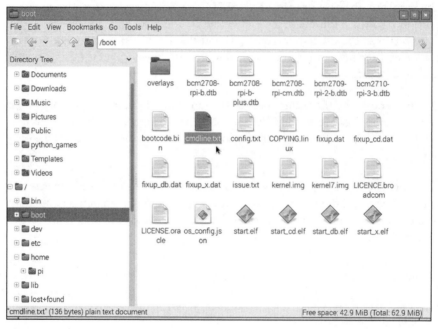

FIGURE 7-4: The `cmdline.txt` file in `/boot`

In a Linux-based desktop or laptop, these options are normally passed to the kernel by a tool known as a *bootloader*, which has its own configuration file. On the Pi, the options are simply entered directly into `cmdline.txt` to be read by the Pi at startup.

Almost any kernel option supported by Linux can be entered into the `cmdline.txt` file to alter things like the appearance of the console or which root file system is loaded. As an example, here is the `cmdline.txt` file from the Raspbian distribution, which should be written in the file as one continuous line:

```
dwc_otg.lpm_enable=0 console=serial0,115200 ↵
 console=tty1 root=/dev/mmcblk0p2 ↵
 rootfstype=ext4 elevator=deadline fsck.repair=yes rootwait
```

The first option, `dwg_otc.1pm_enable`, tells the Pi to disable the *Link Power Management (LPM)* mode of its USB controller to prevent problems that can occur with some peripherals when the functionality is enabled. The majority of Linux distributions for the Pi disable this mode.

The `console` option tells Linux that it should create a serial console—device `serial0`—and at what speed it should operate. In most cases, the speed should be left at the default of 115,200 bps (bits per second). If you're using the Pi to communicate with older devices, this speed can be reduced accordingly.

The second `console` entry creates the device `tty1`, which is the text-filled screen you see when you first boot the Pi. Without this entry, you wouldn't be able to use the Pi without connecting something to the serial console created by the first `console` option.

The `root` option tells the Linux kernel where it can find its *root file system*, which contains all the files and directories required for the system to operate. In the case of the default Raspbian distribution when installed from the official image file, this root file system is on the second partition of the SD card: device `mmcblk0p2`. You can alter it to address an external storage device connected over USB, which can speed up the operation of the Pi considerably, as compared to having the root file system stored on the SD card.

In addition to knowing where to find its root file system, the kernel needs to know what format the partition was created in. Because Linux supports a variety of different file systems, the `rootfstype` option specifically tells the kernel that the Raspbian distribution uses an EXT4 file system.

Finally, the `rootwait` parameter tells the kernel that it should not try to boot the system any further until the device containing the root file system is available. Without this option, the Pi can get stuck as it begins to boot before the relatively slow SD card is fully ready for access.

With the exception of the `dwc_otg` setting, none of these kernel parameters are unique to the Pi. The bootloader configuration of any Linux distribution includes a list of options very similar to those of `cmdline.txt`.

Typically, you should leave the `cmdline.txt` file alone. It's created by the distribution maintainers specifically for that version of Linux and may differ from one distribution to the next. Entries that work on one version of Linux may not work on Raspbian, and vice versa. The options available to `cmdline.txt` depend on what kernel the distribution is using and what features were included when the kernel was built.

If you're a kernel developer, you can use `cmdline.txt` to pass parameters for enabling or disabling new functionality that you've compiled into the kernel. As with `config.txt`, any changes require a reboot to take effect.

Part II
Building a Media Centre or Productivity Machine

Chapter 8
The Pi as a Home Theatre PC

ONE OF THE most popular tasks for a Pi to carry out is that of a home theatre PC, or HTPC. The Broadcom BCM283x system-on-chip module at the Pi's heart was designed to be a multimedia powerhouse, originally developed for use in set-top boxes.

The graphics portion of the BCM283x, a Broadcom VideoCore IV module, is capable of full-speed, high-definition video playback. The chip is also able to play back audio files in a variety of formats, both through the analogue 3.5 mm audio output and digitally via the HDMI port.

The small size, low power draw, and silent operation combine to make the Pi a tempting device for home theatre enthusiasts. A variety of distributions and software packages designed to turn the Pi into a user-friendly home theatre PC have appeared since its launch, but you don't necessarily need to give up your existing operating system to get started.

Playing Music at the Console

If you're a developer, you will likely spend most of your time at the Pi's console. With the majority of music playback software being aimed at desktop use, it can be a quiet experience—but it doesn't have to be.

The Pi supports a powerful text-based music playback package called moc (which stands for *music on console*). Unlike other tools (such as LXMusic), moc can be installed and used even when there is no graphical user interface (GUI) installed on the Pi.

To get started, install the moc package from your distribution's repositories. For the Raspbian distribution, this is as simple as typing the following command at the console or in a terminal window:

```
sudo apt-get install moc
```

If you spend a lot of time outside of the GUI and working at the console, moc is a great choice for music playback. Unlike other tools, it runs in the background, meaning there's no interruption to your music if you start doing something else.

To load moc, the command is mocp rather than moc. The reason for this is that there's another tool which uses the command moc, so a different name was chosen to prevent the operating system from getting confused between the two packages.

To get started, just enter the console—or a terminal window if you're using a desktop environment—and type the following:

mocp

The standard mocp interface is split into two panes (see Figure 8-1). The left pane is a file browser, which allows you to look for music to play. The cursor keys scroll up and down the list, while the Enter key starts playback from the currently highlighted song. If you press Enter on a directory name, the browser enters that directory, while pressing it at the ../ entry at the top of the list goes back one directory level. The right pane shows the current playlist.

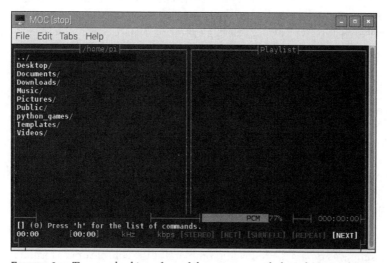

FIGURE 8-1: The standard interface of the mocp console-based music player

Where the power of mocp becomes apparent is when you exit the application by pressing the Q key. If mocp is in the middle of playing back music, it continues to do so even as you use the console or terminal window for other tasks. Running the mocp command again restores the interface, allowing you to change songs, pause, or stop playback. You can also control mocp directly from the terminal, without having to use the interface. Running the mocp command with flags—the options that follow a command, prefixed with a hyphen character—allow you to start, stop, pause, skip, and otherwise change the playback without having to go into the software.

The most commonly used mocp flags are the following:

- **-s**—Stop the current playback
- **-G**—Pause playback, or resume playback if currently paused
- **-f**—Skip to the next song in the directory or playlist
- **-r**—Return to the previous song in the directory or playlist
- **-i**—Print information on the current song to the terminal or console
- **-x**—Stop playback and quit mocp altogether

For more information on controlling mocp, type **man mocp**.

Dedicated HTPC with OSMC

Being able to play music on the Raspberry Pi is one thing, but the BCM283x family can do much more than that. Using the VideoCore IV GPU the Raspberry Pi can decode and play back Full HD 1080p H.264 video, making the Pi a powerful media centre machine in a tiny package and with incredibly low power demands.

To get the most from the Pi as a home theatre PC, however, some additional software is required. This software can be installed in the Raspbian distribution, but there's an easier way to get started: switching to the *OSMC* distribution.

More fully known as the *Open Source Media Centre*, OSMC is based on the popular XBMC software—now known as Kodi—which has been chosen by several device manufacturers to power their commercial set-top box systems.

If you're planning on using the Pi's high-definition video output and decoding capabilities in your home theatre setup, OSMC is an excellent choice and no more complicated to get up and running on the Pi than any other Linux distribution. The easiest way to install the software is via NOOBS as introduced in Chapter 2, "Getting Started with the Raspberry Pi".

Simply find OSMC in the list of operating systems and click on the check box next to it to install it (see Figure 8-2); you can do this alongside any other operating system, including Raspbian, if you don't want to dedicate your Pi to media playback duties.

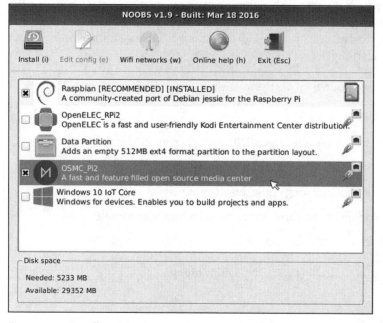

FIGURE 8-2: Installing OSMC via NOOBS

When the NOOBS installer finishes, reboot the Pi. Make sure that your Ethernet cable is connected when you do this, because OSMC needs to download some data from the Internet when it first loads. The initial load of OSMC can take 10 or 15 minutes to complete as it downloads updates, but subsequent loads are significantly faster.

When OSMC has loaded, you are greeted by a setup wizard which walks you through the basic configuration of the software. Use the mouse or keyboard to choose your language and time zone, and then choose a name for your device. You can skip the naming step if you want, but if you plan to have more than one OSMC device on your network, they must have unique names; use the randomisation button to automatically apply a unique suffix to your Pi if you don't want to think of a name yourself.

The wizard will then ask if you want to enable Secure Shell (SSH) support, which is on by default; this is typically safe to leave on if you are connecting the Pi to a secure home network, and allows you to transfer files and control the Pi remotely. Next, read the licence agreement and—assuming you agree to its terms—you can now choose the look and feel of OSMC.

The default is for OSMC to use its own interface, known as a *skin*. The alternative, labelled Classic (Kodi), uses the standard interface supplied with the Kodi media software OSMC uses. There is no difference in functionality between the two; the following instructions use the Classic skin, but choosing the OSMC skin won't affect your experience in anything except the way it looks. Finally, you are given the option to subscribe to the OSMC newsletter; this step is entirely optional.

On each subsequent load, OSMC automatically starts the Kodi software (see Figure 8-3). This provides a custom user interface specifically designed for living room use. Everything is accessible through the keyboard or mouse, with large and easily readable text and categorised menus to make it easier to find things. You can also purchase infrared remote controls, which come with a receiver that plugs into the Pi's USB port and a handheld transmitter that allows for a true home theatre experience with no bulky keyboard or trailing wires.

FIGURE 8-3: The Kodi home screen, loaded by OSMC

Streaming Internet Media

By default, OSMC is configured to play only files it can find on the Raspberry Pi itself. If you choose Add-ons from below the Video menu, you'll be able to add some impressive Internet streaming capabilities to the device, including access to various TV channels and Internet-only streaming services. After clicking Add-ons, choose Get More to access the full list of compatible plug-ins (see Figure 8-4). If nothing appears in the list, click on the tab with the right-facing arrow at the far left of the screen and check for updates in the menu which appears, to load the latest add-on information.

FIGURE 8-4: Adding new video add-ons in OSMC

Scroll through the list with the mouse or cursor keys and click on an entry or press the Enter key to access more information. To install an add-on, just click Install from the pop-up information box that appears when you click on an entry in the list. This step downloads the add-on from the Internet and automatically installs it in OSMC. Watch out for add-ons listed as Broken; these have been reported as not working correctly, and should not be installed until the problem is fixed by the add-on developer.

After you finish choosing and installing video add-ons, click the Home button in the bottom-right corner of the screen to return to the main OSMC interface. Now click the word Video in the centre of the screen or press Enter and then choose Video Add-ons from the options that appear. This provides access to your installed add-ons. Click on one to download a list of files for viewing. If an add-on has various categories, it will download those categories first; in this case, click on an individual category to see the files it contains (see Figure 8-5).

FIGURE 8-5: A list of videos available through the DIY Network OSMC add-on

Similar add-ons are available under the Music and Pictures menus and operate in the same way. Using these add-ons, you can view picture content and stream audio content from sites such as Flickr, Picasa, The Big Picture, Grooveshark, Sky.fm, and SoundCloud.

Streaming Local Network Media

The OSMC software supports the *Universal Plug and Play (UPnP)* media streaming standard, allowing it to connect to a range of devices on your home network. UPnP support is included in most modern mobile phones, games consoles, and *network-attached storage (NAS)* devices for sharing and streaming videos, music, and pictures. Many laptops and desktops also come with support for UPnP or the closely linked *Digital Living Network Alliance (DLNA)* standard. Check your documentation to find out how to enable this feature on your devices.

OSMC isn't just limited to UPnP connections, however; the software can also connect to network servers running the *Network File System (NFS)* standard common to UNIX-based systems, the *Server Message Block (SMB)* standard common to Windows servers, and the *Zeroconf* standard common to OS X devices. No matter what network-attached device you use to store your media content, it's likely that OSMC will support at least one way of connecting to it.

To configure OSMC to connect to a server on your home network, choose the media type— Video, Music, or Pictures— click Files, and then click the Add videos (or Add music, or Add pictures) option. In the window that appears, click Browse to retrieve a list of source types (see Figure 8-6). These source types include local drives connected to the Raspberry Pi, which are highlighted with a blue icon, as well as network devices, which are highlighted with a red icon. Choose the type of server you're trying to connect to from the list, and then click on the server that appears.

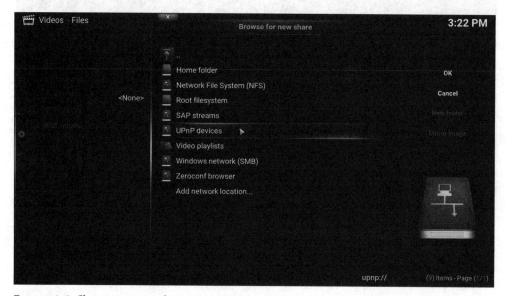

FIGURE 8-6: Choosing a network source in OSMC

If the server you select has multiple folders available—such as folders for different genres, artists, albums, or file types—select the folder you want OSMC to connect to and click OK. This returns you to the Add screen (see Figure 8-7) with the required information filled in. If additional details are required, such as a username and password for a protected server, you need to fill these in before clicking OK.

You can also use the same menu to add an external hard drive as a source to OSMC by selecting its entry in the initial list. Most external drives appear automatically and do not need to be added explicitly. (You need to add a drive as a source only if its contents do not appear in OSMC menus.)

Configuring OSMC

The various settings in OSMC are available from the Programs menu, under My OSMC. Even if you chose the Classic (Kodi) skin during the setup process, this part of OSMC will always appear using its own skin, showing up as a series of icons surrounding the OSMC logo in the centre (see Figure 8-8).

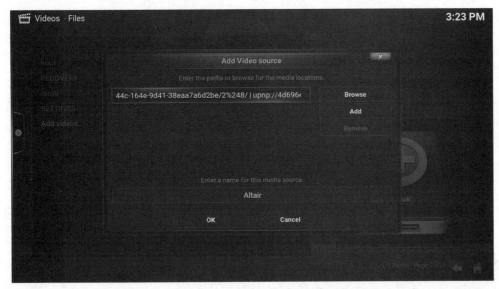

Figure 8-7: Adding a UPnP music source to OSMC

Figure 8-8: Configuring OSMC via My OSMC

The icons, from top running clockwise, are as follows:

- **Updates**—Select this option to check for updates to OSMC and your installed add-ons, and to download and install any as required.

- **Services**—This allows you to enable or disable the SSH service.

- **Overclock**—This allows you to choose from a range of preset overclocks to improve the performance of your Raspberry Pi. Any changes made here will take effect only after a reboot.

- **App Store**—This provides access to additional OSMC applications, which can be downloaded and installed to add new functionality to the software.

- **Network**—Click this option to configure manual network settings.

- **Remotes**—This option allows you to configure a USB-connected remote control receiver, allowing you to control OSMC without using the keyboard or mouse.

- **Pi Config**—This provides access to the Raspberry Pi settings files described in Chapter 7, "Advanced Raspberry Pi Configuration".

- **Log Uploader**—This allows the various log files, containing information about OSMC and the underlying operating system, to be uploaded to the project's servers for use in a bug report. If you're not reporting a bug in OSMC, you shouldn't need to use this.

For more information on configuring OSMC or Kodi, visit the official website at http://osmc.tv.

Chapter 9
The Pi as a Productivity Machine

THE FLEXIBILITY OF the Raspberry Pi makes it a good choice as a low-power, general-purpose desktop computer. Although it will never reach the same level of performance as a standard desktop or laptop, its low cost and environmentally friendly power consumption help to make up for any problems with occasionally sluggish performance.

The Raspbian operating system, available from the Raspberry Pi website, includes the popular LibreOffice productivity suite as standard. This provides equivalents to all the tools you would expect to find in a commercial product such as Microsoft Office: a word processor, spreadsheet, database, presentation tool, and even applications for creating diagrams or mathematical formulae. Alternatively, you can use many of the same cloud-based software through the web browser that you would on any other computer.

Using either of the methods described in this chapter—locally installed applications or cloud-based services—the Pi can be used as a day-to-day machine for office and school work, while not harming its usability as a platform for programming and experimentation.

If you're planning to use the Pi as a pure productivity machine, it's a good idea to reserve more of the memory for general-purpose use and less for the graphics processor. To find out how to change this split, refer to Chapter 6, "The Raspberry Pi Configuration Tool". **TIP**

Using Cloud-Based Apps

If you use your Pi connected to the Internet the majority of the time, either through the integrated Ethernet port, built-in wireless, or through a USB wired or wireless adapter on models without integrated networking, *cloud-based* software offers you a powerful yet lightweight means of using office-centric software on the Pi.

Cloud-based software is so called because it doesn't live locally on your computer like a regular piece of software. Instead, it's stored on powerful servers located in data centres throughout the world and accessed over the Internet using a web browser. By tapping into the processing and storage capabilities of a far more powerful remote server, it's possible for the Pi to work on more complicated documents and tasks without slowing down.

Cloud-based software has other advantages over locally installed applications, too. Any given cloud-based application will look the same on any given device, and many of these applications include mobile-oriented versions designed for access from smartphones and tablets. Files are also stored on the remote servers, making them accessible from any device without taking up any room on the Pi's SD card.

Cloud-based applications aren't perfect, however. They typically lag behind their locally installed counterparts in functionality, and often lack advanced features or support fewer file formats. They are also inaccessible when no Internet connection is available, making them a poor choice for users with unreliable connections.

If you think that the improved performance and saved space on your Pi's SD card is worth the trade-off, continue reading. If not, skip to the next section of this chapter to learn how to use LibreOffice, an open source office suite equivalent to Microsoft Office.

The most popular cloud-based office suites are the following:

- **Google Drive**—Run by the search and advertising giant Google, Google Drive (formerly known as Google Docs) includes a word processor, a spreadsheet, and a presentation tool (see Figure 9-1). Corporate users can also sign up for a Google Apps account, which provides improved functionality. If you have a Gmail web-based email account, it will automatically work for Google Drive. You can access the service at `https://docs.google.com`.

- **Zoho**—With five million registered users, Zoho is another popular choice. As with Google Drive, a word processor, a spreadsheet, and a presentation package are included, but Zoho also offers enhanced business-centric features like a wiki-based knowledge base system, web conferencing, financial management, and even customer relationship management. Many of the advanced features, however, require a paid account. You can access the service at `www.zoho.com`.

- **Office 365**—If you're a Microsoft Office user, Office 365 is a great choice. Based on the same user interface as the current editions of the Microsoft Office suite for desktops, Office 365 is powerful and flexible. Unlike Zoho and Google Drive, Office 365 has no free user level and requires a monthly subscription. Additionally, some features won't work when the software is accessed from a Linux computer. You can subscribe to the service at `http://office365.microsoft.com`.

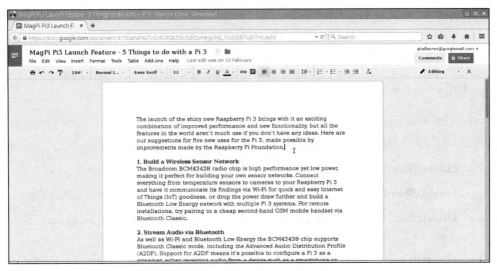

FIGURE 9-1: Google Drive running in Iceweasel on the Raspberry Pi

- **ThinkFree Online**—A web-based interface to the Hancom ThinkFree Office software, ThinkFree Online offers word processing, spreadsheet, and presentation software for free, with 1 GB of storage. The system also ties into ThinkFree Mobile for tablets and smartphones, as well as the enterprise-targeted ThinkFree Server software. You can access the service at `http://online.thinkfree.com`.

Many web-based productivity suites require functionality not present in the Raspbian default browser, however. As a result, to use any of these packages, you have to install a different browser. The following instructions are for installing the Iceweasel browser, which is a version of the popular open source browser Firefox by Mozilla.

To install the Iceweasel browser under Raspbian, open a terminal and type the following:

```
sudo apt-get install iceweasel
```

With Iceweasel installed, using a cloud-based office suite is as simple as visiting the site, signing up for an account—providing your credit card details in the case of premium services like Microsoft Office 365—and logging in. If you find performance slow, changing the memory partitioning to give the ARM processor a larger share can help. Chapter 6 has full instructions for how to do so.

Using LibreOffice

If you prefer not to use a cloud-based service, the alternative is to use LibreOffice. Designed as an open source, cross-platform alternative to the popular Microsoft Office suite and based on the OpenOffice.org project, LibreOffice is powerful and offers just as much functionality as its closed source inspiration.

LibreOffice appears as a series of entries in the Office menu in the Pi's desktop environment. These entries are as follows:

- **LibreOffice Base**—The database application, equivalent to Microsoft Access

- **LibreOffice Calc**—The spreadsheet application, equivalent to Microsoft Excel

- **LibreOffice Draw**—A vector illustration application, designed for drawing high-quality scalable images for use as clipart in other LibreOffice programs

- **LibreOffice Impress**—The presentation application, equivalent to Microsoft PowerPoint

- **LibreOffice Math**—A tool for formatting mathematical formula, equivalent to the Microsoft Equation Editor

- **LibreOffice Writer**—The word processor application, equivalent to Microsoft Word (see Figure 9-2)

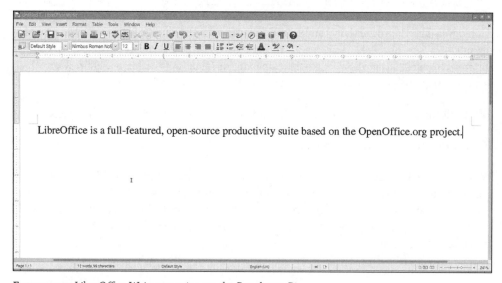

FIGURE 9-2: LibreOffice Writer running on the Raspberry Pi

By default, LibreOffice saves and loads files in a format known as the *Open Document Format (ODF)*. This is a standards-based, royalty-free file format supported by the majority of office suite packages—including newer versions of Microsoft Office.

When saving a file in LibreOffice, you can change the format using a drop-down menu in the Save As dialogue. Under File Type, you can select a variety of formats, including several that are fully compatible with older versions of Microsoft Office. When you're sharing files created on the Pi in LibreOffice with users of older software, remember to change the format to ensure that everyone can open the files. Alternatively, you could convince them to install LibreOffice themselves, which is available for free for Linux, Windows, and OS X.

Image Editing with the Gimp

LibreOffice is a powerful piece of software, but one area where it lacks is in image editing. Although LibreOffice Draw is a highly effective tool for illustrative work, unfortunately, you can't use it to touch up digital photographs. These are known as *bitmapped images*, and they are very different from the vector images Draw is designed to edit.

For image editing, one of the best tools available for Linux is the GNU Image Manipulation Program, usually referred to as the Gimp. The Gimp is one of the most popular projects in the open source world because it offers powerful features for editing bitmapped images with a user interface that is similar to the interface used by the commercial Adobe Photoshop package (see Figure 9-3).

FIGURE 9-3: The Gimp running on the Raspberry Pi

The Gimp is not installed by default in most Raspberry Pi distributions, so you must install it through the package management system (refer to Chapter 3, "Linux System Administration"). The Gimp takes up quite a lot of space on the SD card, so make sure you have enough free space before installing it.

To install the Gimp, open a terminal window and type the following:

```
sudo apt-get install gimp
```

The Gimp can take a little while to get used to because its user interface uses three different windows rather than just one. By default, the window on the left contains the Toolbox; the window on the right displays the Layers, Channels, and Gradients options; and the middle window displays the image you're currently editing. If you open more than one image, you get more than one main window—but still only one each of the Toolbox and the Layers, Channels, and Gradients windows. To simplify things, The Gimp can be switched to a single-window mode more familiar to users of Adobe Photoshop: click on the Windows menu and then Single-Window Mode to activate it.

By default, *the Gimp User Manual* is not installed. For the Pi, this is a good thing. The Gimp is a powerful tool, and its user manual takes up a great deal space on the SD card. If you try to access the manual by pressing the F1 key or choosing Help from the Help menu, you'll be prompted to read an online, web-based version instead. Click the Read Online button to open the user manual in a browser.

The Gimp is a very powerful utility and uses a lot of memory. As a result, it runs relatively slowly on the Raspberry Pi—although it is definitely usable. Be patient with it, especially if you're opening large photographs from a digital camera. It may help to increase the amount of system memory available (refer to Chapter 6 for more details on how this is achieved).

When saving files in the Gimp, you can use a variety of file formats. If you're planning to come back to the file and do more editing, you should use the Gimp's default XCF file format. This keeps important *metadata* intact, uses lossless compression to maximise image quality, and supports images consisting of multiple layers.

If you're planning on uploading your image to the Internet or otherwise sharing it with others, a more portable format such as JPG or PNG is recommended. To save the file in a different format, choose the Export option from the File menu rather than the Save option (see Figure 9-4). This allows you to choose the file format from a wide variety of file types.

FIGURE 9-4: Exporting a file from the Gimp

Part III

Programming the Pi

Chapter 10
An Introduction to Scratch

SO FAR IN this book, you've learned a lot about how to use programs that other people have written on your Raspberry Pi. The chief goal of the Raspberry Pi project is to get people writing their own programs, however—and not just adults. The Raspberry Pi Foundation is working to get the device adopted as an educational tool for all age ranges.

A key requirement for reaching that goal is ensuring that young children can experience the joy of creating their own software, rather than just consuming other people's code. The secret to this is *Scratch*.

Introducing Scratch

Created by the Lifelong Kindergarten group at the Massachusetts Institute of Technology Media Lab in 2006 as an offshoot of the Squeak and Smalltalk languages, Scratch takes the core concepts of programming and makes them accessible to all. Long-winded typing—tiring and dull for younger children—is replaced with a simple jigsaw-like drag-and-drop environment, which nevertheless encourages programmatic thinking and introduces the core concepts used by all programming languages.

Officially considered a program for ages eight and above, but accessible to even younger programmers with a little help and guidance, Scratch is deceptively powerful. Behind its colourful and mouse-driven user interface is a programming language that includes impressive multimedia functionality. It should come as no surprise then that, of the more than five and a half million Scratch projects shared by users of the software on the official website, the majority are games.

Encouraging children to learn how to make their own games can be a great way of sneaking a little learning into their playtimes. Scratch's user-friendly interface and excellent handling of core concepts mean that children are unlikely to get frustrated by a sudden steep learning curve. Better still, the concepts learned in Scratch offer an excellent foundation for progression to a more flexible language like Python (see Chapter 11, "An Introduction to Python").

Even before moving on to another language, Scratch offers more than just a framework for games. It can be used to create interactive presentations and cartoons, as well as to interface with external sensors and motors through the use of add-on hardware such as the PicoBoard and the LEGO WeDo robotics kit, or directly through the Raspberry Pi's GPIO port.

The recommended Raspbian distribution for the Raspberry Pi comes with the latest version of the Scratch development environment preloaded, so if you've been following the recommendations throughout this book, you're ready to start.

Example 1: Hello World

When learning a new programming language, it's traditional to start with a very basic program: one that displays a single line of text. This is typically referred to as a Hello World program, and it's the first step toward learning how to create your own programs.

Unlike a traditional programming language, Scratch doesn't expect the user to memorise the names of instructions such as `print` or `inkey$`. Instead, almost everything is done by dragging and dropping blocks of code and arranging them into a logical pattern.

To begin, load Scratch by double-clicking its icon on the desktop or clicking on its entry in the Programming menu. After a few seconds, the main Scratch interface appears (see Figure 10-1). If it's off-centre or small, click the Maximise button (it's the middle control button located at the far-right of the title bar) to fill the screen.

The Scratch interface is split into multiple panes. At the left is the *block palette*, which holds all the different code blocks you can use to create a program. A list of objects in the program, known as *sprites*, appears at the bottom-right pane along with a control for the *stage* on which the sprites appear. The stage itself is at the top right of the window, which is where you will see the program running. Finally, the middle of the window is where the program is constructed.

To get the user started, a new Scratch project already includes a blank stage and a single sprite. What it lacks is a program, so clicking the green flag icon at the top right of the window achieves nothing, because Scratch doesn't yet know what you want it to do.

For the Hello World program, you need to change the block palette at the left of the screen to the Looks mode by clicking the Looks button. Partway down the list of Looks blocks is one that reads `say Hello!`—click this block and drag it into the empty space in the middle of the window labelled Scripts. If you want to follow the decades of tradition behind this type of program, you can also click on the block where it says `Hello!` and customise it to read `Hello World!` (see Figure 10-2). You can delete blocks by clicking on the block with the right mouse button and then clicking Delete with the left mouse button.

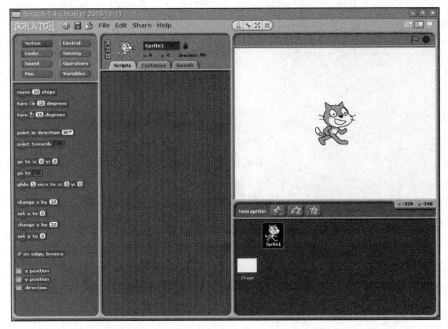

FIGURE 10-1: The main Scratch interface, shown running on the Raspberry Pi

If you click the green flag now, the program still does nothing. That's because although Scratch knows that it is supposed to make the cat sprite say something, it doesn't know when. The event requires a *trigger block*, which you can find in the Control section of the block palette.

Enter this section now by clicking Control and then drag the top entry—marked `when [flag icon] clicked`—and place it just above the purple `say` brick (see Figure 10-3). If you drop it close enough, it should automatically join to the existing brick like a jigsaw piece.

This concept of connecting multiple bricks together is the heart of Scratch. If you look at the Control brick you just placed, you'll see there's no connecting hole at the top. This means that you can't stack another brick on top, because this Control brick is designed to trigger a series of other bricks directly and must come at the start of a stack. The bottom of the `say` brick, meanwhile, has a connector that fits into the top of other bricks, which indicates that more bricks can be placed underneath.

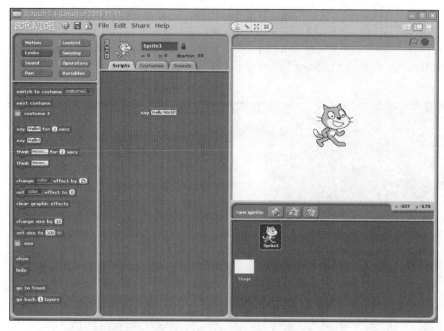

FIGURE 10-2: The first block placed in a Scratch program

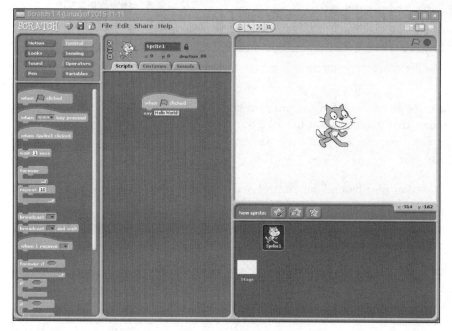

FIGURE 10-3: A Control block joined to a Looks block in Scratch

With the two bricks in place, click the green flag icon at the top right of the screen again. This time a speech bubble appears from the cat's mouth (see Figure 10-4), and the Hello World program is complete.

Before moving on to the next example, take the time to save your work using the File menu. Scratch is designed to have only one project open at a time. So if you create a new blank file, the current file will be closed to make room. Don't worry if you forget about this when you go to create a new file; if there are unsaved changes in the existing file, Scratch prompts you to save the changes before closing it.

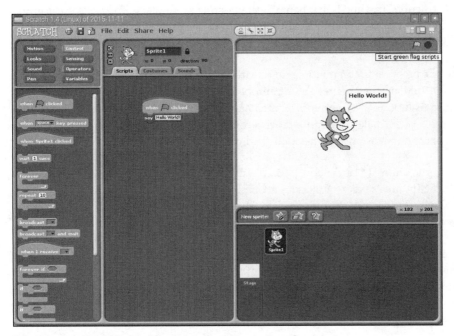

FIGURE 10-4: The Hello World program executing in Scratch

Example 2: Animation and Sound

Hello World is a very traditional example, but it's not particularly interesting. It also fails to show off the true power of Scratch, which lies in its impressive multimedia capabilities and sprite-handling system. This system is particularly well suited to simple animations, which can form the basis of an interactive game.

To begin, start a new project in Scratch by either loading the program afresh or choosing New from the File menu. As with any starter project, Scratch provides a default sprite; it's this sprite that you will be controlling.

To control a simple animation in Scratch, you use the Motion section of the blocks palette. When you start a new project, this is the default palette. Drag the block labelled move 10 steps to the Scripts area. As its name suggests, this block tells the selected sprite to move 10 steps in the direction it is currently facing. The default sprite in Scratch always starts facing directly to the right—thus, the move 10 steps block moves the sprite 10 steps to the right.

Ten steps isn't a very large value, so click on the value 10 and change it to 30. The block then reads move 30 steps. An animation of a cat moving to the right of the stage isn't that interesting, however, so switch to the Sound block palette and drag the play sound meow block to the Scripts area and link it beneath the existing move block. To keep the cat in this position for a while, add a wait 1 secs block from the Control block palette; otherwise, the sprite will appear to flick quickly between its starting position and the target position.

To enable the program to run multiple times without the cat sprite disappearing off the edge of the stage, add another move 10 steps block beneath the wait 1 secs block and modify it to read move -30 steps. Scratch happily allows you to use negative figures like this. If a value of 30 makes the sprite move a certain distance to the right, -30 will make it move the exact same distance in the opposite direction.

Finally, add the when [flag icon] clicked block from the Control block palette to the top of the Script area's stack of blocks to complete the program, as shown in Figure 10-5. Clicking the green flag icon on the top right of the screen triggers the program. Make sure you've got speakers or headphones connected to the Pi for the full effect!

You can extend this simple animation program in a variety of ways. Using the New Sprite option just below the stage on the right side of the Scratch window allows you to add more sprites that can move and play sounds independently. Adding in the say block from the first example—or the similar think block, which creates a thought bubble rather than a speech bubble—allows for the creation of an animated comic strip.

More importantly, even this simple example teaches important programming concepts. Despite being a mere five blocks long, it covers sprite movement in positive and negative distances, sound playback, and the concept of *delays* in a program. To introduce yet another concept—at the risk of driving yourself insane with repetitive noises—try adding a forever block from the Control block palette (see Figure 10-6). This adds a *loop* to the program, causing it to run through its list forever—or at least until the noise becomes too much and you click the red stop button at the top of the stage. You can drag this block between the when flag clicked and move 30 steps block to automatically add your existing blocks to the loop, without having to delete them and start again.

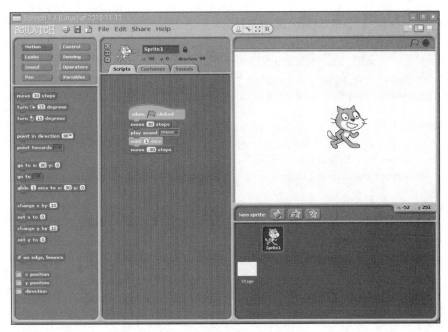

FIGURE 10-5: The completed animation program in Scratch

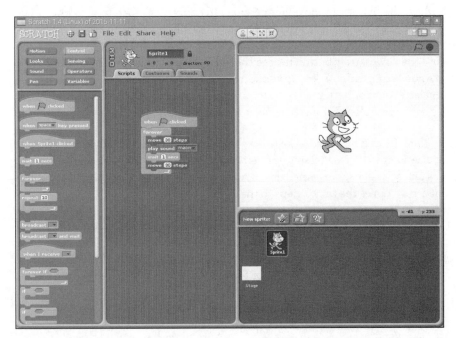

FIGURE 10-6: Adding an infinite loop to the simple Scratch animation

Example 3: A Simple Game

Using Scratch for simple animation is one thing, but the software also allows users to read inputs from the keyboard to introduce interactivity. By combining some simple animation controls to the previously described program, you can create a simple game—and, at the same time, introduce the concepts of *sprite collision, if statements,* and *input*.

For this example, start a new Scratch project—remembering to save the previous example, if you haven't already done so—and begin by dragging a move 10 steps block to the Scripts area. This time, rather than telling the code blocks to execute when the flag icon is clicked, go to the Control block palette and drag a when space key pressed block above the move block.

As the name suggests, the when space key pressed block looks for input from the user—in this instance, the spacebar being pressed—and uses that as the trigger for executing a list of blocks. The block works at any time; if you press the spacebar now, the sprite obeys its instructions and moves 10 steps to the right.

The when space key pressed block also differs from the when [flag icon] clicked block in another important way: it can be customised. Click the down-arrow button next to the word space to see a list of all the keys the block can watch, and then select right arrow from the list to change the block into a when right arrow key pressed block.

A game in which the player can move in only one direction isn't much fun, so drag a new when space key pressed block into the Scripts area. This can't link to the existing block list—you can have only a single trigger block—so start a new list somewhere farther down. As before, use the down-arrow button next to the word space to customise the block, turning it into a when left arrow key pressed block. Finally, switch the block palette back to Motion palette and connect a move 10 steps block beneath the new when left arrow key pressed block before changing it to read move -10 steps.

If you press the left- and right-arrow keys now, you'll see that the cat moves according to your input (see Figure 10-7). Pressing the left arrow moves the cat 10 steps to the left (although, as far as Scratch is concerned, it's moving minus 10 steps to the right), and pressing the right arrow moves the cat 10 steps to the right.

Now that the sprite can be moved by the player, it's time to give the sprite something to do. Because this is just a very simple game, the goal should also be simple: to collect some food. Click the Choose New Sprite From File button, found in the middle of the three buttons above the Sprite palette at the bottom right of the Scratch window. If you're not sure which button is which, hover your mouse cursor over them for a pop-up tip.

A dialog box appears asking you to pick a sprite: double-click the Things folder and then double-click the Cheesy-Puffs sprite (shown in Figure 10-8). This places the sprite as a new entry in the Sprite palette, giving you a new object to control in the game.

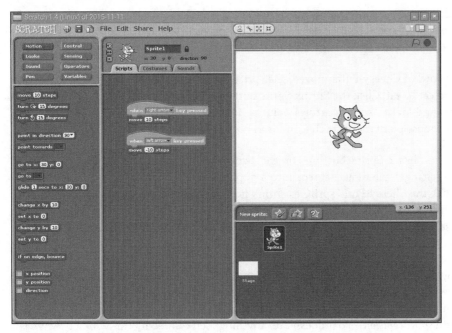

FIGURE 10-7: Using input blocks to control the motion of a sprite in Scratch

FIGURE 10-8: Adding the Cheesy-Puffs sprite to the Scratch game project

The Scratch language is naturally *multithreaded* and partially *object oriented*, which means that each object in the program, including sprites, can have its own code attached and that each section of code runs simultaneously and independently of any other block. Used properly, these features enable you to create quite complex programs.

TIP

By default, any sprite added to a Scratch project appears dead centre on the stage, resulting in the existing cat sprite being obscured. Click the new sprite and drag it to the right of the cat to fix the problem.

With the bowl of Cheesy-Puffs moved, the sprite is still too large for our anthropomorphic two-legged cat to eat. Click the Shrink Sprite button, which is located at the top-right of the Stage area and looks like four arrows pointing inwards. If you're not sure which one it is, hover the mouse pointer over each icon for a short description of what it does.

Clicking the Shrink Sprite button—or the Grow Sprite button, which does exactly the opposite—changes the mouse cursor into a duplicate of the button's icon. Using this new cursor, click the Cheesy-Puffs sprite to shrink it. Keep clicking, and the sprite continues to shrink. Once it's a sensible-looking size, click anywhere outside of the Stage area to return the mouse cursor to normal. You can then drag the bowl closer to the right edge of the stage, if you so choose.

Try using the arrow keys on the keyboard to move the cat sprite towards the Cheesy-Puffs sprite now. As you can see, when the two sprites meet, nothing happens. That's because the programme doesn't contain instructions for what to do when the two sprites overlap—known as a *sprite collision*—so it doesn't do anything. You can rectify this with a new type of block: a *Sensing* block.

With the Cheesy-Puffs sprite currently active (its image should appear at the top of the Scripts pane, but if it doesn't, just double-click the sprite on the stage), switch the Blocks palette into Sensing mode by clicking the Sensing button. From the Sensing palette, drag a touching ? block into the Scripts pane.

Like the when space key pressed block used to control the cat sprite's motion, the touching ? block can be customised. Click the down-arrow button next to the question mark and choose Sprite1 (the cat sprite) from the list. This block will now be activated when the two sprites collide.

TIP	You can name a sprite by clicking the box next to its image in the Scripts pane and typing a name. Giving the sprites sensible names—such as Cat, CheesyPuffs, and so forth—makes it significantly easier to track what's going on in the program.

Look at the shape of the touching Sprite1? block. As you can see, it has no jigsaw-like connectors on the top or the bottom, and it's shaped like a diamond—the same shape used for a decision point in a flowchart. That's no accident. The majority of the Sensing blocks need to be embedded in a Control block in order to operate.

Switch the Blocks palette to Control mode and look for the `if` block—it's shaped like a squished and bumpy letter C. Note that the `if` block has a diamond-shaped indentation— the same shape as the `touching Sprite1?` block. Drag the `if` block onto the Scripts pane and then drag the `touching Sprite1?` block onto its diamond-shaped indentation. The result is a two-coloured block that now reads `if touching Sprite1?` (or whatever name you gave to your sprite earlier).

This represents an *if conditional* in the program. When this point is reached, all code located within its confines is executed if and only if the *condition* is met. In this case, the condition is that Sprite2 is being touched by Sprite1. With the use of *and*, *or*, and *not* logic blocks from the Operators block palette, some complex scenarios can be accommodated.

From the Looks block palette, drag a `say Hello! For 2 secs` block into the centre of the `if touching Sprite1?` conditional. Change the text to read `Don't eat me!`, and then add a `wait 1 secs` Control block, changing the value to 2. Add a `when space key pressed` block to the top, changing the value to read `when right arrow key pressed`. Finally, drag a `hide` block from the Looks palette to the bottom of the loop to end up with the block list that's shown in Figure 10-9.

Double-click the cat sprite on the stage to return to editing its scripts. The script you created for the Cheesy-Puffs sprite disappears. Don't worry, though; it's still present in the background, but appears only when you're editing that particular sprite.

Boolean Logic

Named for George Boole, Boolean logic or Boolean algebra is a key concept to understanding how computers work. In Scratch, Boolean logic is implemented in three Operators bricks: and, or, and not.

The and operator requires that two inputs—in Scratch's case, Sensing blocks—are both true before its own output will be true. If either or both of its inputs are false, its own output will be false; only when both inputs are true will the output be true. You can use this operator to check to see if a sprite is touching two other sprites, as an example.

The or operator requires that one or the other of its two inputs is true. If either input is true, the operator's output will also be true. This is a handy way of reusing code. For example, if you have multiple sprites that are lethal to the player sprite, you can use a single block of code with the or operator to trigger when any of the enemy sprites are touched.

Finally, the not operator is known as an *inverter*; that is, whatever its single input is, it outputs the opposite. If its input is false, the output is true; if the input is true, the output is false.

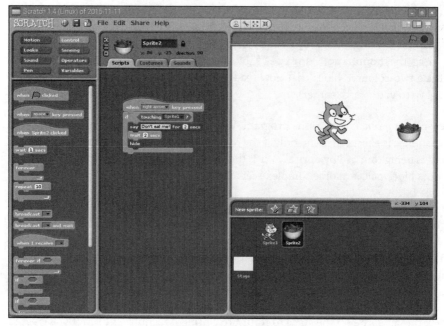

FIGURE 10-9: Controlling the Cheesy-Puffs with a Scratch if block

Drag another `if` block from the Control palette along with another `touching ?` sensing block, and this time, change the Sensing block so that both blocks together read `if touching Sprite2?`. Into this block, insert a `wait 1 secs` Control block with the value changed to 2 and a `say Hello! for 2 secs` Looks block with the message changed to read `Yum-yum-yum!`. Finally, drag the whole stacked block up so that it connects to the bottom of the existing `when right arrow key pressed` block, beneath the `move 10 steps` block. The final code for the cat sprite should look like the blocks in Figure 10-10.

If you move the cat toward the Cheesy-Puffs with the right-arrow key on the keyboard, the game starts. When the cat reaches the Cheesy-Puffs, the dialogue exchange takes place, and the bowl should disappear.

Although this example is effective for introducing some important programming concepts, it's hardly the best way to code the game. Scratch includes a *message broadcast* system that allows code attached to one object to communicate with code attached to another, which enables you to create much neater collision results that to make sense don't rely on carefully timed pauses.

To experiment with broadcasting, try using the `broadcast` and `when I receive` blocks from the Control palette. A message created for a broadcast block in any object can trigger code in any other object using the `when I receive` flag, meaning you can use it to link multiple objects and their code together.

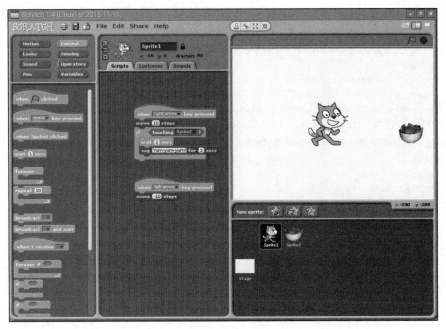

FIGURE 10-10: The completed code for the simple Scratch game's cat sprite

Interfacing Scratch with Hardware

Scratch may have been designed with ease of accessibility in mind, but it's also a fully-functional programming language—and that includes the ability to control external hardware, typically using the Raspberry Pi's *GPIO port*. This port, found at the top edge of each Raspberry Pi board, allows you to interface with external hardware—from complex add-on boards to individual switches and LEDs—and is fully described in Chapter 14, "The GPIO Port".

Interfacing with the GPIO port through Scratch requires an extra step compared to simply making things onscreen move around: enabling the GPIO server software. This can be done in two ways: you can click on the Edit menu and choose Start GPIO Server, or you can include a broadcast message reading `gpioserveron` to enable it within your Scratch program then disable it with `gpioserveroff` when it is no longer required.

With the GPIO server enabled, each pin of the GPIO header can be controlled individually. This is done using the GPIO pin numbering scheme, rather than the physical pin number; see the pinout diagrams in Chapter 14 for reference: physical Pin 11, as an example, is addressed in Scratch as GPIO Pin 17, as indicated on the diagrams.

> **WARNING**　It's possible to damage the Raspberry Pi by connecting to the wrong pins of the GPIO header, or using external hardware which operates on voltages above the Pi's 3.3V. Always make sure you have correctly identified the pin numbers and voltages in use before connecting anything to the GPIO header.

To experiment with using the GPIO header in Scratch, first turn to Chapter 14 and build the circuit described under the section "GPIO Output: Flashing an LED". Rather than using the Python program, however, build a new Scratch sketch with the following blocks (see Figure 10-11):

```
when flag clicked
broadcast gpioserveron
broadcast config17out
forever
   broadcast gpio17on
   wait 2 secs
   broadcast gpio17off
   wait 2 secs
```

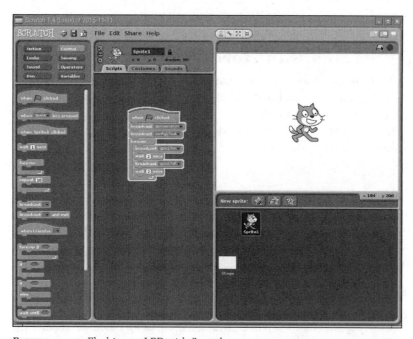

FIGURE 10-11: Flashing an LED with Scratch

Run this program by clicking the flag and you'll see the LED connected to physical Pin 11—GPIO Pin 17—flash on and off in 2-second intervals. If it doesn't, double-check your wiring (paying close attention to the pin numbering, making sure you have connected the LED to physical Pin 11 on the GPIO header) and the orientation of the LED.

To experiment with inputs, turn to Chapter 14 and build the circuit described under the section "GPIO Input: Reading a Button". This time, use the following blocks for your Scratch program (see Figure 10-12):

```
when flag clicked
broadcast gpioserveron
broadcast config18in
forever
  if gpio18 sensor value = 0
  say Button pressed! for 2 secs
```

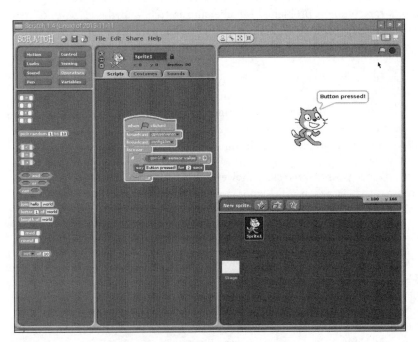

FIGURE 10-12: Reading an input with Scratch

Run this program by clicking the flag, and every time you press the physical button, you will see your message appear on the screen. To further expand your skills, try combining both programs together: have the LED start flashing only when the button is pressed.

Further Reading

This chapter serves as a brief introduction to Scratch and is far from exhaustive on the subject. It's also a little verbose for younger readers, who tend to learn more quickly when their lessons are accompanied by lots of colourful pictures.

The Support section of the official Scratch website, hosted by MIT at `http://scratch.mit.edu/help/`, includes a link to a *Getting Started Guide* in PDF format. The guide describes how to work with Scratch in a colourful, child-friendly manner, and is a great educational tool. This learning experience can be enhanced even further when combined with Scratch Cards, which are downloadable flash cards containing explanations for each of the block types found in Scratch. Note, however, that these documents are based on a newer version of Scratch than is provided with Raspbian at present; while the techniques are the same, the user interface has been changed between the versions.

MIT also runs a user forum for Scratch, allowing enthusiasts of the software to learn together and share solutions for common problems. Membership is free, and the site works well using the web browser included in the Raspbian distribution for the Raspberry Pi. You can access the forums at `http://scratch.mit.edu/discuss`.

To learn more about using the GPIO port from within Scratch, visit `https://raspberrypi.org` and view the official documentation under Help. This provides examples for GPIO interfacing, chaining Scratch programs to other software running on the Pi, and even using add-on hardware such as the Sense HAT, described in Chapter 16, "Add-On Hardware", from within the programming environment.

The easiest way to advance your Scratch skills, however, is to play. The name Scratch has its roots in turntablism—that is, when a DJ spins a record, the needle creates a scratching sound. Just as DJs remix existing songs into something new, Scratch enthusiasts are encouraged to submit their creations to the official website for others to download, examine, modify, and remix. The official Scratch site currently hosts more than 5.5 million Scratch programs, making it a perfect source for learning how Scratch is being used to create projects and for sharing your own ideas with others. You can find a list of the most recently shared projects at `http://scratch.mit.edu/exploreprojects/all`, but be aware that the very newest are written in Scratch 2.0. This newer version of Scratch is incompatible with the version included on the Raspberry Pi; look for projects that state they have been created in Scratch 1.4 to be sure they are compatible with the Pi.

Chapter 11
An Introduction to Python

THE RASPBERRY PI gets the first half of its name from a long-standing tradition of using fruit to name new computing systems (from classic microcomputers like the Acorn, Apricot, and Tangerine to more recognisably modern brands including Apple and BlackBerry), but the second half comes courtesy of the Python programming language.

Introducing Python

Flexible and powerful, Python was originally developed in the late 1980s at the National Research Institute for Mathematics and Computer Science by Guido van Rossum as a successor to the ABC language. Since its introduction, Python has grown in popularity thanks to what is seen as a clear and expressive syntax developed with a focus on ensuring that code is readable.

Python is a *high-level language*. This means that Python code is written in largely recognisable English, providing the Pi with commands in a manner that is quick to learn and easy to follow. This is in marked contrast to *low-level languages*, like assembler, which are closer to how the computer "thinks" but almost impossible for a human to follow without experience. The high-level nature and clear syntax of Python make it a valuable tool for anyone who wants to learn to program. It is also the language that is recommended by the Raspberry Pi Foundation for those looking to progress from the simple Scratch (described in Chapter 10, "An Introduction to Scratch") to more "hands-on" programming.

Python is published under an open source licence and is freely available for Linux, OS X, and Windows computer systems. This cross-platform support means that software written using Python on the Pi can be used on computers running almost any other operating system as well—except where the program makes use of Pi-specific hardware such as the GPIO (general-purpose input/output) port. To find out how Python can be used to address this port, see Chapter 14, "The GPIO Port".

Example 1: Hello World

As you discovered in Chapter 10, the easiest way to learn a new programming language is to create a project that prints "Hello World!" on the screen. In Scratch, you just had to drag and drop blocks of prewritten code, but in Python, you need to write this program entirely by hand.

A Python project is, at heart, nothing more than a text file containing written instructions for the computer to follow. This file can be created using any text editor. For example, if you enjoy working at the console or in a terminal window, you can use nano; if you prefer a graphical user interface (GUI), you can use Leafpad. Another alternative is to use an integrated development environment (IDE) such as IDLE, which provides Python-specific functionality that's missing from a standard text editor, including syntax checking, debugging facilities, and the ability to run your program without having to leave the editor. This chapter gives you instructions on how to create Python files using IDLE, but of course, the IDE or editor that you choose to use for programming is up to you. This chapter also includes instructions for running your created files directly from the terminal, which can be used in conjunction with any text editor or other IDE.

To begin the Hello World project, open Python 2 (IDLE) from the Programming menu in the Raspbian distribution's desktop environment. If you're not using IDLE, create a blank document in your favourite text editor and skip the rest of this paragraph. By default, IDLE opens up in *Python shell* mode (see Figure 11-1), so anything you type in the initial window will be immediately executed. To open a new Python project that can be executed later, click on the File menu and choose New File to open a blank file.

> **TIP** Choosing Python 3 (IDLE) from the Programming menu instead of Python 2 (IDLE) loads the Python 3 version. This uses a subtly different form of the language, or *syntax*, which can cause problems with programs written for Python 2. The examples in this chapter are all written with Python 2 in mind, so be sure to load Python 2 (IDLE) and not Python 3 (IDLE).

It's good practice to start all Python programs with a line known as a *shebang*, which gets its name from the # and ! characters at the beginning of the line. This line tells the operating system where it should look for the Python interpreter. Although this is not entirely necessary for programs that will run from within IDLE or that will call Python explicitly at the terminal, it *is* required for programs that are run directly by calling the program's filename.

To ensure the program runs regardless of where the Python executable is installed, the first line of your program should read as follows:

```
#!/usr/bin/env python
```

FIGURE 11-1: The IDLE Python Shell window

This line tells the operating system to look at the *$PATH* environment variable—which is where Linux stores the location(s) of files that can be executed as programs—for the location of Python, which should work on any Linux distribution used on the Pi. The *$PATH* variable contains a list of directories where executable files are stored and is used to find programs when you type their names at the console or in a terminal window.

To print a message, you should use Python's `print` statement. As its name suggests, this statement prints text to an output device—by default, to the console or terminal window from which the program is being executed. Its usage is simple. Text following the word `print` and placed between quotation marks will be printed to the standard output device. Enter the following line in your new project:

```
print "Hello, World!"
```

The final program should look like this:

```
#!/usr/bin/env python
print "Hello, World!"
```

If you're creating the example program in IDLE rather than a plain text editor, notice that the text is multicoloured (see Figure 11-2, where colours are represented as differing shades of grey in the print edition). This is a feature known as *syntax highlighting* and is a feature of IDEs and the more-advanced text editing tools. Syntax highlighting changes the colour of sections of the text according to their function to make the program easier to understand at a glance. It also makes it easy to spot so-called *syntax errors* caused by forgetting to put an end-quote in a `print` command or forgetting to comment out a remark. For this short example, syntax highlighting isn't necessary; in larger programs, though, it can be an invaluable tool for finding errors.

FIGURE 11-2: Syntax highlighting in IDLE

Before you run your program, save it as `helloworld.py` using the File menu. If you're using IDLE, the file is given the extension `.py` automatically. If you're using a text editor, be sure to type `.py` at the end of the filename (not `.txt`) when you save it. This extension indicates that the file contains Python code—although Python is clever enough to run the program even if it's saved with a different file extension.

How you run the file depends on whether you're using IDLE or a text editor. In IDLE, simply choose Run Module from the Run menu or press the F5 key on the keyboard. This switches

IDLE back to the Python shell window and runs the program. You should then see the message `Hello, World!` appear onscreen in blue (see Figure 11-3). If not, check your syntax; in particular, check that you have quotation marks at both the beginning and end of the message on the `print` line.

FIGURE 11-3: Running helloworld.py in IDLE

If you created the `helloworld.py` program in a text editor, you need to open a terminal window from the Accessories menu on the desktop. If you saved the file anywhere except your home directory, you must also use the `cd` command to change to that directory (refer to Chapter 3, "Linux System Administration"). Once you're in the right directory, you can run your program by typing the following:

```
python helloworld.py
```

This tells the operating system to run Python and then load the `helloworld.py` file for execution. Unlike the Python shell in IDLE, Python quits when it reaches the end of the file and returns you to the terminal. The result, however, is the same: the message `Hello, World!` is printed to the standard output (see Figure 11-4).

FIGURE 11-4: Running helloworld.py at the terminal

Making Python Programs Executable

Normally, the only way to run a Python program is to tell the Python software to open the file. With the shebang line at the top of the file, however, it's possible to execute the file directly without having to call Python first. This can be a useful way of making your own tools that can be executed at the terminal: once copied into a location in the system's $PATH environment variable, the Python program can be called simply by typing its name.

First, you need to tell Linux that the Python file should be marked as executable—an attribute that means the file is a program. To protect the system from malware being downloaded from the Internet, this attribute isn't automatically set, since only files that are marked as executable will run. To make the helloworld.py file executable, use the chmod command (described in detail in Chapter 3) by typing the following:

chmod +x helloworld.py

Now try running the program directly by typing the following:

./helloworld.py

Despite the fact that you didn't call the Python program, the `helloworld.py` program should run just the same as though you'd typed `python helloworld.py`. The program can be run only by calling it with its full location—`/home/pi/helloworld.py`—or from the current directory by using `./` as the location. To make the file accessible in the same way as any other terminal command, you need to copy it to `/usr/local/bin` with the following command:

sudo cp helloworld.py /usr/local/bin/

The `sudo` prefix is required because, for security reasons, nonprivileged users cannot write to the `/usr/local/bin` directory. With the `helloworld.py` file located in `/usr/local/bin`, which is included in the `$PATH` variable, it can be executed from any directory by simply typing its name. Try changing to a different directory and then run the program by typing the following:

helloworld.py

To make your custom-made programs seem more like native utilities, you can rename them to remove the `.py` file extension. To change the `helloworld.py` program in this way, just type the following line at the terminal as a single line:

sudo mv /usr/local/bin/helloworld.py ↩

   /usr/local/bin/helloworld

Once renamed, the program can be run simply by typing `helloworld` at the terminal or console.

Example 2: Comments, Inputs, Variables, and Loops

Although the Hello World program is a useful, gentle introduction to a language, it's not terribly exciting. By its nature, it covers only the basics and fails to introduce some of the concepts required for creating useful or interesting programs. The next example, however, uses some of the basic tools required to make interactive programs in Python.

As in Example 1, begin by opening a new blank document in IDLE or your text editor and then start the program with the following shebang line:

```
#!/usr/bin/env python
```

As previously discussed, this line isn't strictly necessary unless the program is going to be made executable, but it does no harm and is a good habit to develop.

Next, add a comment to the program to provide context if you need to open the file at a later date. Note that this needs to be entered as a single line, as with all code lines that end in a ↵ symbol:

```
# Example 2: A Python program from the ↵
 Raspberry Pi User Guide
```

In Python, anything following a hash symbol—with the exception of the shebang line (which can only occur on the very first line of the program)—is treated as a comment. When a comment is found, Python ignores it and skips to the next line. Commenting your code is good practice because although you may know what a particular section of code does now, things might not be so clear when you open the file again six months down the line. Comments also help make code more maintainable, and if you decide to share your code with other people, your comments help them understand what each section is supposed to do. For simple programs, it's not strictly necessary to include comments; as with adding the shebang line, though, it's a very good habit to get into. Comments can be on their own line, as with the preceding comment, or at the end of a line, in which case Python runs the code line up until it reaches the hash symbol.

Next, ask the user for his or her name using the following line:

```
userName = raw_input("What is your name? ")
```

This small line actually achieves quite a lot. The first part, userName =, tells Python to create a new *variable*—a location for storing a piece of information—called userName. The equals symbol tells Python that the variable should be set to whatever follows. However, in this case what follows isn't just a piece of information, but another function: raw_input. This tool is designed to accept *string* (text) input from the keyboard, and allows for a message to be printed to the default output so the user knows what to type. This helps keep the program simple: without the ability to print a prompt telling the user what to type, a preceding line with a print command is required. Remember to leave a space at the end of the prompt; otherwise, the user's input will begin immediately after the question mark.

WARNING When asking the user to type text, always use raw_input. This provides security that the input command alone does not. If you just use input, a user may *inject* his or her own code into your program and have it crash or work contrary to your intentions.

With the user's name now stored safely in the `userName` variable, the program can begin to get clever. Welcome the user using the following line:

```
print "Welcome to the program,", userName
```

This line demonstrates a secondary function of the `print` command introduced in Example 1: the ability to print the contents of variables. This `print` command is split into two sections: the first section prints everything between the two quotation marks, and the second comma tells `print` that more should be printed to the same line. Simply typing the variable name `userName` is enough for Python to know that it should print the contents of that variable, resulting in a message customised to the user's own name.

This example program takes the form of a simple but friendly calculator. Unlike Example 1, it continues to run until the user tells it otherwise. This is achieved using a loop, just as in Scratch. Begin the loop by typing the following two lines:

```
goAgain = 1
while goAgain == 1:
```

The first line creates a new variable called `goAgain` and sets it to 1. The second line begins the loop and tells Python that `while` the `goAgain` variable is equal to 1, it should continue to loop through the following code. As the next few lines are written, they need to be *indented*, which you do by inserting four spaces at the start of each line. These spaces tell Python which lines are part of the loop and which lines are outside the loop. If you're using IDLE, the spaces are inserted automatically; if you're using a text editor, remember to insert the spaces manually.

Why ==?

Previously, you've been using a single equals symbol to set the value of variables. The `while` loop, however, uses two. Using two equals symbols next to each other performs an *evaluation*, which compares a variable's value to whatever follows. A single equals symbol instead sets the variable to the value that follows.

There are other evaluations as well as the double-equals, which is true only if the variable matches the given value exactly: `>` means greater than, `<` means less than, `>=` means greater than or equal to, `<=` means less than or equal to, and `!=` means not equal to.

Using these evaluation symbols, you can control the flow of a program according to the rules of Boolean logic. For more information on Boolean logic, refer to Chapter 10.

In its most basic form, a calculator takes two numbers as input and performs a mathematical operation on them. To make your calculator work, first take the two numbers from the user with the following lines:

```
firstNumber = int(raw_input("Type the first number: "))
secondNumber = int(raw_input("Type the second number: "))
```

These lines not only use the `raw_input` instruction to ask for two numbers, but they also use int. Short for *integer*, the `int` instruction tells Python to treat input as a number rather than a string. Obviously, this is important for a calculator program since it won't be calculating words.

With the two numbers stored as variables, the program can perform its calculations. Type the following lines, which add, subtract, and multiply the two numbers and send the output to the user:

```
print firstNumber, "added to", secondNumber, "equals", ↵
firstNumber + secondNumber
print firstNumber, "minus", secondNumber, "equals", ↵
firstNumber - secondNumber
print firstNumber, "multiplied by", secondNumber, "equals", ↵
firstNumber * secondNumber
```

Notice that while the addition and subtraction operations use the expected plus and minus symbols, multiplication uses the * symbol. Also notice that there are no formatting spaces between the quotation marks. This is because Python automatically adds spaces where required when it prints integers and strings together. Finally, note that there is no division operation (which would be indicated with the / symbol). This is because the example calculator program uses *integers*, which can be only whole numbers, with no decimal places or fractions allowed.

Although the calculation part of the program is now complete, it will run forever because there is currently nothing to tell Python when it's time to exit the loop. To provide the user with a way to exit the program, add the following line:

```
goAgain = int(raw_input("Type 1 to enter more numbers, ↵
or any other number to quit: "))
```

This allows the user to change the goAgain variable, which controls the `while` loop. If the user enters the number 1, the goAgain variable is still equal to 1, and the loop will run again. However, if the user enters any other number, the evaluation is no longer true (goAgain is no longer equal to 1), and the loop will end.

The finished program should look like this (remember that anything marked with ↵ should be entered on a single line):

```
#!/usr/bin/env python
# Example 2: A Python program from the Raspberry Pi User Guide
userName = raw_input("What is your name?   ")
print "Welcome to the program,", userName
goAgain = 1
while goAgain == 1:
    firstNumber = int(raw_input("Type the first number: "))
    secondNumber = int(raw_input("Type the second number: "))
    print firstNumber, "added to", secondNumber, "equals", ↵
    firstNumber + secondNumber
    print firstNumber, "minus", secondNumber, "equals", ↵
    firstNumber - secondNumber
    print firstNumber, "multiplied by", secondNumber, "equals", ↵
    firstNumber * secondNumber
    goAgain = int(raw_input("Type 1 to enter more numbers, or ↵
    any other number to quit: "))
```

Save the program as calculator.py, and run it by choosing Run Module from the Run menu in IDLE or by typing python calculator.py at the terminal. Enter your username when prompted; then provide the numbers that you want to calculate (see Figure 11-5) until you get bored and then type any number other than 1 to exit the program.

FIGURE 11-5: Running calculator.py in IDLE

For more short programs that introduce important Python concepts, visit the official Python Simple Programs wiki page at `https://wiki.python.org/moin/SimplePrograms`.

Example 3: Gaming with pygame

To illustrate the power of Python, this example creates a fully functional arcade game based on the classic game of Snake or Nibbles. To do so, it uses an external Python library called *pygame*.

Originally written by Pete Shinners, pygame is a collection of python *modules* designed to add new functionality to the language—functionality specifically designed to make it easy to write a game in Python. Each pygame module provides functionality required by a modern game, including sound, graphics, and even networking support. Although it's possible to write a game in Python without using pygame, it's a lot easier if you take advantage of the code already written in the pygame library.

If you are running Raspbian, the pygame library is already installed and ready to use. For other distributions, you can download the pygame source files from the official pygame website at `www.pygame.org/download.shtml`. Instructions for installation are provided on the same page.

Starting a pygame program is the same as starting any other Python project. Open a new blank document in either IDLE or a text editor and add the following shebang line to the top:

```
#!/usr/bin/env python
```

Next you need to tell Python that this program uses the pygame modules. To do this, you use an `import` instruction, which tells Python to load an external module (another Python file) and make it accessible from the current program. Type the following two lines to import the necessary modules into your new project:

```
import pygame, sys, time, random
from pygame.locals import *
```

The first line imports the main `pygame` module along with the Python modules `sys`, `time`, and `random`, which will also be used in this program. Typically, a module must then be called by typing its name followed by a full stop and the name of the instruction from within the module, but the second line in the preceding code tells Python to load all the instructions from the `pygame.locals` module as though they're native instructions. As a result, you can do less typing when using these instructions. Other module names—such as pygame. clock, which is separate from pygame.locals—will still need to be typed in full.

Enter the next two lines to set up pygame so that it's ready to use in the example program:

```
pygame.init()
fpsClock = pygame.time.Clock()
```

The first line tells pygame to initialise itself, and the second line sets up a new variable called fpsClock, which will be used to control the speed of the game. Next, set up a new pygame display surface—the canvas onto which in-game objects will be drawn—with the following two lines:

```
playSurface = pygame.display.set_mode((640, 480))
pygame.display.set_caption('Raspberry Snake')
```

Next, you should define some colours for the program to use. Although this step isn't strictly necessary, it again saves on typing. For example, if you want to set a particular object to be red, you can simply use the redColour variable rather than having to call the pygame. Color instruction and remember the three colour values for red, green, and blue. To define the colours for this example program, type the following lines:

```
redColour = pygame.Color(255, 0, 0)
blackColour = pygame.Color(0, 0, 0)
whiteColour = pygame.Color(255, 255, 255)
greyColour = pygame.Color(150, 150, 150)
```

The next few lines initialise some of the game's variables so they're ready for use. Note the use of the US English spelling of "color," an artefact of Pygame's US development; make sure you don't type "colour," as it won't be recognised. Initialising these variables is an important step, because if these variables are left blank when the game begins, Python won't know what to do. Don't worry about what each variable does for now; just type the following lines (but make sure you get all the commas and square brackets in the right places):

```
snakePosition = [100,100]
snakeSegments = [[100,100],[80,100],[60,100]]
raspberryPosition = [300,300]
raspberrySpawned = 1
direction = 'right'
changeDirection = direction
```

Notice that three of the variables—`snakePosition`, `snakeSegments`, and `raspberry Position`—are set to a list of comma-separated values. This causes Python to create the variables as *lists*—a number of different values stored in a single variable name. Later, you'll see how you can access individual values stored in a list.

Next, you need to define a new function—a fragment of Python code that can be called upon later in the program. Functions are useful for avoiding code repetition and making the program easier to understand. If you have a particular set of instructions that are needed at multiple points in the same program, using `def` to create a function means you have to type them only once—and have to change them in only a single place if you alter the program later. Type the following lines to define the `gameOver` function:

```
def gameOver():
    gameOverFont = pygame.font.Font ↵
    ('freesansbold.ttf', 72)
    gameOverSurf = gameOverFont.render ↵
    ('Game Over', True, greyColour)
    gameOverRect = gameOverSurf.get_rect()
    gameOverRect.midtop = (320, 10)
    playSurface.blit(gameOverSurf, gameOverRect)
    pygame.display.flip()
    time.sleep(5)
    pygame.quit()
    sys.exit()
```

As with loops, the code for a function should be indented. Every line after the `def` instruction should have four spaces at the start—if you're using IDLE, these spaces are inserted automatically, but if you're using a text editor, you must insert the spaces yourself. After the final line of the function—`sys.exit()`—you can stop indenting.

The `gameOver` function uses a selection of pygame's commands to perform a simple task: write the words `Game Over` to the screen in a large font, pause for five seconds, and then quit both pygame and Python. It may seem strange to set up the instructions for quitting the game before the game has even begun, but functions should always be defined before they are called. Python won't execute these instructions until it is told to do so using the newly created `gameOver` instruction.

With the beginning of the program complete, it's time to start the main section. This takes place in an infinite loop—a `while` loop that never exits. This is so that the game can continue to run until the player dies by hitting a wall or eating his or her own tail. Begin the main loop with the following line:

```
while True:
```

Without anything to evaluate, Python checks to see if `True` is true. Because that's always the case, the loop will continue to run forever—or at least until you tell Python to quit running by calling the `gameOver` function.

Continue the program with the following lines, paying attention to the indentation levels:

```python
for event in pygame.event.get():
    if event.type == QUIT:
        pygame.quit()
        sys.exit()
    elif event.type == KEYDOWN:
```

The first line, which comes right after the `while` loop begins, should be indented four spaces—but it's a loop of its own, using a `for` instruction to check for pygame events such as key presses. As a result, the line under `for` needs to be indented an additional four spaces for a total of eight—but that line is using an `if` instruction to check whether the user has pressed a key. As a result, the next line—`pygame.quit()`—is indented an additional four spaces for a total of 12 spaces. This logical progression of indentation tells Python where each loop block begins and ends, which is important because, if the wrong number of spaces is used, the program won't work correctly. This is why using a development environment like IDLE, which attempts to automatically indent code where required, can be easier than using a plain text editor to create Python programs.

An `if` statement tells Python to check to see if a particular evaluation is true. The first check, `if event.type == QUIT`, tells Python to execute the indented code below if pygame reports a `QUIT` message (which happens when the user presses the Escape key or when the user clicks the X button at the top-right to close the window). The two lines beneath that should be familiar from the `gameOver` function: they tell pygame and Python to close down and exit.

The line beginning `elif` extends `if` checks. Short for *else if*, an `elif` instruction is evaluated when a previous `if` instruction was found to be false. In this case, the `elif` instruction is used to see if pygame is reporting a `KEYDOWN` event, which is returned when the user is pressing a key on the keyboard. As with the `if` instruction, code to be executed when an `elif` is true should be indented by an additional four spaces plus whatever indentation the `elif` instruction itself has. Type the following lines to give the `elif` instruction something to do when the user presses a key:

```python
if event.key == K_RIGHT or event.key == ord('d'):
    changeDirection = 'right'
if event.key == K_LEFT or event.key == ord('a'):
    changeDirection = 'left'
```

```
if event.key == K_UP or event.key == ord('w'):
    changeDirection = 'up'
if event.key == K_DOWN or event.key == ord('s'):
    changeDirection = 'down'
if event.key == K_ESCAPE:
    pygame.event.post(pygame.event.Event(QUIT))
```

These instructions modify the value of the changeDirection variable, which is used to control the direction the player's snake is travelling during the game. Using or with an if statement allows more than one evaluation to be made. In this case, it provides two ways of controlling the snake: the player can use the cursor keys or the W, A, S, and D keys to make the snake go up, left, down, or right. Until a key is pressed, the snake travels to the right according to the value set for direction at the start of the program.

The variable direction is used alongside changeDirection to see whether the instruction the user has given is valid. The snake should be prevented from turning immediately back on itself; if it does, the snake dies and the game is over. To prevent this from happening, the direction requested by the player—stored in changeDirection—is compared to the current direction in which the snake is travelling—stored in direction. If they are opposite directions, the instruction is ignored, and the snake continues in the same direction as before. Type the following lines to set up the comparisons, alternating between indentations of four spaces and eight spaces:

```
if changeDirection == 'right' and not direction == 'left':
    direction = changeDirection
if changeDirection == 'left' and not direction == 'right':
    direction = changeDirection
if changeDirection == 'up' and not direction == 'down':
    direction = changeDirection
if changeDirection == 'down' and not direction == 'up':
    direction = changeDirection
```

With the user's input checked to make sure it makes sense, the snake—which appears on the screen as a series of blocks—can be moved. During each turn, the snake moves a distance equal to the size of one of its blocky segments. With each segment measuring 20 pixels, you can tell pygame to move the snake a single segment in any direction. Type the following code:

```
if direction == 'right':
    snakePosition[0] += 20
if direction == 'left':
    snakePosition[0] -= 20
```

```
if direction == 'up':
    snakePosition[1] -= 20
if direction == 'down':
    snakePosition[1] += 20
```

The += and -= operators change the value of a variable by a certain amount: += sets the variable to its previous value plus the new value, and -= sets the variable to its previous value minus the new value. By way of example, snakePosition[0] += 20 is a shorthand way of writing snakePosition[0] = snakePosition[0] + 20. The number in square brackets following the snakePosition variable name is the position in the list being affected. The first value in the snakePosition list stores the snake's position along the x-axis, and the second value stores the position along the y-axis, with 0,0 representing the upper-left corner. Python begins counting at zero, so the x-axis is controlled with snakePosition[0] and the y-axis with snakePosition[1]. If the list were longer, additional entries could be affected by increasing the number: [2], [3], and so on.

Although the snakePosition list is always two values long, another list created at the start of the program is not: snakeSegments. This list stores the location of the snake's body, behind the head. As the snake eats raspberries and grows longer, this list increases in size and provides the difficulty in the game: as the player progresses, it becomes harder to avoid hitting the body of the snake with the head. If the head hits the body, the snake dies, and the game is over. Type the following line to make the snake's body grow:

```
snakeSegments.insert(0,list(snakePosition))
```

This uses the insert instruction to insert a new value into the snakeSegments list: the current position of the snake. Each time Python reaches this line, it increases the length of the snake's body by one segment and locates that segment at the current position of the snake's head. To the player, it will look as though the snake is growing. However, you want this to happen only when the snake eats a raspberry; otherwise, the snake will just grow and grow. Type the following lines:

```
if snakePosition[0] == raspberryPosition[0] ↵
and snakePosition[1] == raspberryPosition[1]:
    raspberrySpawned = 0
else:
    snakeSegments.pop()
```

The first instruction checks the X and Y coordinates of the snake's head to see if they match the X and Y coordinates of the raspberry—the target the player is chasing. If the values match, the raspberry is considered to have been eaten by the snake—and the raspberrySpawned variable is set to 0. The else instruction tells Python what to do if the raspberry has not been eaten: pop the "oldest" value from the snakeSegments list.

The pop instruction is simple but clever. It returns the last value from the list but also removes it, making the list one item shorter. In the case of the snakeSegment list, it tells Python to delete the portion of the snake's body farthest away from the head. To the player, it will look as though the entire snake has moved without growing, whereas in reality, it grew at one end and shrank at the other. Because of the else statement, the pop instruction runs only when a raspberry has not been eaten. If a raspberry has been eaten, the last entry in the list doesn't get deleted—so the snake grows in size by one segment.

At this point in the program, it's possible that the player has eaten a raspberry. A game in which only a single raspberry is available is boring, so type the following lines to add a new raspberry back to the playing surface if the player has eaten the existing raspberry:

```
if raspberrySpawned == 0:
    x = random.randrange(1,32)
    y = random.randrange(1,24)
    raspberryPosition = [x*20,y*20]
    raspberrySpawned = 1
```

This section of code checks to see whether the raspberry has been eaten by testing if the **raspberrySpawned** variable is set to 0, and if so, the code picks a random location on the playing surface using the random module you imported at the start of the program. This location is then multiplied by the size of a snake's segment—20 pixels wide and 20 pixels tall—to give Python a place on the playing field to position the new raspberry. It's important that the location of the raspberry is set randomly. Doing so prevents the player from learning where the raspberry will appear next and keeps the game interesting. Finally, the **raspberrySpawned** variable is set back to 1, to make sure that there will be only a single raspberry on the playing surface at any given time.

Now you have the code required to make the snake move and grow, and to cause raspberries to be eaten and created—a process known in gaming as *respawning*. However, nothing is being drawn to the screen. Type the following lines:

```
playSurface.fill(blackColour)
for position in snakeSegments:
    pygame.draw.rect(playSurface,whiteColour,Rect ↵
    (position[0], position[1], 20, 20))
pygame.draw.rect(playSurface,redColour,Rect ↵
    (raspberryPosition[0], raspberryPosition[1], 20, 20))
pygame.display.flip()
```

These lines tell pygame to fill in the background of the playing surface in black, draw the snake's body segments in white, and finally, draw the raspberry in red. The last line, **pygame.display.flip()**, tells pygame to update the screen; without this instruction, items will be invisible to the player. Every time you finish drawing objects onto the screen, remember to use pygame.display.flip() so the user can see the changes.

Currently, it's impossible for the snake to die. A game where the player can never die would rapidly get boring, so enter the following lines to set up some scenarios for the snake's death:

```
if snakePosition[0] > 620 or snakePosition[0] < 0:
    gameOver()
if snakePosition[1] > 460 or snakePosition[1] < 0:
    gameOver()
```

The first if statement checks to see whether the snake has gone off the playing surface horizontally, and the second if statement checks whether the snake has gone off the playing surface vertically. In either case, it's bad news for the snake; the gameOver function, defined earlier in the program, is called to print a message to the screen and quit the game. The snake should also die if its head hits any portion of its body, so add the following lines:

```
for snakeBody in snakeSegments[1:]:
    if snakePosition[0] == snakeBody[0] and ↩
    snakePosition[1] == snakeBody[1]:
        gameOver()
```

The for statement runs through each of the snake segments' locations, from the second list entry to the end of the list, and compares it to the current position of the snake's head. It's important to start the comparison at the second entry using snakeSegments[1:] and not the first. The first entry is always set to the position of the head, and starting the comparison there would result in instant death for the snake as soon as the game begins.

Finally, all that is required for the game to be complete is to control the update speed using the fpsClock variable. Without the variable, which you created at the start of the program, the game would run too quickly to play. Type the following line to finish the program:

```
fpsClock.tick(20)
```

If you think the game is too easy or too slow, you can increase this number (to update the game at a higher number of *frames per second*); or if the game is too hard or too fast, decrease the number. Save the program as raspberrysnake.py and run it either by using IDLE's Run Module option in the Run menu or from the terminal by typing **python raspberrysnake.py**. The game will start as soon as it's loaded (see Figure 11-6), so make sure you're ready!

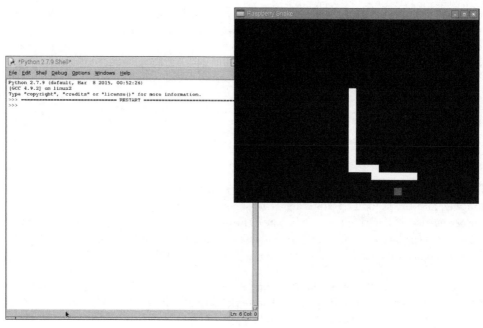

FIGURE 11-6: Playing Raspberry Snake on the Raspberry Pi

A full copy of the program listing for Raspberry Snake is included in Appendix A, "Python Recipes", and on the Raspberry Pi User Guide website at `www.wiley.com/go/ raspberrypiuserguide4`. Downloading the source code from the website will save you some typing, but entering the code by hand is a good way of ensuring that you understand what each section does. In addition to the functions you've used in Raspberry Snake, pygame provides lots of features not used in this program, including audio playback, sprite handling for better graphics, and mouse control. The best place to learn about pygame's more-advanced functions is on the official website, `www.pygame.org/wiki/tutorials`, where you can download tutorials and example programs to get a handle on how things work.

Example 4: Python and Networking

So far, you have learned how to use Python to create standalone programs, but the language can also be used to create programs that communicate with the outside world over a computer's network connection. This next example, written by Tom Hudson, offers a brief glimpse of these possibilities with a tool for monitoring the users connected to an Internet Relay Chat (IRC) channel.

As usual, create a new project in IDLE or a text editor and enter the shebang line along with a comment describing the purpose of the program:

```
#!/usr/bin/env python
# IRC Channel Checker, written for the ↵
Raspberry Pi User Guide by Tom Hudson
```

Next, import the modules required by the program—sys, socket, and time—with the following line:

```
import sys, socket, time
```

You used the sys and time modules previously in the Raspberry Snake program, but you have not yet used socket. The socket module provides Python with the ability to open, close, read from, and write to network sockets—giving Python programs rudimentary networking capabilities. It's the socket module that provides this example with its ability to connect to a remote IRC server.

There are some *constants* needed for this program to operate. Constants are like variables in that they can have values assigned to them. Unlike variables, however, the value in a constant shouldn't change. To help differentiate a constant from a variable, it's good practice to use all-capital letters for their names; that way it's easy to see at a glance whether a particular section of the code is using a constant or a variable. Note, though, that Python makes no distinction itself; using upper- or lower-case typography is there simply as an aid to the programmer. Type the following two lines into the program:

```
RPL_NAMREPLY = '353'
RPL_ENDOFNAMES = '366'
```

These are IRC *status codes*, provided by the server to indicate when particular operations have completed. The program uses these codes to determine when it has received the required list of names from the IRC server. Next, set up the variables for the server connection by entering the following lines:

```
irc = {
    'host': 'chat.freenode.net',
    'port': 6667,
    'channel': '#raspiuserguide',
    'namesinterval': 5
}
```

The first line tells Python to create a *dict* data type. Short for dictionary, this allows multiple variables to be stored in a single master variable—in this case, `irc`. These individual variables can then be recalled later in the program. Although you could write this program without using dicts to store variables, it would make the program significantly more difficult to read. The dict begins with the opening curly brace and ends with the closing curly brace on the final line.

Set the `host` variable to the fully qualified domain name (FQDN) of the IRC server to which the program will connect. In this example, `chat.freenode.net` is used, but if you want to customise the program to use a different server, change the domain name here. The `port` variable tells the program which network port IRC is running on, which will usually be 6667. The `channel` variable tells Python which channel to join in order to monitor the users, and `namesinterval` controls how long the program waits to refresh the list of users, measured in seconds.

Set up a second dict to store the user-specific variables by typing the following lines:

```
user = {
    'nick': 'botnick',
    'username': 'botuser',
    'hostname': 'localhost',
    'servername': 'localhost',
    'realname': 'Raspberry Pi Names Bot'
}
```

As with `irc`, all these variables are stored within a dict called `user` to make it clear which variables pertain to which section. The `nick` variable should be set to the IRC nickname the program will use. Don't use your usual nickname if you're planning to connect to the IRC server at the same time; instead, try appending `-bot` to the end of your name to make it clear that the user is a program rather than a real person. Do the same with `username`, and fill in the `realname` variable with a descriptive message about whom the bot belongs to. The `hostname` and `servername` variables can be left set to `localhost` or altered to match your Internet address.

The `socket` module requires the user to create a socket *object*. This object provides network connectivity to the rest of the program. Create the socket object by typing the following line:

```
s = socket.socket(socket.AF_INET, socket.SOCK_STREAM)
```

Next, you need to tell the program to try connecting to the IRC server specified in the variables at the start of the program. Type the following lines:

```
print 'Connecting to %(host)s:%(port)s...' % irc
try:
    s.connect((irc['host'], irc['port']))
except socket.error:
    print 'Error connecting to IRC server ↵
    %(host)s:%(port)s' % irc
    sys.exit(1)
```

The `try` and `except` commands are included in this code for *error handling*. If the system fails to connect to the server—because the Pi isn't connected to the Internet, for example, or because the server is down for maintenance—the program will print an error message and gracefully exit. The `s.connect` line tells the socket module to try connecting to the IRC server, using the `host` and `port` variables held in the `irc` dict.

If the program doesn't quit from the exception, it has successfully connected to the IRC server. Before you can get a list of names in a channel, however, you need to identify yourself to the server and issue some commands using the `send` function of the `socket` module. Type the following lines into the program:

```
s.send('NICK %(nick)s\r\n' % user)
s.send('USER %(username)s %(hostname)s ↵
 %(servername)s :%(realname)s\r\n' % user)
s.send('JOIN %(channel)s\r\n' % irc)
s.send('NAMES %(channel)s\r\n' % irc)
```

The send function works in almost exactly the same way as the `print` function, except that instead of printing to the standard output—usually the terminal window or console—it sends the output through the network connection. In this case, the program is sending strings of text to the IRC server, followed by carriage return (\r) and newline (\r) characters, simulating the user pressing the Enter key, which tell it to register the program using the nickname held in the `nick` variable and the user details held in the `username`, `hostname`, `servername`, and `realname` variables. Next, the program sends the command to join the channel specified in the `channel` variable, and finally, it sends the command to receive the list of users in that channel. Although this example is tailored to IRC, the same basic principle can be used to issue commands to any network service—with modifications, this program could be used to list the files on an FTP server or unread emails on a POP3 server.

Receiving data from the socket is a little more complicated. First, you need to create an empty string variable that will act as the *receive buffer*, holding data from the server as it's received until it can be processed. Initialise the buffer by typing the following line:

```
read_buffer = ''
```

Note that there are two single quotes after the equals sign, not one double quote.

Next, create an empty list, which will be used to store the names of users, by typing the following line:

```
names = []
```

The list data type is the same as you used to store the locations in the Raspberry Snake game. Unlike a normal variable, it can store multiple values—in this case, the names of users present in the IRC channel.

The next step is to create an infinite loop, during which the program continuously queries the server for usernames and prints them to the screen. Start the loop by typing the following:

```
while True:
    read_buffer += s.recv(1024)
```

The first line of the loop, following `while True:`, tells the `socket` module to receive (up to) 1024 bytes (1K) of data from the IRC server and place it in the `read_buffer` variable. Because the `+=` operator is used, rather than just `=`, the received data will be appended to anything already in the buffer. The value of 1024 bytes is more or less arbitrary.

The next step is to split the buffer into individual lines of text, using the following program lines:

```
    lines = read_buffer.split('\r\n')
    read_buffer = lines.pop();
```

The first line sets the `lines` variable to full lines of text from the receive buffer by using the `split` function to find *end-of-line* characters—signified by \r\n. These characters occur only at the end of a line, so when the buffer has been split in this way you know that `lines` contains only full-line responses from the server. The `pop` instruction in the second line makes sure that only full lines are removed from the `read_buffer`; because responses from the server are read in 1K chunks, it's likely that at any given time, the end of the buffer will contain a fraction of a line. When that's the case, the fraction is left in the buffer ready to receive the remainder of the line the next time the loop runs and the next 1K chunk is received from the server.

At this point, the `lines` variable contains a list of full responses—full lines—received from the server. Type the following to process these lines and find the names of channel participants:

```
for line in lines:
    response = line.rstrip().split(' ', 3)
    response_code = response[1]
    if response_code == RPL_NAMREPLY:
        names_list = response[3].split(':')[1]
        names += names_list.split(' ')
```

This runs through every line found in the `lines` variable and looks for the numerical IRC response code provided by the server. Although there are plenty of different response codes, this program is interested in only the two defined as constants at the start of the program: 353, which means a list of names follows; and 366, which means the list has ended. The `if` statement looks for the first of these responses, and then uses the `split` function to retrieve these names and add them to the `names` list.

Now, the `names` list contains all the names received from the server in response to the program's query. This may not be all the names, however, because until the 366 response, which signals the end of the member names, is received, the list is incomplete. That is why the last line—`names += names_list.split(' ')`—is appending the newly received names to the existing list, rather than blanking it out entirely: each time that section of the code runs, the program is likely to have received only a subsection of the entire member list. To tell Python what to do when the full list has been received, enter the following lines, making sure to start with eight spaces:

```
    if response_code == RPL_ENDOFNAMES:
        # Display the names
        print '\r\nUsers in %(channel)s:' % irc
        for name in names:
            print name
        names = []
```

This tells Python that when the 366 response has been received, it should print the now-complete list of names to the standard output before blanking the `names` list again. This last line—`names = []`—is important. Without it, each time the loop runs, it will add users' names to the list, even though they already exist from an earlier run.

Finally, finish the program by entering the following lines:

```
time.sleep(irc['namesinterval'])
s.send('NAMES %(channel)s\r\n' % irc)
```

This tells Python to wait the `namesinterval` number of seconds before sending another request for usernames and beginning the loop again. Be careful to set `namesinterval` to a reasonable value; if the IRC server receives too many requests in too short a space of time, it may forcibly disconnect you for *flooding*.

Save the program as `ircuserlist.py` and run it either by using IDLE's Run Module option in the Run menu or from the terminal by typing **python ircuserlist.py.** When the program first runs, it might take a while to connect to the server; once connected, however, the list of names (see Figure 11-7) should refresh quickly. To quit the program, press Crtl+C.

FIGURE 11-7: Using Python to list users in an IRC channel

A full copy of the program listing for the IRC user list is included in Appendix A and on the Raspberry Pi User Guide website at `www.wiley.com/go/raspberrypiuserguide4`. Downloading the source code from the website will save you some typing, but entering the code by hand is a good way of ensuring that you understand what each section does.

Further Reading

I hope this chapter has given you a taste of what you can do with Python. The information in this chapter is far from exhaustive. To do the language full justice would take a considerably larger book; however, plenty of resources are out there for learning more about the Python language, including the following:

- The official *Beginner's Guide to Python*, which you can access at `http://wiki.python.org/moin/BeginnersGuide`.

- A free, interactive tutorial that runs entirely in your browser is available at `www.learnpython.org`.

- Zed A. Shaw's *Learn Python The Hard Way* (Shavian Publishing, 2012) offers great insight into best-practice coding for Python, and despite the name, it's suitable for beginners. This book is commercially available, or you can read it for free at `http://learnpythonthehardway.org`.

- Although somewhat outdated and since replaced by *Dive Into Python 3* (Apress, 2009), *Dive Into Python* by Mark Pilgrim (Apress, 2004) does a good job of addressing the basics of writing programs in Python. It's available for free download at `www.diveintopython.net` or for purchase in printed format from all good booksellers.

- If you prefer hands-on learning with other interested individuals, a list of local Python User Groups—sometimes called PIGgies—can be found at `https://wiki.python.org/moin/LocalUserGroups`.

- For learning pygame, Al Sweigart's book *Making Games with Python & Pygame* (CreateSpace, 2012) is a great introduction with practical examples. You can purchase the hardcopy book or download it for free at `http://inventwithpython.com`.

Chapter 12
Minecraft Pi Edition

MINECRAFT, THE CREATION of the Swedish software development firm Mojang, has become a cultural phenomenon. Blending survivalist gaming with a LEGO-inspired creative approach, the game gives players the tools to explore, mine, and build in an open-world environment and has sold millions of copies worldwide across computers, consoles, and even smartphones. Now, it's also available for the Raspberry Pi—and brings with it educational elements that let interested parties learn through play.

Introducing Minecraft Pi Edition

The creation of Mojang's Aron Nieminen and Daniel Frisk, Minecraft Pi Edition is at its heart a cut-down version of the smartphone-oriented Minecraft Pocket Edition. Although missing many of the features of the full game—such as survival mode, which pits the player against numerous foes in a deadly world—it is very well suited to casual and creative play, particularly by younger children.

Although a very early test release, known as an *alpha*, Minecraft Pi Edition has already proved popular in education for a number of reasons. The game provides a means for the player to experiment with building by using blocks constructed from a variety of materials, making it a good choice for teaching geographical or architectural concepts. The game is also free, unlike its other variants, with those who own a Pi able to download and make use of the title as they see fit without having to pay a licence fee.

The biggest reason that Minecraft Pi Edition has attracted so much interest in education, however, lies in its *application programming interface (API)*. The Minecraft Pi Edition API allows users to control the in-game environment using programs they have written. Most commonly accessed from Python (not coincidentally the same language chosen by the Raspberry Pi Foundation for its educational programmes), the API allows users to send and receive messages, control the placement of in-game blocks, and even control the player character directly—and it's a great way to get children already conversant in Minecraft interested in the more serious pursuit of programming.

Installing Minecraft

If you're using the latest version of the Raspbian operating system, Minecraft Pi Edition is already installed and ready to use. If you're using any other distribution, you'll need to open your web browser and enter the address **pi.minecraft.net** to access the official Minecraft Pi Edition website. To download the Minecraft Pi Edition package, find the blue highlighted link labelled Download and when prompted choose to open the file.

After a brief pause as the file downloads, a new window appears showing the content of the Minecraft Pi Edition software archive: a single folder named mcpi. Choose the extract the folder from the archive then place it somewhere you can easily find it, either in your home directory or on your desktop.

Click the Extract button and wait briefly while the Pi uncompresses Minecraft Pi Edition. Unlike installing software through a package manager like Apt, installing from an archive in this manner is a one-time operation. So, if a new version of Minecraft Pi Edition is released in the future, you won't receive automatic upgrades. Instead, you just follow the preceding steps again to download the new version and extract it over the existing copy. If you're using Raspbian, any available updates will be installed when you run apt-get update, as usual.

Running Minecraft

Minecraft Pi Edition is installed as standard in the latest versions of the Raspbian distribution, and is compatible with any model of Raspberry Pi as long as it is connected to an external display. The game runs within the graphical user interface, known as the desktop, rather than at the text-based console. If your Pi is not set to boot into the desktop automatically, you'll need to manually load it by typing the following command at the console:

```
startx
```

When the graphical user interface (GUI) has loaded, click the Menu button at the top-left of the screen and scroll down to Games. Hover the mouse cursor over this option to load the submenu, and you'll find an entry called Minecraft Pi. Simply click Minecraft Pi to load the game (see Figure 12-1).

FIGURE 12-1: Running Minecraft Pi Edition

By default, Minecraft Pi Edition loads in a window on the desktop (see Figure 12-2). It's best to play the game entirely within this window, although you can click the Maximise button to enlarge the screen but will find the game difficult to play should you choose to do so.

A bug in the software—which is, at the time of writing, still an early alpha release—means that the mouse will not track your movements properly and the game will be impossible to play while in full screen mode. You'll also find that it's impossible to take screenshots while playing the game. Minecraft Pi Edition interfaces with the Pi's graphics accelerator at a very low level to achieve reasonable performance, and attempts to take a screenshot result in a black box where the Minecraft window should be.

To experiment with Minecraft, click Start Game to load the World Selection screen. Minecraft works by generating a random world each time you start a new game. This world is populated with blocks of various materials and typically features a sea, a mountain, beaches, and trees. The first time you click Start Game, no worlds appear on the World Selection screen, so click Create New to build a new one. The next time you load the game, you'll have the choice of creating a new random world or loading the existing world you created by clicking and dragging the world to the centre of the screen and then clicking on it.

Worlds in Minecraft Pi Edition operate independently from each other. If you build a house in one world, it won't be present in any other world stored on the same Pi. This is especially important when using the World Selection screen to delete existing worlds. Make sure you are deleting the right world because anything created in that world will be lost for good when you do so.

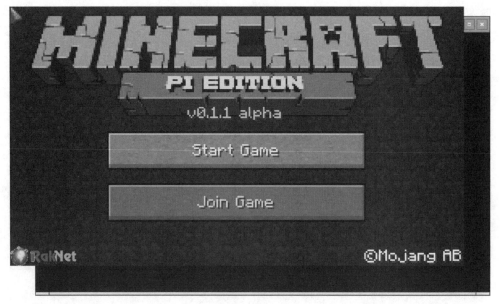

FIGURE 12-2: Minecraft Pi running in Raspbian

Exploration

Minecraft works very similar to a traditional first-person shooter (FPS) game, although Minecraft is considerably less violent. In fact, in the Pi Edition, there are no enemies at all, nor is there a time limit, so it's a great stress-free introduction to gaming for younger or less experienced players.

You start the game at a random location in the world (see Figure 12-3). You move your character by using the W, A, S, and D keys to move to the left, the right, backward, and forward, respectively. These keys don't turn your character; you achieve that by moving the mouse. Unlike most games, Minecraft also gives the player the ability to fly: the Space key jumps, and double-tapping the key engages flight mode. While flying, Space increases your altitude and Shift sends you back down to the ground; double-tapping the Space key again cancels flight mode.

Unlike the main game's Survival mode, Minecraft Pi Edition starts the player with infinite supplies of all the block types available in the game. As a result, there's no need to mine for resources, and you can begin to build your first structures immediately. The blocks available for building are displayed across the bottom of the Minecraft window, with the currently active block highlighted. Scrolling with a mouse wheel or pressing the 1 through 8 keys on the keyboard allows you to choose different blocks, each of which has different properties. You can access additional blocks by bringing up the full inventory with the E key. Experimenting is the best way to see what happens when block types are combined.

FIGURE 12-3: Exploring in Minecraft Pi Edition

Click the right mouse button to place a block, and hold that button down while moving the mouse to place multiple blocks at once. You can destroy any block in the world—including those that you didn't place—by clicking the left mouse button and holding that button down and moving the mouse deletes swathes of blocks.

Construction is simply a question of placing and removing blocks until your chosen edifice—whether it's a tree house, a mansion, or a full-scale replica of a spaceship—is complete. When you quit the game, your progress is saved and can be loaded from the World Selection screen the next time you start a Minecraft Pi game. It's a good idea to spend a while experimenting with the world of Minecraft, in particular how various blocks interact with one another, before moving on to using the application programming interface (API).

Hacking Minecraft

The secret to Minecraft Pi Edition's educational success is its API, which allows various aspects of the game to be modified by programs that you write. The Minecraft API is a powerful tool, but one that makes it as easy as possible to get started.

If you're currently playing a game of Minecraft Pi Edition, quit it now by pressing the Escape key, selecting Quit to Title, and then clicking on the window's X close button at the top right. Alternatively, press Escape, hold down the Alt key, and press F4 to instantly quit.

If you're running Raspbian, you can begin using the Minecraft API immediately. Those running on other distributions will need to create a copy of the Minecraft API outside the main Minecraft directory. This step ensures that what you do won't affect your main Minecraft Pi Edition installation, which gives you the freedom to experiment without worrying about breaking something. Type the following commands in your system's terminal to do so:

```
mkdir ~/minecraftcode
cp -r ~/mcpi/api/python/mcpi ~/minecraftcode/minecraft
```

This creates a new directory called `minecraftcode` and copies the Python version of the Minecraft Pi Edition API into that folder. This is the folder in which you will create your scripts to modify how Minecraft operates.

If you're running Raspbian, you simply need only create a directory in which to store your programs. Do so by loading the Terminal by clicking the Menu button and scrolling down to Accessories before clicking on the Terminal option, then typing the following command:

```
mkdir ~/minecraftcode
```

If multiple people will be using your Pi and will all log in under the same user account, you can create a folder for each by modifying the name `minecraftcode` in the preceding commands to (for example, `minecraft-steve`, `minecraft-bob`, `minecraft-sara`).

Although the Minecraft Pi Edition API supports multiple programming languages, the easiest way to get started is by using Python. For full details on getting started with Python programming on the Raspberry Pi, refer to Chapter 11, "An Introduction to Python". If you've already read that chapter, you can get started with Minecraft modification straightaway.

Begin by loading the IDLE programming environment, by clicking on the Menu button, scrolling down to Programming, and then clicking on Python 2 (IDLE). Make sure you click on the entry marked Python 2, and not Python 3; the latter uses a different version of the Python programming language that does not work with the Minecraft API. In the window that appears, click the File menu and click New File. A blank Python file to edit appears. Begin by clicking File and Save As to save the file. In the Save As dialogue that appears, double-click the `minecraftcode` folder and name the file **testing.py** before saving it (see Figure 12-4).

Start your first Minecraft Python program by entering the usual shebang line at the top of the file:

```
#!/usr/bin/env python
```

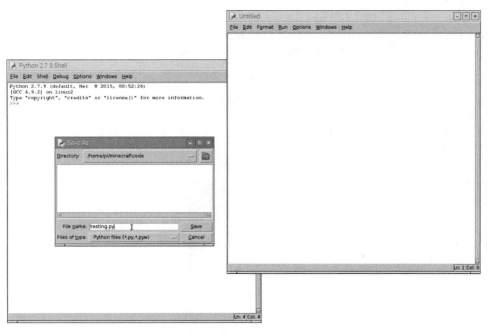

FIGURE 12-4: Saving your first Minecraft Python program

This allows you to run your program without loading IDLE, if you so desire. It's not strictly required, but it's a good habit to form and helps identify your scripts as Python programs, even if they are renamed and lose the .py file extension. Next, you import the Minecraft API library to provide the various commands you need to modify the game from within Python. Type the following two lines into IDLE:

```
import mcpi.minecraft as minecraft
import mcpi.block as block
```

Next, set up a simple way to send commands to Minecraft with the following line:

```
mc = minecraft.Minecraft.create()
```

This sets Python up so that, instead of having to type the command for accessing the Minecraft API every time you want to reference it in your program, you can simply type the letters *mc*. This not only saves on typing but also makes the finished program a lot easier to read and understand. It also connects the program to the running Minecraft game, ready for the API to take instructions.

The Minecraft Pi Edition API is extremely powerful, and exploring its many features is beyond the scope of this introductory chapter. The following lines offer a brief example of its basic usage, however, and you can enter them into IDLE (see Figure 12-5):

```
playerPos = mc.player.getTilePos()
mc.setBlock(playerPos.x+1, playerPos.y+1, playerPos.z,
  block.STONE)
mc.postToChat("Stone block
created")
```

FIGURE 12-5: The finished Minecraft Pi Edition Python program

The first line retrieves the player's current position, relative to the nearest block surface—known as a *tile*. The second creates a new stone block, shifted one block away from the player on the X and Y coordinates and at the same Z coordinate. All locations in Minecraft are recorded in this three-dimensional format, with Y representing the vertical plane, and learning how to address the precise location you need is the secret of success with the Minecraft API.

The final line uses the in-game chat system to confirm the creation of the stone block (this system was originally designed for multiplayer use, to allow players to communicate over the Internet even when they're not in the same physical room). This message confirms that the script has run correctly. Without this message, you might not notice the appearance of the stone block—because its location might be behind you rather than in front of you.

Save the file by clicking the File menu and then clicking Save. Load Minecraft Pi Edition again and click Start Game. Either load an existing world or generate a new one, and then press the Alt and Tab keys to release the mouse focus from the Minecraft window. This shift returns the control of the mouse to you, and moving it now moves the onscreen cursor rather than the viewpoint of the Minecraft character, allowing you to swap back to the IDLE window containing your text program.

In IDLE, click the Run menu and click Run Module or press the F5 key on the keyboard to run the example program you created. After a few seconds, the message "Stone block created" should appear in the Minecraft window (see Figure 12-6). Press Alt and Tab again to return your focus to the game, holding the Alt key and pressing Tab until the Minecraft entry is highlighted in the list, and use the mouse to look around. The stone block your program created will have appeared nearby. If you move your character, go back to IDLE with Tab and click Run Module again, another stone block will be created. Alternatively, you can change the X, Y, and Z coordinates within the program to create a block somewhere else without moving your character. You can even create one in the sky, if you so wish.

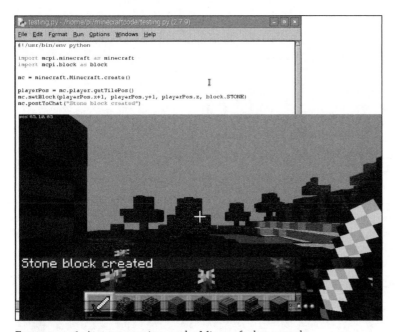

FIGURE 12-6: A message prints to the Minecraft chat console

As with Minecraft, the best way to master the API is by experimentation. *The MagPi*, the official magazine of the Raspberry Pi Foundation, has run tutorials on Minecraft Pi Edition available at `www.raspberrypi.org/magpi`. You can quickly find other resources by searching for Minecraft Pi Edition on the Internet. Examining others' programs and modifying them to see what happens will quickly lead to proficiency in the API—and, as an added bonus, it's a great way to practice general Python programming techniques, too.

Part IV

Hardware
Hacking

Chapter 13
Learning to Hack Hardware

IN EARLIER CHAPTERS, you learned how the Raspberry Pi can be turned into a flexible platform for running a variety of software. In this respect, it's not alone: any desktop or laptop can run the same software, and in many cases, run it far faster than the Pi's low-power processor can manage.

The Pi has another trick up its sleeve, though, which places it above and beyond the capabilities of the average PC: its *general-purpose input-output (GPIO)* port, located on the top-left of the Pi's printed circuit board.

The GPIO enables the Pi to communicate with other components and circuits and allows it to act as a controller in a larger electronic circuit. Through the GPIO port, it's possible to have the Pi sense temperatures, move servos, and talk to other computing devices using a variety of different *protocols,* including *Serial Peripheral Interface (SPI)* and *Inter-Integrated Circuit (I^2C).* Chapter 14, "The GPIO Port", provides details on working with the GPIO pins.

Before you can get started building circuits to use with the Pi's GPIO port, however, you need some additional equipment and an understanding about some of the language surrounding the world of electronics.

Electronic Equipment

To start building circuits that can be controlled by the Pi's GPIO port, you need various components and tools. The following is a sample shopping list for getting started with electronics:

- **Breadboard**—An electronic breadboard provides a grid of holes spaced at 2.54 mm intervals into which components can be inserted and removed. Below each grid is a series of electrical contacts which allow components in the same row to be connected together without wires. A breadboard is a valuable tool for electronics work, especially prototyping, because it allows you to quickly make mock-up circuits that can be modified without the need for soldering or desoldering.

- **Wires**—While a breadboard allows some components to be joined without wiring, you still need wires to connect one row to another, or to connect the breadboard to the Pi's GPIO port. These are known as *jumper wires*, and if you're working on a breadboard, it's a good idea to get solid-core wire rather than stranded-core wire. Solid-core wire is easier to insert into the breadboard's holes than stranded-core wire. It's also helpful to get various colours so you can colour-code each connection according to its purpose.

- **Resistors**—The vast majority of electrical circuits use components called *resistors*, and the example projects in this chapter are no exception. Resistors are measured in *ohms*, written as the symbol Ω. Always try to have a handful each of a variety of common values: 2.2 KΩ, 10 KΩ, and 68 Ω are good values to start with. Some retailers carry *resistor kits*, which include a wide range of useful values.

- **Push-buttons**—A very common input component, a *push-button* completes an electrical circuit when pushed. At the most basic level, a keyboard is little more than a collection of push-buttons. If you're designing a circuit to provide a simple input to the Pi, pick the button labelled *momentary switch*.

- **LEDs**—*Light-emitting diodes* (LEDs) are the most common output device in existence. An LED lights up when voltage is applied, giving you visual feedback on whether a pin on the Pi's GPIO port is high or low. When you're buying LEDs for use with the Pi, opt for low-power ones. The GPIO port isn't that powerful, and high-current LEDs—such as bright-white or bright-blue models—require an external power supply and an extra component known as a *transistor*.

Additionally, if you're planning on making something more permanent once you finish your breadboard prototype (which you'll learn about later in this chapter), you'll also need the following:

- **Stripboard**—This can be thought of as a single-use breadboard. As with breadboards, holes are arranged in a 2.54 mm grid. Unlike breadboards, the components need to be soldered into place, after which you have a permanent electronic circuit.

- **Soldering iron**—When you need to connect a component permanently into a circuit, you must solder the component. You don't have to spend a fortune on a soldering iron, but if your budget stretches to a temperature-controlled model, it's a wise investment. Make sure any soldering iron you buy has a small, pointed tip or swappable tips; chisel-tip irons aren't suitable for delicate electronic work.

- **Solder**—Your soldering iron needs solder. Solder is a mixture of conductive metals with a relatively low melting point, mixed with a cleaning substance known as *flux*. Make sure the solder you buy is suitable for electronics work; thick, plumbing solder is cheap but may damage delicate circuits because it requires too much heat to melt.

- **Stand and sponge**—It's important to have somewhere to put the hot soldering iron when it's not in use and a way of cleaning the tip of the iron while you're using it. Some soldering irons come with a stand with a built-in cleaning sponge; if yours didn't, buy a separate stand-and-sponge set.

- **Side cutters**—Through-hole components have long legs, which are left sticking out after you've soldered them in place. *Side cutters* allow you to cleanly and quickly trim these excess legs without damaging the solder joint.

- **Tweezers**—Electronic components can be small and fiddly, and a good pair of tweezers is invaluable. If you're thinking of using surface-mount components, instead of the easier-to-solder through-hole components, tweezers are an absolute necessity; without tweezers, you'll burn your fingers if you try to hold the component and solder it at the same time!

- **Work stand**—Commonly referred to as *helping hands*, these are weighted stands with clamps or clips that hold the item to be soldered in place. Some work stands include an integrated magnifying glass for delicate work, while the most expensive work stands add a light to help illuminate the work area.

- **Multimeter**—Multimeters are test meters that have multiple functions, including voltage, resistance, and capacitance measurement, along with continuity testing for finding breaks in circuits. Although a multimeter is not an absolute necessity, it can be very useful for diagnosing issues with circuits. Professional multimeter units can be quite expensive, but a simple model is fairly inexpensive and is a sound investment for anyone getting started in electronics.

- **Desoldering wick**—Mistakes happen, but they don't have to be permanent. A desoldering wick is a braided metal tape that can be placed over a solder joint and heated, pulling the solder away from the component and into the wick. With practice, it's possible to use a desoldering wick to salvage components from discarded electronic equipment—a handy way to gather common components cheaply.

Reading Resistor Colour Codes

Most electronic components are clearly labelled. For example, *capacitors* will have their *capacitance*, measured in *farads*, printed directly on them or illustrated via a numeric code, while *crystals* will have their *frequency* likewise marked.

The major exception is a resistor, which typically has no writing on its surface. Instead, the resistance value in ohms is calculated from the colour bands that adorn the resistor's surface. Learning to decode these bands is an important skill for a hardware hacker to learn, because once a resistor is removed from its packaging, the only way to figure out its value is to use a multimeter, which is an awkward and slow measuring tool for this particular job.

Thankfully, the resistor colour codes follow a logical pattern. Figure 13-1 shows a typical four-band resistor. A high-resolution colour version of this diagram is available on the *Raspberry Pi User Guide* website at `www.wiley.com/go/raspberrypiuserguide4e`. The first two bands are assigned a colour that equates to a resistance value in ohms. The third band is the *multiplier,* by which the first two numbers are multiplied to arrive at the actual resistance value. The final band indicates the *tolerance* of the resistor, or how accurate it is. A resistor with a lower tolerance will be closer to its marked value than a resistor with a higher tolerance, but you'll pay more for the component.

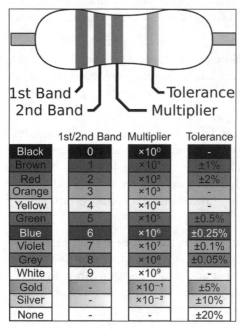

	1st/2nd Band	Multiplier	Tolerance
Black	0	$\times 10^0$	-
Brown	1	$\times 10^1$	±1%
Red	2	$\times 10^2$	±2%
Orange	3	$\times 10^3$	-
Yellow	4	$\times 10^4$	-
Green	5	$\times 10^5$	±0.5%
Blue	6	$\times 10^6$	±0.25%
Violet	7	$\times 10^7$	±0.1%
Grey	8	$\times 10^8$	±0.05%
White	9	$\times 10^9$	-
Gold	-	$\times 10^{-1}$	±5%
Silver	-	$\times 10^{-2}$	±10%
None	-	-	±20%

FIGURE 13-1: A four-band resistor and the decoding table for its colour code

To read the example resistor, first take the two resistance bands starting from the left. These are coloured red and red. Red, on the table included in Figure 13-1, equates to the value 2, so the initial reading is 22. The next band is green, which is the multiplier and equates to 10^5 or 100,000 (10 followed by five zeros). Multiplying 22 by 100,000 equals 2,200,000, which is the resistance value in ohms: 2,200,000 Ω.

There are 1,000 ohms in a *kiloohm* and 1,000 kiloohms in a *megaohm*. Thus, 2,200,000 Ω would typically be written as 2.2 MΩ. The final band, located on the right side of the resistor, is gold and details the tolerance, or accuracy, of the resistor, which is plus or minus 5 percent in the example shown in Figure 13-1 (i.e., it could have a value as low as 2.09 MΩ or as high as 2.31 MΩ).

There are also five-band resistors. You read these in the same way as a four-band resistor, except that the first three bands offer resistance figures, the fourth the multiplier, and the fifth the tolerance.

Sourcing Components

If you haven't dabbled in electronics before, it can be difficult to find components and tools. Thankfully, there are plenty of online and offline sources that specialise in the hard-to-find components you might need to complete your project.

Online Sources

Two of the largest retailers of electronic components and tools in the world are *RS Components* and *Farnell*. Both operate offices and warehouses across the world, and both have a substantial selection of hardware from which to choose. These were the first two companies to receive licences to produce and sell the Raspberry Pi, and still make them available to purchase. It's also possible to buy Raspberry Pi units from third-party companies, many of which offer lower pricing for smaller orders.

Both RS Components and Farnell focus on *business-to-business* transactions, meaning that their main source of income is from electronics companies buying large quantities of components. However, both will happily allow consumers to register with their respective web stores and place orders as small as individual components.

When you're placing small orders, be aware that additional charges may be incurred. RS Components charges for its next-day delivery service, and while the charge is quite reasonable for larger orders, it can cost significantly more than the components themselves for smaller orders. On the other hand, Farnell doesn't charge for next-day delivery as long as the order total is above a minimum value, which varies from country to country.

Depending on where you live, you may be able to reserve items for collection at one of RS Components' or Farnell's trade counters. This saves on the cost of postage and gets you the goods faster, but it may not be an option at your location. Here are the websites for both retailers:

RS Components: `www.rs-online.com`

Farnell: `www.farnell.com`

Offline Sources

You may find that you need a component immediately, and even next-day delivery is not soon enough. Or you may need only a single resistor or a small length of wire and can't justify a high delivery cost or minimum order value for one of the online retailers. Thankfully, there are brick-and-mortar stores that specialise in electronic components. Although there are not as many of these types of stores as in previous decades, most major towns and cities will include at least one physical shop that stocks the most commonly required tools and components.

In the UK, the most popular chain of electronic component shops is Maplin Electronics. Established in Essex in 1972, the company has grown from a small mail-order outlet to include more than 200 stores across the UK. Inhabitants of most cities will find themselves within reach of a Maplin Electronics store, which can be a handy source of hardware if you're running low on common parts.

Maplin Electronics also offers a mail-order and click-and-reserve service through its website, but be aware of its *business-to-consumer* focus. Many components are significantly more expensive when ordered from Maplin than from RS Components or Premier Farnell because the company relies on mark-up rather than high-volume trade to make a profit.

In the U.S. and other countries, Radio Shack remains the most popular chain of electronics stores. Founded in 1921 and boasting over 7,150 stores across the world, the company stocks a wide selection of common electronic components and tools that can be purchased in person or ordered for delivery through its website.

As with Maplin Electronics in the UK, Radio Shack is a *business-to-consumer* operation. As a result, buyers can expect to pay more for components purchased at Radio Shack than for the same parts ordered from RS Components or Farnell. However, the numerous Radio Shack stores make it a convenient choice for buyers who are in a hurry or who are looking for one-off items.

Both Maplin and Radio Shack also have the advantage of being staffed by people to whom you can speak. Many employees of both companies have significant knowledge in electronics and are happy to offer advice and assistance if you're unsure about what parts you need for a given project. Here are the websites for both retailers:

Maplin Electronics: www.maplin.co.uk

Radio Shack: www.radioshack.com

Hobby Specialists

In addition to the major chains, there are smaller companies that specialise in working with hobbyists. Although their selection is dwarfed by those of the larger chains, it's typically hand-picked and comes with the personal recommendation of the people behind the company.

Many of these hobby shops sprang up in the wake of the Arduino, an open-source project to create an education-friendly microcontroller prototyping platform. With the Raspberry Pi appealing to much of the same "maker" audience as the Arduino—albeit for very different tasks—the majority are investigating support for the Pi in addition to their existing product lines.

Buying from a hobby specialist has several advantages. If the products are sold as working with the Pi, then they've been tested for that specific reason—taking much of the guesswork out of the equation. Several companies also design their own add-on hardware for various platforms, with the Pi being no exception. These devices, designed to address a need in the community, may include additional ports and/or extra hardware, or can otherwise extend the functionality of the target device.

In the UK, one of the most popular hobby specialists is oomlout. Founded by open-source enthusiasts working with Arduino hardware, oomlout is an excellent source of add-on kits as well as common components including push-buttons, displays and transistors. Unlike the larger retailers, oomlout equips its components with all necessary extras—such as pull-up resistors for the push-buttons—and a circuit schematic for easy assembly. Where possible, sample source code is also provided to get you up and running as quickly as possible.

In the U.S., Adafruit offers a similar service. Founded with the intention of making open-source add-ons for the Arduino boards, Adafruit offers a wide selection of components and kits, and was responsible for designing and producing one of the first add-on boards designed specifically for the Raspberry Pi.

Here are the websites for both retailers:

oomlout: oomlout.co.uk

Adafruit: www.adafruit.com

Moving Up from the Breadboard

Solderless breadbards are excellent for quickly creating prototype circuits for experimentation. They're fast and reusable, and they don't damage components.

However, breadboards also have some disadvantages. They're bulky, expensive, and prone to loose connections—which can result in critical components falling out, especially while the breadboard is being transported from place to place. Figure 13-2 demonstrates this perfectly. Despite best efforts, the push-button component is only loosely secured in the breadboard and is likely to fall out if the circuit is handled roughly.

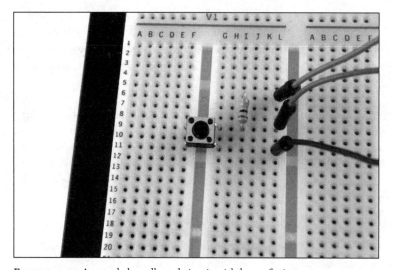

FIGURE 13-2: A sample breadboard circuit with loose-fitting components

This, among other reasons, is why the Raspberry Pi is built on a *printed circuit board (PCB)* rather than a breadboard, although the breadboard method was certainly used in the early days of prototyping the device. It's possible to print and etch your own PCBs at home, but there is a simpler intermediate step you can take: using *stripboard* to create permanent stand-alone circuits.

At first glance, stripboard looks similar to breadboard because its surface is covered in small holes at 2.54 mm spacing. Unlike a breadboard, however, there's no clever mechanism for ensuring that electronic components placed into these holes stay in place; instead, you have to solder them onto the stripboard. Stripboard is often referred to by the trade name *Veroboard*, which is a trademark of Vero Technologies in the UK and Pixel Print in Canada.

Creating a stripboard circuit has many advantages over using a breadboard. A sheet of stripboard is significantly cheaper than an equivalently sized breadboard, and stripboard can be snapped to size for smaller circuits. This also allows a single, large piece of stripboard to be used in the creation of several smaller, independent circuits.

Because components are soldered onto stripboard, it's also significantly more robust than a breadboard prototype. A stripboard circuit can be carried around from place to place with little risk that one of its components will become dislodged and lost. Figure 13-3 shows a piece of stripboard flipped to show the copper tracks on its underside.

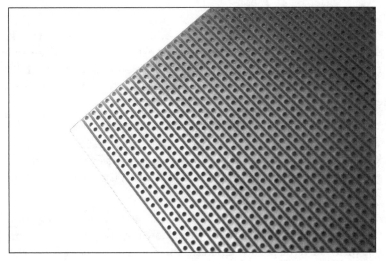

FIGURE 13-3: The copper tracks on the underside of a piece of stripboard

Stripboard is extremely easy to use, which makes it a great stepping-stone to custom circuit board design and manufacturing. However, you should be aware of the following before you buy stripboard:

- There are different types of stripboard. Some stripboards have copper tracks on the underside which go all the way across a row or down a column, while other stripboards are split into two separate rows with a gap in the middle like a breadboard. Yet another type of stripboard, often called a *project board*, has no copper tracks at all and requires the use of wires to join components together electrically.

- Stripboard can be made in different thicknesses and with different materials, and one type of stripboard may be more suited to a particular project than another. For example, a heatproof stripboard is good for a circuit that is going to be in a high-temperature environment, while thicker stripboard should be used for circuits that may be exposed to rough handling.

- To make the component layout on a stripboard neater, it's possible to break the tracks on the underside to separate components electrically. Doing so avoids wasted board space and is an absolute necessity in more complex circuits, but to achieve the neatest results, you need a small handheld tool called a *track cutter*. Remember to add that to your shopping list if you're planning on using stripboard, although a small drill bit can also be used.

There are also some tricks to handling stripboard that, if ignored, can make things harder than necessary:

- The copper tracks on the underside of stripboard are not usually coated in any way. If you touch the tracks, you will tarnish the copper and make it difficult to solder. Avoid touching the underside of stripboard unless you're going to use it immediately; if it's too late, get some steel wool and give the copper a gentle brush to remove the corrosion before attempting to solder.

- Unlike a printed circuit board, stripboard has no *solder mask*—a substance that prevents solder from going anywhere it isn't supposed to. As a result, soldering is somewhat trickier than it is on a PCB. It's all too easy to accidentally join tracks together with a blob of solder that is too large. If this happens, use your desoldering wick to remove the excess solder and try again.

- The holes in stripboard make it easy to snap it into custom sizes, but ragged edges are left, so after snapping stripboard, take the time to file down the edges before assembling your circuit. Make sure you wear a facemask when doing so because the dust from stripboard isn't particularly healthy to breathe.

A Brief Guide to Soldering

Having a soldering iron is one thing, but you also need to know how to use it. Soldering, like any skill, takes practise to become proficient. If you follow the tips in this section and keep practising, you'll create clean, tidy solder joins in no time.

WARNING This may seem obvious, but it's worth pointing out: soldering irons get extremely hot during use. Make sure you don't touch any exposed metal surface, even away from the tip, and be careful where you put the iron down. If possible, buy an iron with a stand or obtain a separate heatproof stand. Never leave a hot iron unattended, and if you drop an iron, don't be tempted to try to catch it!

Soldering works by melting a small quantity of metal to form a joint between two components. If you turn the Raspberry Pi over, you'll see plenty of evidence of this. All the larger components are connected using what's called *through-hole soldering*, where the components' leads are passed through holes in the printed circuit board and then soldered into place. Smaller components are attached via *surface-mount soldering*.

Solder isn't pure metal—it also contains a substance called *flux*, which is designed to etch away any tarnish on the surfaces to be soldered in order to ensure as clean a join as possible. Most electronic solders include three to five *cores* of flux. You can also buy flux separately as a paste or in liquid form, although for most hobby soldering, this isn't necessary.

When you're starting a soldering project, make sure you have a clean, well-lit workspace. Also, make sure the area is well ventilated. Solder fumes aren't very healthy, and while they're extremely unlikely to build up to dangerous levels in low-volume hobby soldering, it's still a good idea to keep exposure to a minimum.

In addition, you should protect the work surface in some way. It's not uncommon for small blobs of molten solder to fall, which can burn and mark tables. You can purchase an anti-static workmat (see Figure 13-4 for an example), but a glossy magazine works just as well. Don't be tempted to use a few sheets of cheap newspaper—solder can burn through thin paper before it cools.

FIGURE 13-4: An example soldering work area with a protective antistatic workmat

If you're doing delicate, close-up work, you should wear protective glasses. Sometimes the boiling flux inside the solder can cause it to spit upward, and if it hits you in the eye, you'll be in for a world of pain. The glasses will also help protect you when clipping the leads of through-hole components.

Don't let these warnings put you off soldering, however. Although solder is extremely hot, it cools quickly, and burns are not only rare but also nearly always inconsequential. Respect the equipment, but don't fear it.

With your work surface chosen and protected, lay out your equipment. Place the iron on the side of your dominant hand, and position it so that the cable isn't trailing across your work area. Make sure you can move the iron freely before plugging it in. If the cable gets caught on something, you may end up burning yourself.

Dampen your soldering sponge with water—it should be damp, but not dripping wet. This is important: the damp sponge will be used to clean the iron, and if it's dry, it will burn and may damage the iron's delicate tip.

It will take a few minutes for the soldering iron to reach its operating temperature. If you've purchased a temperature-controlled iron, the operating temperature is normally indicated either by a light that switches on or off or by a numerical temperature read-out. (See the operating manual that came with your soldering iron to find out how temperatures are indicated on it.)

Once the operating temperature is reached, it's time to prepare the soldering iron using a process known as *tinning*. Follow these steps:

1. Push the tip of the solder against the tip of the iron, allowing a small amount to melt onto the iron. Be careful not to melt too much onto the iron. This is not only a waste of solder but can also cause excess solder to fall onto the work area.

2. Wipe the tip of the iron onto the sponge. If it hisses and spits, the sponge is too wet. Allow it to cool; then remove it from the stand and wring it out.

3. Keep wiping the tip of the iron until it is coated with a silver layer of solder (see Figure 13-5). If necessary, apply more solder to the tip.

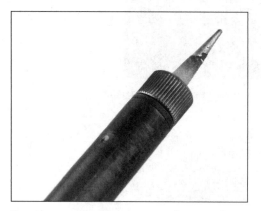

FIGURE 13-5: A soldering iron tip that is in the process of being tinned with solder

This process of tinning the tip protects it against damage and ensures that it will efficiently transfer heat onto the surfaces to be soldered. Failure to properly tin the iron's tip is one of the most common causes of bad solder joints. You may need to repeat this process more than once if you're soldering a lot of connections, and you'll need to do it again at the end of the soldering session (to keep the tip protected after the soldering iron cools down). In general, if the tip of the soldering iron loses its shiny coating, repeat the tinning process.

With the iron prepared, it's time to start soldering. Place the items to be soldered—such as a printed circuit board and the legs of a component—onto the work stand and ensure that you have a good view. Extend a length of solder from the container or reel and begin to solder the components using these basic steps:

1. If you're soldering through-hole components into a printed circuit board, stripboard, or similar through-hole board, place the legs of the component through the holes and bend them outward so the component doesn't fall out when the board is flipped over.

2. With the board secured in the work stand, push the tip of the iron against both the component and the copper contact on the board. It's important that the iron touches both items. If the iron is in contact with only one, the finished joint will be bad.

3. It takes only a few seconds for the area to heat up. Count to three and then push the solder against the component and copper contact (see Figure 13-6). If the solder doesn't melt, withdraw it, count a couple of seconds more and then try again. If it still doesn't melt, try repositioning the soldering iron.

FIGURE 13-6: Soldering a through-hole component into a printed circuit board

4. As the solder flows, you'll see it drawn down into the hole in the board. This is an indication that the area is hot enough for a good solder joint. If the solder floats, the area is not yet hot enough.

5. Remove the solder from the joint first, followed by the iron. (If you remove the iron first, the solder will harden and leave your spool of solder stuck to the contact!)

If all went well, you're left with a solid solder joint that will last for many years. If not, don't be disheartened; just press the iron against the joint to reflow the solder and use the desoldering wick if you need to clean up a spill or any excess. A perfect solder joint should be shaped somewhat like a volcano, rising up from the surface of the board to meet the leg of the component.

Never leave the iron in contact with the parts for more than a few seconds. This is especially important when soldering heat-sensitive components like integrated circuits, which can be damaged by prolonged contact with a hot soldering iron. If you're using a temperature-controlled solder station, make sure the temperature is set to an appropriate level for the solder being used (check the solder's packaging or data sheet for details).

When you finish, remember to re-tin the tip of the iron. If you don't, the tip may corrode in storage and need to be replaced much sooner than would otherwise be the case.

TIP Remember to heat both surfaces with the iron. Heating only one surface results in what is known as a *dry joint* or *cold joint,* where the solder is not properly mated to one surface. Over time, these joints will fail and need to be soldered again.

Like any skill, soldering takes practice. Many electronics shops sell kits that include a printed circuit board and a selection of components which you can use to practice soldering through-hole components. Some add-on boards for the Raspberry Pi are provided as kits, while the Raspberry Pi Zero itself requires some soldering to make full use of the GPIO header and composite video output capabilities.

Chapter 14
The GPIO Port

THE RASPBERRY PI'S *general-purpose input-output (GPIO)* port is located on the top left of the printed circuit board. The port is fitted with two rows of 20 2.54 mm male header pins, except in the case of the Raspberry Pi Zero where header pins must be soldered; this is explained at the end of this chapter. The spacing of these headers is particularly important: 2.54 mm pin spacing (0.1 inches in imperial measurements) is a very common sight in electronics and is the standard spacing for prototyping platforms that include stripboards and breadboards.

Identifying Your Board Revision

All modern Raspberry Pis, bar the industrial-friendly Raspberry Pi Compute Module design, feature a standardised 40-pin GPIO header. If you have a Raspberry Pi Model A+, Model B+, Raspberry Pi 2, Raspberry Pi 3, or Raspberry Pi Zero, you have the most recent version of the GPIO port design and should use the full-size GPIO pinout diagram shown as Figure 14-1 under "GPIO Pinout Diagrams".

There are two other types of GPIO port design, exclusive to older Raspberry Pi hardware. These are immediately distinguishable from the newer 40-pin design, as they have only 26 pins laid out in two rows of 13. This shorter GPIO header can be found on the Raspberry Pi Model A and Model B. If you own an original Raspberry Pi Model A, you should use the pinout diagram found in Figure 14-2.

For owners of the Raspberry Pi Model B, you need to distinguish which revision you own. The later revisions, which are distinguished by the presence of an unpopulated P5 header just below the GPIO header itself, should use the pinout found in Figure 14-2, as with the Raspberry Pi Model A. If there is no P5 header, you have an original Raspberry Pi Model B Revision 1, which is the only model to use the pinout layout found in Figure 14-3.

For more details on the board revisions and how to tell them apart, see Chapter 1, "Meet the Raspberry Pi".

GPIO Pinout Diagrams

Each pin of the GPIO port has its own purpose, with several pins working together to form particular interfaces. Figure 14-1 shows the layout of the GPIO port.

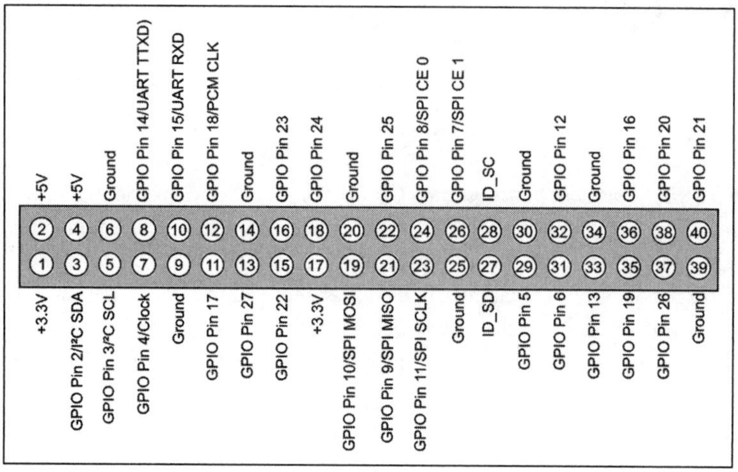

FIGURE 14-1: The Raspberry Pi's GPIO port and its pin definitions

The GPIO port is the same across the Raspberry Pi Model A+, Model B+, Raspberry Pi 2, Raspberry Pi 3, and Raspberry Pi Zero. If you have one of these models, use the diagram in Figure 14-1 to determine which pins perform which task. Always refer to this diagram before connecting anything to the Raspberry Pi's GPIO header; connecting a device to the wrong pins can damage both the device and the Raspberry Pi.

If you have a Raspberry Pi Model A or Model B Revision 2 or later, refer to the diagram in Figure 14-2. You may notice that it is identical to the first 26 pins of the newer 40-pin layout above. This is a deliberate design choice to provide forward compatibility; devices designed to connect to the 26-pin GPIO port will work fine when connected to the first 26 pins of the newer 40-pin GPIO port.

The final GPIO port variant is found on only one model of Raspberry Pi: the very original Model B Revision 1. If you have one of these, first congratulations on owning what is now a collector's item; second, use the pinout diagram found in Figure 14-3.

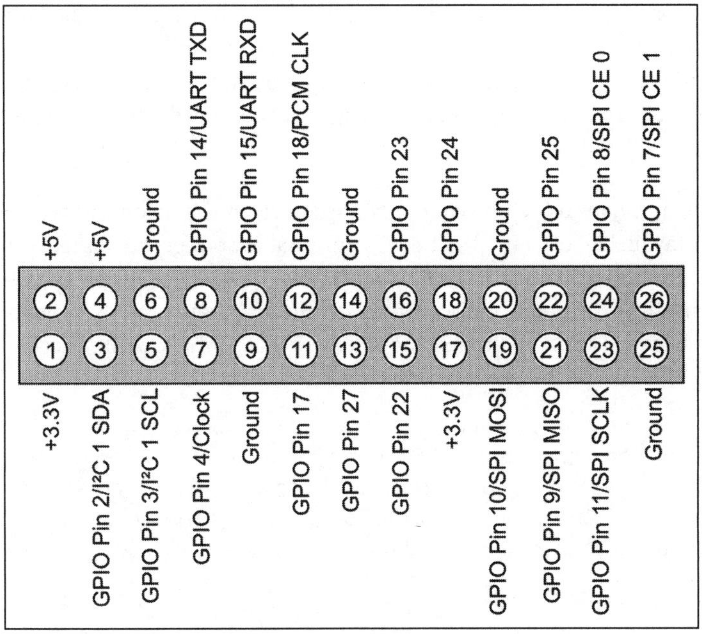

FIGURE 14-2: The older 26-pin Raspberry Pi GPIO port pinout

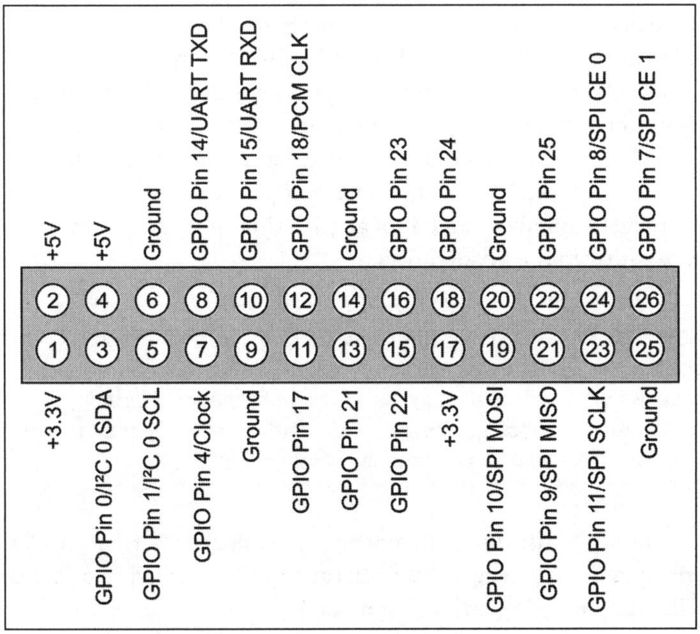

FIGURE 14-3: The original Raspberry Pi Model B Revision 1 pinout

Pin numbers for the GPIO port are split into two rows, with the bottom row taking the odd numbers and the top row the even numbers. It's important to keep this in mind when working with the Pi's GPIO port—most other devices use a different system for numbering pins, and because there are no obvious markings on the Pi, it's easy to get confused as to which pin is which.

Although the Pi's GPIO port provides a 5V power supply, tapped from the incoming power on the micro-USB socket (available on Pin 2), the Pi's internal workings are based on 3.3V logic. This means that the components on the Pi work from a 3.3V power supply (available on Pin 1). If you're planning on creating a circuit that will interface with the Pi through its GPIO port, make sure you are using components compatible with 3.3V logic or are passing the circuit through a *logic level converter* before it reaches the Pi.

> **WARNING** Connecting a 5V supply to any pin on the Raspberry Pi's GPIO port or directly shorting either of the power supply pins (Pin 2 and Pin 4) to any other pin will damage the Pi. Because the port is wired directly to pins on the Broadcom BCM283x SoC (system on a chip) processor, you cannot repair any damage you do to it. Always be extra careful when working around the GPIO port.

GPIO Features

Depending on the model of Raspberry Pi you have, the GPIO port provides at least eight pins for general-purpose use by default: Pin 7, Pin 11, Pin 12, Pin 13, Pin 15, Pin 16, Pin 18, and Pin 22. These pins can be toggled between three states: *high*, where they are providing a positive voltage of 3.3V; *low*, where they are equal to ground or 0V; and *input*. The two outputs equate to the 1 and 0 of binary logic and can be used to turn other components on or off. You find out more about this topic later in the chapter. Raspberry Pis featuring the newer 40-pin GPIO header provide a number of additional general-purpose pins, which are outlined in its pinout diagram earlier in this chapter.

> **WARNING** The Pi's internal logic operates at 3.3V, which is in contrast to many common microcontroller devices, such as the popular Arduino and its variants, which typically operate at 5V. Devices designed for the Arduino may not work with the Pi unless a *level translator* or *optical isolator* is used between the two. Likewise, connecting pins on a 5V microcontroller directly to the Raspberry Pi's GPIO port will not work and may permanently damage the Pi.

In addition to these general-purpose pins, the GPIO port has pins dedicated to particular *buses*. These buses are described in the following subsections and can be enabled or disabled as described in Chapter 6, "The Raspberry Pi Configuration Tool".

UART Serial Bus

The *Universal Asynchronous Receiver/Transmitter (UART) serial bus* provides a simple two-wire serial interface. When a serial port is configured in the `cmdline.txt` file (as described in Chapter 7, "Advanced Raspberry Pi Configuration"), it's this serial bus that is used as the port for the messages. Connecting the Pi's UART serial bus to a device capable of displaying the data reveals messages from the Linux kernel. If you're having trouble getting the Pi to boot, this can be a handy diagnostic tool—especially if nothing is showing on the display.

The UART serial bus can be accessed on Pins 8 and 10, with Pin 8 carrying the *transmit* signal and Pin 10 carrying the *receive* signal. You can set the speed in the `cmdline.txt` file—the speed is usually 115,200 bits per second (bps).

I²C Bus

As the name suggests, the *Inter-Integrated Circuit (I²C) bus* is designed to provide communications between multiple *integrated circuits (ICs)*. In the case of the Pi, one of those integrated circuits is the Broadcom BCM2835 SoC processor at the heart of the system. These pins are connected to *pull-up resistors* located on the Pi, meaning no external resistors are required to access the I²C functionality.

The I²C bus can be accessed on Pins 3 and 5, with Pin 3 providing the *Serial Data Line (SDA)* signal and Pin 5 providing the *Serial Clock Line (SCL)* signal. The I²C bus available on these pins is actually only one of two provided by the BCM2835 chip itself, and is bus 0 on a Raspberry Pi Model B Revision 1 and bus 1 on all other Raspberry Pis. The second I²C bus is reserved for use by the Raspberry Pi Camera Module and Touchscreen Display.

SPI Bus

The *Serial Peripheral Interface (SPI) bus* is a synchronous serial bus that offers improved performance compared with I²C. SPI is a four-wire bus with multiple *Chip Select* lines, which allow it to communicate with more than one target device.

The Pi's SPI bus is available on Pins 19, 21, and 23, with a pair of Chip Select lines on Pin 24 and Pin 26. Pin 19 provides the *SPI Master Output, Slave Input (MOSI)* signal; Pin 21 provides the *SPI Master Input, Slave Output (MISO)* signal; Pin 23 provides the *Serial Clock (SLCK)* used to synchronise communication; and Pins 24 and 26 provide the *Chip Select* signals for up to two independent slave devices.

Although additional buses are present in the Raspberry Pi's BCM283x SoC processor, they are not brought out to the GPIO port and thus aren't available for use.

Using the GPIO Port in Python

With the theory out of the way, it's time to get practical. In this section, you learn how to construct and program two simple electronic circuits that demonstrate how to use the GPIO port for input and output.

As you saw in Chapter 11, "An Introduction to Python", Python is a friendly yet powerful programming language. It's not, however, the perfect choice for every scenario. Although it works fine for the simple circuits you create in this chapter, it does not offer what is known as *deterministic real-time operation*. For the majority of users, this doesn't matter. If you're planning on using the Pi at the heart of a nuclear reactor or a complex robotics platform, however, you may want to investigate a lower-level language such as C++ or even *assembler* running on a dedicated real-time microcontroller.

If true real-time operation is required for your project, the Pi may be a bad choice. Instead, consider using a microcontroller platform such as the popular open source Arduino or one of the MSP430 family of microcontrollers from Texas Instruments. Both of these devices can interface with the Pi either through the GPIO header (using the aforementioned buses) or over USB and provide a specialised real-time environment for control and sensing.

GPIO Output: Flashing an LED

For the first example, you need to build a simple circuit consisting of an LED and a resistor. The LED provides visual confirmation that the Pi's GPIO port is doing what your Python program tells it to do, and the resistor limits the current drawn by the LED to protect it from burning out.

To assemble the circuit, you need a breadboard, two jumper wires, an LED, and an appropriate current-limiting resistor (as described in the "Calculating Limiting Resistor Values" sidebar). Although it's possible to assemble the circuit without a breadboard by twisting wires together, a breadboard is a sound investment and makes assembling and disassembling prototype circuits straightforward.

Assuming the use of a breadboard, assemble the circuit in the following manner to match Figure 14-4:

1. Insert the LED into the breadboard so that the long leg (the *anode*) is in one row and the shorter leg (the *cathode*) is in another. If you put the LED's legs in the same row, it won't work.

2. Insert one leg of the resistor into the same row as the LED's shorter leg, and the other resistor leg into an empty row. The direction in which the resistor's legs are placed doesn't matter, as a resistor is a *nonpolarised* (direction-insensitive) device.

3. Using a jumper wire, connect Pin 11 of the Raspberry Pi's GPIO port (or the corresponding pin on an interface board connected to the GPIO port) to the same row as the long leg of the LED.

4. Using another jumper wire, connect Pin 6 of the Raspberry Pi's GPIO port (or the corresponding pin on an interface board connected to the GPIO port) to the row that contains only one leg of the resistor and none of the LED's legs.

Be very careful when connecting wires to the Raspberry Pi's GPIO port. As discussed earlier in the chapter, you may do serious damage to the Pi if you connect the wrong pins. **WARNING**

Calculating Limiting Resistor Values

An LED needs a *current limiting resistor* to protect it from burning out. Without a resistor, an LED will likely work only for a short time before failing and needing to be replaced. Knowing a resistor is required is one thing, but it's also important to pick the right resistor for the job. Too high a value, and the LED will be extremely dim or fail to light at all; too low a value, and it will burn out.

To calculate the resistor value required, you need to know the *forward current* of your LED. This is the maximum current the LED can draw before being damaged, and it's measured in milliamps (mA). You also need to know the *forward voltage* of the LED. This latter value, measured in volts, should be 3.3V or lower—any higher, and the LED requires an external power supply and a switching device known as a *transistor* before it will work with the Pi.

The easiest way to determine how large a resistor is required is with the formula $R = (V-F)/I$, where R is resistance in ohms, V is the voltage applied to the LED, F is the forward voltage of the LED, and I is the maximum forward current of the LED in amps (with a thousand mA being equal to one amp).

Taking a typical red LED with a forward current of 25 mA and a forward voltage of 1.7 V, and powering it using the 3.3 V supplied by the Pi's GPIO port, you can calculate the resistor needed as $(3.3 - 1.7) / 0.025 = 64$. Thus, a resistor of 64 KΩ or higher will protect the LED. These figures rarely come out to match the common resistor values as sold, so when you're choosing a resistor, always round up to ensure the LED is protected. The nearest commonly available value is 68 KΩ, which will adequately protect the LED.

If you don't know the forward voltage and forward current of your LEDs (for example, if the LEDs did not come with documentation or were salvaged from scrap electronics), err on the side of caution and fit a reasonably large resistor. If the LED is too dim, you can revise downward—but it's impossible to repair an LED that has been blown.

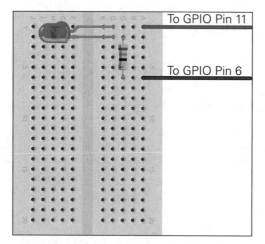

To GPIO Pin 11

To GPIO Pin 6

FIGURE 14-4: A breadboard circuit for a simple LED output

At this point, nothing will happen. That's perfectly normal: by default, the Raspberry Pi's GPIO pins are switched off. If you want to check your circuit immediately, move the wire from Pin 11 to Pin 1 to make the LED light up. Be careful not to connect it to Pin 2, though. A current-limiting resistor suitable for a 3.3 V power supply is inadequate for protecting the LED when connected to 5 V. Remember to move the wire back to Pin 11 before continuing.

To make the LED do something useful, start a new Python project. As with the projects in Chapter 11, you can use a plain text editor or the IDLE software included in the recommended Raspbian distribution for this project as well.

Before you can use the Raspberry Pi GPIO port from Python, you must import a library into your Python project. Accordingly, start the file with the following line:

```
import RPi.GPIO as GPIO
```

Remember that Python is case-sensitive, so be sure to type RPi.GPIO exactly as it appears. To allow Python to understand the concept of time (in other words, to make the LED blink, rather than just turning it on and off), you also need to import the time module. Add the following line to the project:

```
import time
```

With the libraries imported, it's time to address the GPIO ports. The GPIO library makes it easy to address the general-purpose ports through the instructions GPIO.output and GPIO.input. However, before you can use them, you need to set the GPIO library in board mode—which numbers the pins according to their physical position on the

Raspberry Pi—and initialise the pins as either inputs or outputs. In this example, Pin 11 is an output, so add the following line to the project:

```
GPIO.setmode(GPIO.BOARD)
GPIO.setup(11, GPIO.OUT)
```

The last line tells the GPIO library that Pin 11 on the Raspberry Pi's GPIO port should be set up as an output. If you were controlling additional devices, you could add more `GPIO.setup` lines into the project. For now, however, one suffices.

With the pin configured as an output, you can switch its 3.3 V supply on and off in a simple demonstration of binary logic. The instruction `GPIO.output(11, True)` turns the pin on, and `GPIO.output(11, False)` switches it off again. The pin will remember its last state, so if you only give the command to turn the pin on and then exit your Python program, the pin remains on until told otherwise.

Although you could just add `GPIO.output(11, True)` to the Python project to switch the pin on, it's more interesting to make it blink. First, add the following line to create an infinite loop in the program:

```
while True:
```

Next, add the following lines to switch the pin on, wait 2 seconds, and then switch it off again before waiting another 2 seconds. Make sure each line starts with four spaces to signify that it is part of the infinite `while` loop:

```
    GPIO.output(11, True)
    time.sleep(2)
    GPIO.output(11, False)
    time.sleep(2)
```

The finished program should look like this:

```
import RPi.GPIO as GPIO
import time
GPIO.setmode(GPIO.BOARD)
GPIO.setup(11, GPIO.OUT)
while True:
    GPIO.output(11, True)
    time.sleep(2)
    GPIO.output(11, False)
    time.sleep(2)
```

Save the file as `gpiooutput.py`. If you're using a Python development environment such as IDLE, you can run the program from directly within the development environment using the Run menu. If you're at the terminal, you can directly run the file with the command `python gpiooutput.py` to get it started. If all has gone well, you should see the LED begin to blink on and off at regular intervals—and you've created your first homemade output device for the Pi. You can quit this program by pressing Ctrl+C on the keyboard.

If things don't work, don't panic. First, check all your connections. The holes in a breadboard are quite small, and it's easy to think you've inserted a component into one row only to find it's actually in another. Next, check that you've connected the circuit to the right pins on the GPIO port; with no labelling on the Pi, mistakes are unfortunately easy to make. Finally, double-check your components: if the forward voltage of your LED is higher than 3.3 V or if your current limiting resistor is too large, the LED won't light up.

Although this example is basic, it's a good demonstration of some fundamental concepts. To extend its functionality, the LED could be replaced with a buzzer to make an audible alert, or a servo or motor as part of a robotics platform if combined with additional components. The code used to activate and deactivate the GPIO pin can be integrated into other programs, causing an LED to come on when new email arrives or a flag to be raised when a friend joins an IRC channel.

GPIO Input: Reading a Button

Being able to use the GPIO as an output is undeniably useful, but it becomes significantly more so when you can combine that with one or more inputs. In the following example, you see how to connect a push-button switch to another pin on the GPIO port and read its status in Python.

If you've already built the GPIO output example, you can either disconnect that from your Pi or leave it connected; this example uses different pins, so both can coexist quite happily. If you do leave the previous example connected, be sure to use different rows on the breadboard for the new components, or you'll find things don't work quite as planned.

Build the circuit as follows, matching Figure 14-5:

1. Insert the push-button switch into the breadboard. Most switches have either two or four legs. You need to worry about only two of the legs in the circuit. If the button has four legs, they'll be set up in pairs: check the push-button's data sheet to find out which legs are paired together.

2. Connect a 10 KΩ resistor to the same row as one of the push-button's legs and an unused row. This is a pull-up resistor and provides the Pi with a reference voltage so it knows when the button is pressed.

3. Connect the unused leg of the pull-up resistor to Pin 1 of the Raspberry Pi's GPIO port. This provides the 3.3 V reference voltage.

4. Connect the unused leg of the push-button switch to Pin 6 of the Raspberry Pi's GPIO port. This provides the ground connection.

5. Finally, connect Pin 12 of the Raspberry Pi's GPIO port to the other leg of the push-button switch in the same row as the 10 KΩ resistor. Your breadboard should now look like Figure 14-5.

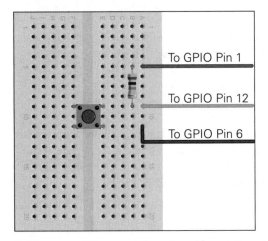

FIGURE 14-5: The example breadboard layout for a simple push-button input

The circuit you just built creates a situation whereby the input pin, which in this instance is Pin 12 of the Raspberry Pi's GPIO port, is constantly *high* thanks to the pull-up resistor connected to a 3.3 V supply. When the push-button is pressed, the circuit is grounded and becomes *low*, providing the cue for your Python program to know that the button has been activated.

You may wonder why the resistor is required at all, and why the switch does not simply connect Pin 12 to Pin 6 or Pin 1 directly. While this is possible, it creates what is known as a *floating* pin, which is a pin that doesn't know whether it's high or low. As a result, the circuit may act as though the button is being pressed even when it isn't, and may fail to detect the button being pressed even when it is.

Open a new Python file, either in a text editor or by using one of the Python integrated development environments (IDEs) available on the Raspberry Pi. Begin by importing the same GPIO library as in the previous GPIO output example:

```
import RPi.GPIO as GPIO
```

You don't need to import the time library, because this example doesn't require timing instructions. Instead, you can get right to enabling board mode and setting up Pin 12 as an input, which is done in the same way as setting a pin as an output, with just the final part of the instruction changed accordingly:

```
GPIO.setmode(GPIO.BOARD)
GPIO.setup(12, GPIO.IN)
```

If you're not using Pin 12, make sure you change the pin number in the preceding instruction.

As with the previous example, the next step is to create an infinite loop that constantly checks the input pin to see if it's been brought low (in other words, if it's been pressed). Begin the loop with the following code line:

```
while True:
```

Reading the status of an input pin is very similar to setting the status of an output pin, with one exception. Before you can do anything useful with the resulting value, you need to store it in a variable. The following instruction tells Python to create a new variable called input_value (as described in Chapter 12) and set it to the current value of Pin 12:

```
input_value = GPIO.input(12)
```

Although the program could be executed now and work, it doesn't do anything useful. To make sure you know what's going on, add the following print instruction to get feedback:

```
if input_value == False:
    print("The button has been pressed.")
    while input_value == False:
        input_value = GPIO.input(12)
```

The last two lines—the second while and the second input_value, an *embedded loop*—are important. Even on the Raspberry Pi's processor, which is relatively underpowered when compared to high-performance desktop and laptop processors, Python runs very quickly. This embedded loop tells Python to keep checking the status of Pin 12 until it's no longer low, at which point it knows the button has been released. Without this loop, the program will loop while the button is being pressed—and no matter how quick your reflexes, you'll see the message printed to the screen multiple times, which is misleading.

The final program should look like this:

```
import RPi.GPIO as GPIO
GPIO.setmode(GPIO.BOARD)
GPIO.setup(12, GPIO.IN)
while True:
    input_value = GPIO.input(12)
    if input_value == False:
        print("The button has been pressed.")
        while input_value == False:
            input_value = GPIO.input(12)
```

Save the file as gpioinput.py and then execute it from the terminal with python gpioinput.py. At first, nothing will happen, but if you press the push-button switch, the program prints the message from line seven to the terminal (see Figure 14-6). Release the button and press it again, and the message repeats until you press Ctrl+C.

FIGURE 14-6: The output of the gpioinput.py program

As with the previous input example, this is a deceptively simple program that can be used for many purposes. In addition to being able to read when a switch is pressed, the same code can be used to read when the pins of a separate device—such as a sensor or external microcontroller—have been pulled high or low.

By extending the code to look for multiple push-buttons, each on an individual GPIO pin, you could even create a simple four-button game controller. For example, you could combine the preceding code with the Raspberry Snake game from Chapter 12 to turn the Raspberry Pi into a simple games console. You can also combine both input and output examples into a single program, which waits for the button to be pushed and then turns on the LED by sending the output pin high. To ensure that you understand the concepts in this section, try creating the combined program now. If you get stuck or want to check your method, turn to Appendix A, "Python Recipes", for a sample solution.

Soldering the Raspberry Pi Zero's GPIO Header

The Raspberry Pi Zero is unique in the mainstream Pi family, and not just because of its small size: it's the only model to be sold with an *unpopulated* GPIO header, meaning that it doesn't have the pins found on most models. This offers increased flexibility: if you only need a few pins in your project you can solder wires directly to the header to save space; if you don't need the GPIO header at all, it makes the Pi Zero the thinnest model by far.

If you want to use the Pi Zero with existing Raspberry Pi hardware and add-on boards, though, you'll want to solder your own headers. For this, you need the following equipment (see Figure 14-7):

- A soldering iron and solder
- A Raspberry Pi Zero
- 2.54 mm male pin headers

FIGURE 14-7: Equipment for soldering a GPIO header to a Pi Zero

Using male pin headers makes the Pi Zero compatible with any HAT or other add-on board designed for the Raspberry Pi family. Alternatively, you can use female headers to make it easier to connect the Pi Zero to a breadboard using standard male-to-male jumper wires. If you're not sure where to pick up the tools and materials, turn to Chapter 13, "Learning to Hack Hardware," for a list of suppliers.

Pin headers are typically supplied in long rows. A specialist Raspberry Pi supplier will likely offer a set in a 2 x 20 layout suitable for immediate use with the Pi Zero; other suppliers may offer them in 1 x 36 or longer strips. If you have the latter, count off 20 pins and snap between the last pin and the remainder of the strip where the plastic is indented. Do the same with another strip, and place a strip through each row of holes in the Pi Zero's GPIO header (see Figure 14-8).

FIGURE 14-8: Placing male headers into a Pi Zero

Soldering irons get extremely hot during use, and the solder itself contains chemicals hazardous to your health. Always take care when using a soldering iron, make sure your work area is clear, clean of flammable materials and well ventilated, and wash your hands before and after using solder.

WARNING

Begin by inserting your 2.54 mm pins through the Pi Zero, from the top of the board where the main ports are. Flip the Pi Zero over, holding the pins in place. (You might find some tape or sticky putty helpful here, or use a breadboard to hold the pins steady.) The black plastic of the pins should be flat against the top surface of the Pi Zero, with the pins sticking throught the bottom surface—now facing upwards. Make sure that the pins are as flat and straight as possible, as soldering them in at an angle now will make it very difficult to attach hardware to them.

When your iron has come to temperature, clean and tin the tip (see Chapter 13, "Learning to Hack Hardware"). Hold the tip against one of the pins, making sure it's touching both the pin and the circular copper solder point surrounding the hole in the circuit board. After 3 or so seconds, push your solder against the pin and solder point (not the tip of the iron) and allow it to melt (see Figure 14-9). If you have a good contact, the solder should appear to be sucked into the base of the pin; if not, reposition your iron and try again.

FIGURE 14-9: Soldering the Pi Zero's GPIO header pins

With one pin soldered, repeat the process on the remaining 39 pins to fully secure the GPIO header. Clean and tin your soldering iron's tip again, unplug it, and allow both the iron and the Pi Zero to cool. If you used tape or putty to secure the pins, you can clean it off now. If you would like a cleaner finish, you can also wash the flux residue from the solder off the base of the Pi Zero with any commercial flux cleaner.

Before plugging the Pi Zero back in, look carefully at the solder points to make sure you haven't shorted any pins out by using too much solder. If you have, heat up your iron and use it to melt the solder then remove any excess with either desoldering braid or a desoldering pump to avoid damage to the Pi Zero.

Chapter 15
The Raspberry Pi Camera Module

DESIGNED BY ENGINEERS working for the Raspberry Pi Foundation, the Raspberry Pi Camera Module is the most compact way of adding the ability to record still images and video to your project. Designed to connect to the *Camera Serial Interface (CSI)* of the Raspberry Pi, the Camera Module measures just 25 mm on its longest edge and weighs just 3 grams (see Figure 15-1).

FIGURE 15-1: The Raspberry Pi Camera Module, pictured without its ribbon cable

Since its release, the Camera Module has found a place in projects ranging from simple home security systems to more complex computer vision experiments that track a user's face or hand gestures. The module has even reached near-space as the result of photography projects that tether a Raspberry Pi to a weather balloon and release it to gather live high-altitude images.

The Camera Module is built around an 8-megapixel sensor of a type commonly used in smartphones, located behind a fixed-focus lens. The module works in tandem with the Raspberry Pi's graphics processor to ensure that high-resolution video and stills can be captured smoothly without overloading the Pi's main processor or requiring too much memory.

Why Use the Camera Module?

If you have no need to capture images or video, you don't need the Camera Module. It's an optional extra, and the Pi works just fine without one. It's also possible to add vision to your Pi using alternative products, such as webcams, which connect to a free USB port.

The Pi has only a limited number of USB ports, however, and these are often used for more critical functions such as a keyboard, mouse, or wireless network adapter. This is particularly important in the Raspberry Pi Model A, which has just one USB port available for use.

The official Camera Module has other advantages over a traditional webcam: it draws considerably less power, meaning it doesn't strain the Raspberry Pi's power supply or drain the batteries in a portable or solar-powered project; it offers image capture at a resolution of up to eight megapixels and video capture at a Full HD resolution and 30 frames per second; and it is considerably smaller than USB-connected cameras.

The Camera Module is compatible with all models and revisions of Raspberry Pi, so if you haven't decided whether you'll need a camera in your project, don't worry; you can pick up any Pi model now and add the Camera Module at a later date.

Choosing a Camera Module

There are two main variants of the Raspberry Pi Camera Module: the standard variant, and the NoIR variant. The standard variant is the model you need if you're planning to take colour pictures or video in a well-lit environment, or to provide your own visible lighting to illuminate the scene.

The NoIR Camera Module is a modified version of the standard variant, which has an infrared filter removed from its construction. In daylight, this results in a slightly degraded image over the standard variant. In darkness, however, it allows you to illuminate a scene with infrared light that is invisible to the human eye; to the camera, the light is bright enough to create a black-and-white image or video of the surrounding area. Note that the NoIR Camera Module is sold without infrared LEDs of its own; you'll need to buy the LEDs, or an off-the-shelf infrared torch or similar, separately to enable this night-vision mode.

Additionally, there are two major revisions of Camera Module currently available. Any version marked as v1.0 or higher to v1.9 feature a 5-megapixel image sensor; versions marked as v2.0 or higher replace this with a higher-resolution 8-megapixel image sensor, allowing for higher-quality still images to be captured. Both revisions are available in standard and NoIR variants.

Installing the Camera Module

The Raspberry Pi Camera Module, like the Raspberry Pi itself, is supplied as a bare circuit board. Although this is reasonably robust, you must take care when handling it so as not to damage any of its components, particularly the plastic lens located over the camera sensor.

The Camera Module connects to the Pi through a *ribbon cable*, a thin, semi-rigid cable that should be inserted into the Raspberry Pi's CSI connector. When you receive the camera, one end of the cable will already be inserted into the module, one side of the other end is coloured blue, and the other side has visible silver contacts. These contacts connect to pins in the Pi's CSI connector, transferring power and data between the Pi and the Camera Module.

The CSI connector is labelled S5 or CAMERA and is located towards the right side of the board, near where the USB ports are located (see Figure 15-2). The CSI connector of a Raspberry Pi Model B is located just to the left of the Ethernet port; on a Model A, it is found in the same place, just to the left of the gap on the board below the USB port(s). Some models may have the CSI connector covered by a protective piece of plastic film, which you should peel off before you try to install the camera.

There's a similar-looking connector located on the left side of the Raspberry Pi. This is the *Display Serial Interface (DSI)* connector, and it's designed for connecting the Pi to liquid crystal display panels. The two ports aren't interchangeable; if you connect the camera to the DSI port rather than the CSI port, it won't work.

Before inserting the cable, small *lugs* on either side of the connector must be gently lifted, which you can do with your fingernails, but be careful. They should lift easily and stop moving once they're a couple of millimetres above the rest of the CSI connector (see Figure 15-3). This then allows you to gently tilt the lugs away from the HDMI connector (which gives you more room to insert the cable).

FIGURE 15-2: The Raspberry Pi's CSI connector, pictured on a Raspberry Pi 3 Model B

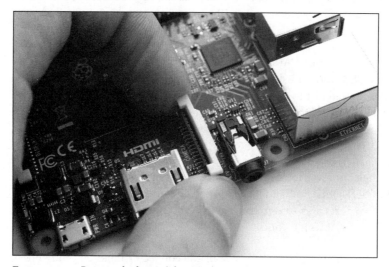

FIGURE 15-3: Raising the lugs of the CSI connector prior to inserting the ribbon cable

Insert the free end of the ribbon cable into the CSI port, making sure that the silver contacts are facing towards the left of the Pi and the blue portion of the cable to the right. Gently push the cable home, making sure not to bend it, and then push the lugs back down to secure them in place (see Figure 15-4). When properly inserted, the cable should be coming out of the connector perfectly straight and should withstand a gentle tug. Don't pull the cable too hard while testing it, however, as it can be damaged.

FIGURE 15-4: The Camera Module's ribbon cable securely inserted into the CSI connector

The ribbon cable included with the Raspberry Pi Camera Module is reasonably robust and will prove reliable even with daily use. It is, however, susceptible to damage if folded. When inserting the cable or moving the camera, be sure not to fold the ribbon cable back on itself. If you do damage your ribbon cable, replacements (including longer ribbon cables) are available from most Pi stockists.

WARNING

When using the Camera Module with a Raspberry Pi case, you'll usually have to thread the ribbon cable through a thin slot or in between layers of plastic. Some cases are not directly compatible with the Camera Module. In these cases, you may need to leave the lid of the case off to route the ribbon cable. Position the Camera Module with the ribbon cable at the bottom. If this isn't possible, you'll learn a software option to flip the captured image upside down later in this chapter.

The final step in the camera's physical installation is to remove the small protective piece of plastic film found over the lens. You can simply peel it off by pulling gently upwards on the tab that extends out from the lens. Although it's tempting to leave it in place to protect the lens, doing so will give everything you capture an unpleasant blue hue.

Enabling Camera Mode

The software to drive the Raspberry Pi Camera Module is included in the Raspbian distribution by default. If you're using a particularly old release, you may find that the files are missing; if so, update your system using the following command at the terminal or console (see Chapter 3, "Linux System Administration" for details):

```
sudo apt-get update && sudo apt-get upgrade
```

You will need to change some system settings in order for the Camera Module to work correctly, however. In particular, recording video requires that the graphics processing portion of the Pi's BCM283x processor has at least 128 MB of memory available. With any less than that, still image capturing will work, but video recording will fail. For details on how to change this split, see Chapter 6, "The Raspberry Pi Configuration Tool".

The easiest way of ensuring that your Pi is camera-ready is to use the Raspberry Pi Configuration tool `raspi-config`. At the terminal, type the following command to load the tool:

```
sudo raspi-config
```

In the menu that appears, select option 6—Enable Camera—using the cursor keys and pressing Enter. Choose Enable in the screen that appears and press Enter again (see Figure 15-5). If Camera Mode was disabled previously, you are prompted to reboot the Pi, which you confirm by pressing Enter.

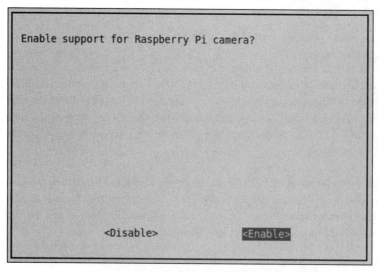

FIGURE 15-5: Enabling Camera Mode in the Raspberry Pi Configuration tool `raspi-config`

If you can't find a camera option in `raspi-config`, you might be running an outdated version. **TIP** Use the `sudo apt-get update && sudo apt-get upgrade` command to update your software; then reboot the Pi and try running `raspi-config` again.

Once the Pi reboots, your Camera Module is ready to use.

An optional final step, if you want to view captured images from the Raspbian console without having to load the graphical user interface, is to install the *framebuffer image viewer* `fbi`. To do so, type the following command:

```
sudo apt-get install fbi
```

To view images using the tool (see Figure 15-6), simply type the command followed by the name of the image:

```
fbi -a imagename.jpg
```

To quit `fbi`, press the Q or Escape key.

FIGURE 15-6: Viewing captured images using the `fbi` package

Capturing Stills

The best way to test that the camera is working correctly is to try capturing an image. The Camera Module uses a custom software package called `raspistill` to capture still images, which are saved, by default, in the *Joint Photographic Experts Group (JPEG)* file format—the same format used by most digital cameras and smartphones.

The software for the Raspberry Pi camera is run from the terminal or console. For best results, run the software at the console without using the `startx` command to load the graphical user interface (see Chapter 3 for details).

The `raspistill` command accepts a number of optional arguments that control settings such as the horizontal and vertical resolution of the captured image, the exposure mode of the camera, the file type saved and the level of compression applied to the final image. If these options are left out of the command, defaults are used.

To test the camera, run the `raspistill` application at the console by typing its name as the command:

```
raspistill -o testcapture.jpg
```

This shows a 5-second live preview (see Figure 15-7), during which time a red light on the front of the camera illuminates. This is an activity light, designed to provide confirmation that the camera is working. If you wave your fingers in front of the camera during this five-second period, they will appear in the preview window. When the five seconds are up, the light extinguishes, and the preview window disappears.

> **TIP** Sometimes the position of the Camera Module's cable makes it difficult to place the camera the right way up. If your preview appears upside-down, use the `-vf` (vertical flip) and `-hf` (horizontal flip) options to correct the image. Just add the option to the command line along with any other options you are using.

When the preview finishes, the `-o` (output) option saves a JPEG file with the name `testcapture.jpg`. When using the `-o` option, you can change the type of file saved with `-e` (encoding). Currently supported file types include *bitmap (BMP)*, *Portable Network Graphics (PNG)*, and *Graphics Interchange Format (GIF)* images. To save a PNG, for example, use the following command:

```
raspistill -o testcapture.png -e png
```

FIGURE 15-7: The raspistill capture application showing a live preview image

Altering png to read bmp, gif, or jpg allows access to the other supported formats. If you forget the -e option, a file will still be saved, but regardless of its extension, the content will be JPEG data.

Another pair of commonly used options adjusts the width and height of the captured image. This is good for capturing low-resolution stills as part of a computer vision project, or simply to save space.

The width of the captured image is adjusted with the -w option, and the height is adjusted with -h. These options are most commonly used together to set the overall resolution of the image. To capture an image of 1,920 pixels wide by 1,080 pixels high—the same resolution as a Full HD high-definition TV or Blu-ray film—type the following command:

```
raspistill -w 1920 -h 1080 -o fullhdcapture.jpg
```

The final basic option to know is -t, which controls the preview timeout. By default, raspistill shows a 5-second live preview before capturing an image, but the -t option overrides this default. The required delay should be specified in milliseconds. To capture an image after a 10-second delay, use the following command:

```
raspistill -t 10000 -o tensecondcapture.jpg
```

To minimise the delay and capture almost immediately—a useful trick if you're running the software from a *shell script*, as demonstrated later in this chapter—use a value of 1, as in the following command:

```
raspistill -t 1 -o instantcapture.jpg
```

The filename after the output (-o) option can be anything you want it to be, with the preceding commands merely using example filenames. When writing the filename, always be sure to add the extension appropriate to your file type: .jpg for JPEG images, .png for Portable Network Graphics, .bmp for bitmap images, and .gif for the Graphics Interchange Format.

For a full description of all options available to raspistill, turn to Appendix B, "Raspberry Pi Camera Module Quick Reference". Alternatively, type the following command to see a list of options:

```
raspistill --help | less
```

Recording Video

Just as there is a dedicated application for capturing still images through the Raspberry Pi Camera Module, there is another one for capturing video: raspivid. Using raspivid is similar to using raspistill, but there are several differences you need to know about before forging ahead.

The most important difference between raspivid and raspistill is in the -t option. In raspistill, the -t option provides the time-out for the preview before the image is captured; in raspivid, the -t option provides a limit for the overall length of the recorded video. If a value of 0 is given, the video records forever—rapidly filling your SD card or external storage device.

As with raspistill, the default for the -t option is five seconds. So, to check the camera is working and record a short video, you can type the command's name along with the -o (output) option and a filename:

```
raspivid -o testvideo.h264
```

This records a 5-second video and saves it in a format known as *h.264*. Unlike raspistill, there is no option to save the file in a different format: raspivid uses the hardware acceleration available in the Pi's BCM283x processor to do the recording, and only h.264 is supported as a capture format.

If you play the video back, you'll find that there's no sound. Unfortunately, the Raspberry Pi Camera Module does not include a microphone input. Although it's possible to record audio by connecting certain USB microphones or sound cards to the Raspberry Pi, this will need to be captured using separate software and combined with the video file later using a video editing package.

Other options supported by raspistill are also supported by raspivid. For example, to set the width and height of the recorded video to 1,280 x 720, use the -w and -h options as in the following command:

```
raspivid -w 1280 -h 720 -o hdvideo.h264
```

To record a longer video, adjust the -t option by specifying your required length of video in milliseconds. To record a minute of video, type the following command:

```
raspivid -t 60000 -o minutelongvideo.h264
```

> **TIP** Although h.264 is a reasonably efficient video format, recording at high resolutions can take up considerable disk space. If you're recording longer videos, be sure that you have enough free space on your SD card or consider connecting a USB storage device like an external hard drive.

You can read more options for raspivid in Appendix B or see a list of available options with the following command:

```
raspivid --help | less
```

Command-Line Time-Lapse Photography

So far, you've learned the basics of how to use the Raspberry Pi Camera Module. Now it's time to find a practical use for the project. The key advantage of the Raspberry Pi over a dumb network-connected camera is the capability that Raspberry Pi provides for easily programming different tasks. In this example, you can turn your Raspberry Pi and connected Camera Module into a time-lapse photography system.

The raspistill software has a built-in time-lapse option: -tl. Using this, it's possible to set a time in milliseconds between automated image captures. The value you choose will depend largely on exactly what you're trying to capture: if you want a time-lapse series of a day's weather, you may want to capture as often as every ten seconds; if you want to document a building going up over a period of several months, half an hour may be more appropriate.

When choosing how often to capture images, think about how many images you will generate: a month-long capture set to trigger every ten seconds will generate around 242,000 images, which at higher resolutions may be enough to fill up your Pi's storage. Also think about how long your final video will be: capturing thousands of images for a 30 second final video is a waste, but capturing only a hundred for an hour-long final video will not give a smooth finished product.

To begin, open a terminal or use the console and create a folder for your images:

```
cd ~
mkdir timelapse
cd timelapse
```

In your new folder, begin the capture process with the following command:

```
raspistill -o frame%08d.jpg -tl 10000 -t 600000
```

While `raspistill`, by default, outputs to a single file—and thus would overwrite your captured image each time it is triggered by the time-lapse timer—the filename here contains an instruction, `%08d`, which tells it to insert an incrementing number into the filename each time it runs. These numbers are padded with zeros to make them eight digits long, which ensures that they are kept in order even if you capture as many as 10,000,000 images. The `-tl 10000` option instructs the software to capture one image every ten seconds—a good starting point for experimentation—while the `-t` option tells it to run for ten minutes (600 seconds, or 600,000 milliseconds) in total.

As you experiment with time-lapse photography, you can vary both of these values: a shorter `-tl` delay will generate more images for a smoother final result, while a longer delay will let you take images over a longer period of time without filling up your storage. The `-t` delay should be set to however long you need in order to capture the entire event; if in doubt, set it to a longer delay than you need, and if necessary, cancel the ongoing capture with Ctrl+C. You won't lose any of your already-captured images.

Time-lapse photography is often used to compress a long or complex task into an entertaining video. Commercial time-lapse photography rigs, which can be extremely expensive, are often used to film the growth of plants, the construction of buildings, or the flow of traffic. A Raspberry Pi can do all of these things, but at a fraction of the cost.

The images you've captured can be transformed into a video, either using video editing software or the `avconv` tool. Although `avconv` can be run on the Raspberry Pi itself, it's a resource-hungry program that takes a considerable time to run if you have a large number of high-resolution images to convert. If you have the patience to do the conversion on the Pi itself, install avconv with the following command:

```
sudo apt-get install libav-tools
```

Then collate the images by typing the following:

```
avconv -r 10 -i frame%08d.jpg -r 10 -vcodec libx264 timelapse.mp4
```

This creates a video with images showing at a rate of ten per second from the JPEG images raspistill saved earlier. To speed the video up still further, you can adjust the -r option: -r 15 will show 15 images per second and -r 20 will show 20 images per second and so forth. The finished video can then be shared directly or uploaded to a video streaming site such as YouTube or Vimeo.

Chapter 16
Add-On Hardware

THE RASPBERRY PI is more than a single-board computer; it's an entire ecosystem. The Pi's low cost, ready availability, and onboard expansion headers have sparked an explosion of creativity in which engineers and enthusiasts from around the world have built hundreds of add-on devices compatible with the Pi, many of which connect through the multifunction general-purpose input/output (GPIO) header.

As well as these third-party accessories, the Raspberry Pi Foundation has designed, produced, and released a range of first-party add-ons designed to expand the capabilities of the Raspberry Pi. Some of these – such as the Raspberry Pi Camera Module and the Raspberry Pi Wi-Fi Adapter – have been discussed earlier in this book. The remainder are covered in this chapter, complete with instructions for their installation and use.

At the time of writing, the Foundation has released the following add-on hardware for the Raspberry Pi:

- **Universal Raspberry Pi power supply**—Provides high-quality power for any model or Raspberry Pi or other micro-USB device; see Chapter 2, "Getting Started with the Raspberry Pi".

- **Raspberry Pi Wi-Fi adapter**—Used to add wireless networking capabilities to a Raspberry Pi via a USB port; see Chapter 5, "Network Configuration".

- **Raspberry Pi Zero adapter kit**—Converts the Pi Zero's micro-USB OTG and mini-HDMI ports into their full-size equivalents and provides male pin headers for soldering to the GPIO port; see Chapter 14, "The GPIO Port".

- **Raspberry Pi Camera Module**—Connects to the Raspberry Pi's Camera Serial Interface (CSI) header to capture video and still images; see Chapter 15, "The Raspberry Pi Camera Module".

- **Official Raspberry Pi case**—A five-part plastic case designed to house a Raspberry Pi model B+, Raspberry Pi 2, or Raspberry Pi 3 while offering access to all ports and connections.

- **Raspberry Pi 7" touchscreen display**—Connects to the Raspberry Pi's Display Serial Interface (DSI) header to provide full-colour video output and touch-sensing input.

- **Sense HAT**—A multifunction Hardware Attached on Top (HAT) module that provides orientation, pressure, humidity, and temperature sensing along with an 8x8 LED matrix display.

All of these add-on accessories are available from the official Raspberry Pi partners Element14 and RS Components now, and may also be available from local and third-party online electronics outlets.

Official Raspberry Pi Case

Designed to protect the Raspberry Pi without blocking access to any of its ports or features, the Official Raspberry Pi case (see Figure 16-1) is made up of five parts. The bottom and top of the case hold the Pi clamped securely in place, and removable side and top panels can either close off the inside or provide access to the Pi's GPIO header and any attached HAT module.

FIGURE 16-1: The Official Raspberry Pi case

The Official Raspberry Pi case is compatible with the Raspberry Pi Model B+, the Raspberry Pi 2, **WARNING** and the Raspberry Pi 3. The case can also be used with the Raspberry Pi Model A+, although the shorter length of the A+ makes the board's single USB port more difficult to reach. The case is not compatible with the Raspberry Pi Zero or Compute Module, nor with the original Raspberry Pi Model B or Model A.

Installation

Using the case is simple: no tools are required, as the case has been designed to snap into place with little physical effort and there are no screws or bolts. Begin by removing the two side panels. Separate the top half from the bottom by squeezing the two indentations, marked with triangles pointing upwards, at the end of the case with the Raspberry Pi logo, and pulling upwards. The top half will lift at an angle; when the front is clear, you can pull the back two retaining clips free.

At this point, you can also remove the top lid by pushing it out from underneath the upper section of the case; if you don't need vertical access to the GPIO header and are not planning to mount a HAT module, you can leave this in place.

With the casing split into its five parts, mount your Raspberry Pi by placing it inside the bottom section of the case and lining up the small plastic pins with the mounting holes on the Raspberry Pi (see Figure 16-2). The Pi will simply rest on top of the rear mounting pins, closest to the microSD Card slot and DSI header; gently flex and push the case to make the front mounting pins appear through the Pi's mounting holes to secure it in place. If you have a HAT module, attach it to the Pi's GPIO header now.

FIGURE 16-2: Mounting the Raspberry Pi inside the official case

Take the top half of the case, with or without its top-most cover, and line the rear retaining clips up with their matching holes in the bottom half before pushing the front of the case down over the Pi's USB and Ethernet ports (see Figure 16-3). Make sure the two side retaining clips are lined up before pushing the front home with a gentle click.

FIGURE 16-3: Assembling the top of the case

Attach the first side panel, which has cutouts for the power, HDMI, and analogue AV ports, by gently pushing it into place until you hear a clicking noise. Attach the second, featureless, side panel the same way, or leave it off to provide easy access to the GPIO header. Finish by admiring your handiwork!

Raspberry Pi 7" Touchscreen Display

The Raspberry Pi 7" touchscreen display turns any Raspberry Pi into a tablet-like device, offering 10-point multitouch finger tracking and a full-colour 800x480 resolution display. Using the touchscreen display, it's possible to interact with a Raspberry Pi with no external accessories such as a keyboard or mouse (see Figure 16-4) while still retaining access to the Pi's GPIO header.

Support for the Raspberry Pi 7" touchscreen display is automatic in Raspbian and derived distributions. If you're running an alternative operating system, check its website or support forum for information on compatibility before purchasing and installing the display.

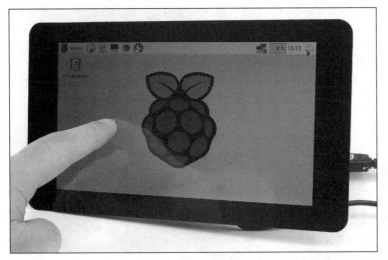

FIGURE 16-4: Using the Raspberry Pi 7" touchscreen display

Installation

Begin by unpacking the display from its packaging, taking particular care of the edges of the display panel and the thin ribbon cable which attaches the converter board on the back of the chassis to the display's internals (see Figure 16-5). Any damage to this cable will render the touchscreen display unusable, and the edges of the panel can be cracked if not handled carefully. The front of the touchscreen display is protected by a layer of plastic; to avoid scratching the panel, leave this in place until you've finished installing your Pi.

FIGURE 16-5: The thin and fragile ribbon cable on the touchscreen display

Take the flat ribbon cable from the packet and turn it so that the shiny silver contacts are facing upwards. Find the DSI connector on the left edge of the converter board at the back of the screen, and gently pull on the sticking-out tabs at either side to release its catch. Slide one end of the ribbon cable into the DSI connector with the silver contacts facing upwards, and then gently push the tabs to secure the catch into place (see Figure 16-6). Give the ribbon cable a gentle tug to ensure it's properly secured; if it comes free, pull the tabs to release the catch and try again. Don't worry if you can still see some silver when the ribbon cable is in place, as this is perfectly normal.

FIGURE 16-6: Installing the ribbon cable to the adapter board

If the screws supplied with your touchscreen display are already attached to the metal stand-off pillars, undo them using a cross-blade screwdriver. If the pillar starts to spin, pinch it between your fingers to hold it steady while you remove the screw, and then twist it gently to tighten it back up. Take your Pi and place it so the mounting holes are on top of the pillars with the HDMI port facing down and the DSI connector closest to the ribbon cable coming out of the adapter. Place the screws through the mounting holes and tighten, but don't over-tighten (because this can damage both the Pi and the display).

If your Pi doesn't have a micro-SD card inserted, insert it now before lifting the tabs on the DSI connector's catch to open it. Take the free end of the ribbon cable and insert it into the Pi's DSI connector with the silver contacts facing towards the body of the Pi (see Figure 16-7); it should form a smooth curve between the Pi and the adapter board with no twist or turn. Push the tabs down to secure the cable, and again give it a gentle tug to check it is firmly gripped.

FIGURE 16-7: Installing the ribbon cable to the Raspberry Pi

To power the touchscreen display, insert a micro-USB cable connected to a good quality 5V power supply into the micro-USB connector at the bottom of the adapter board. You can then either use a second micro-USB cable and 5V power supply to power the Pi, or you can have it draw power from the adapter board. The major advantage to the latter approach is that you need only one cable running to the display and only one wall socket.

There are two ways to have the Pi draw power from the touchscreen display. The easiest is to place the large end of a micro-USB cable into the USB port found on the right side of the adapter board, and then place the smaller end into the Pi's micro-USB power input. An alternative method is to use the bundled female-to-female jumper cables to wire the adapter board directly to the Pi's GPIO header, if you don't plan to use any add-on hardware: take the black jumper cable and connect it between the right-most pin on the adapter board's GPIO header and Pin 6 of the Raspberry Pi's GPIO header, and then use the red jumper cable to connect the leftmost pin of the adapter board's GPIO header and Pin 4 of the Raspberry Pi's GPIO header (see Figure 16-8). Make sure to double-check your connections to avoid damage to either device; for a reminder of which pin is which, see Chapter 14.

To finish, connect the touchscreen display—and Pi, if you're not drawing its power from the adapter board—to its power supply. The Pi will boot and automatically use the display as its primary display. The touchscreen display can track up to 10 fingers simultaneously and doesn't require calibration; drag your finger over the screen to move the mouse cursor and tap to click.

FIGURE 16-8: Power the Pi from the touchscreen display's GPIO port

Sense HAT

The Sense HAT is a multifunction input and output board, designed for use in the Astro Pi programme and currently orbiting the Earth as part of a science bundle sent up to the International Space Station. Its onboard sensors provide information about the board's orientation and position via a gyroscope, accelerometer, and magnetometer, as well as the ambient air pressure, temperature, and humidity levels. An onboard 8x8 matrix of LEDs provides an output, and interaction is possible through the use of the Sense HAT's five-way joystick (see Figure 16-9).

The Astro Pi programme offers a wealth of resources for users of the Sense HAT, with example projects provided for using the device in both Python and Scratch. You can find these projects on the official website, `http://astro-pi.org`, along with information about how the Sense HAT is being used to gather information on the International Space Station.

> **WARNING** The Sense HAT is compatible with the Raspberry Pi Model A+ and Model B+, Raspberry Pi 2, and Raspberry Pi 3. It is also compatible with the Raspberry Pi Zero provided a USB network adapter is used during installation or a microSD card with the software preinstalled is inserted and GPIO headers have been soldered into place. It is not compatible with the original Raspberry Pi Model A or Model B, nor the Compute Module. For more information on the differences between models see Chapter 1, "Meet the Raspberry Pi".

FIGURE 16-9: The Sense HAT

Installation

Begin by affixing the four mounting pillars included with the Sense HAT to the mounting holes on your Raspberry Pi using a cross-head screwdriver and four of the bundled screws. Place one of the screws through a mounting hole on the Raspberry Pi, and then hold it in place while you screw the mounting pillar over the top without overtightening (see Figure 16-10). If you're using a Pi Zero, you'll only be able to attach two of the four pillars; these should be inserted in the top two mounting holes. Next, push the Sense HAT over the Pi's GPIO pins, making sure to line the pins up carefully with the female header on the underside of the Sense HAT. Finally, secure the Sense HAT with the four remaining screws, again being careful not to overtighten.

Unlike other devices included in this chapter, the Sense HAT requires the installation of additional software before it can be used (see Figure 16-11). Make sure your Raspberry Pi has an active Internet connection. (If you're using a Model A+ or Pi Zero, you need to either use a USB network adapter or temporarily install your microSD card into a Model B+, Pi 2, or Pi 3 for this step.) Then type the following command at the console or terminal to install the Sense HAT's software:

```
wget -O - http://www.raspberrypi.org/files↵
/astro-pi/astro-pi-install.sh --no-check-certificate | bash
```

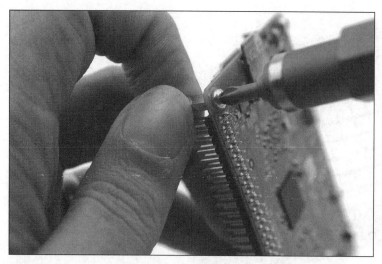

FIGURE 16-10: Installing the brass mounting pillars

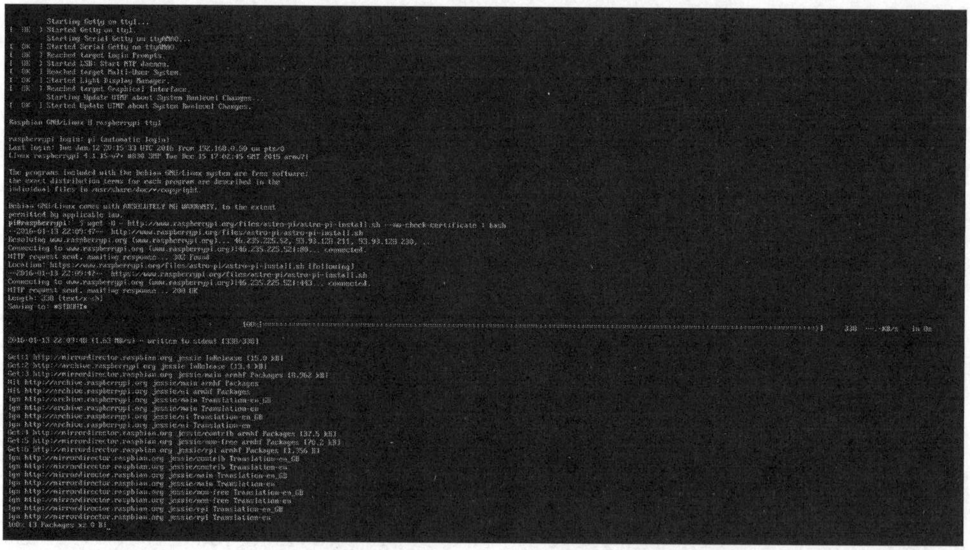

FIGURE 16-11: Installing the Sense HAT software

The installation process will take up to 20 minutes to complete on the Raspberry Pi Model A+ and B+, and around five minutes on the faster Raspberry Pi 2 and Pi 3, so be patient. When the process has finished, you need to reboot your Pi with the following command:

```
sudo reboot
```

When the Pi has rebooted, the Sense HAT is ready to use.

Programming the Sense HAT

The fastest way to get started with programming the Sense HAT is with Python. Begin by testing the Sense HAT with a simple output-only example. Create a new Python file (see Chapter 11, "An Introduction to Python", for how to do this) with the following contents:

```
#!/usr/bin/env python
from sense_hat import SenseHat
sense = SenseHat()
sense.show_message("Hello, world!")
```

Save the file and run it, and you'll see your message scrolled across the Sense HAT's LED display (see Figure 16-12). The `sense.show_message` function is the natural way to get output from the Sense HAT without having to connect a display, although it can also be used in other ways such as to cycle through various colours.

FIGURE 16-12: Scrolling a message across the Sense HAT LED matrix

To read from the Sense HAT's onboard sensors, create a new Python file with the following contents:

```
#!/usr/bin/env python
from sense_hat import SenseHat
sense = SenseHat()
while True:
    temperature = sense.get_temperature()
    pressure = sense.get_pressure()
    humidity = sense.get_humidity()
    sense.show_message("The temperature is %d, the
    pressure is %d, and the humidity is %d." % (temperature,
    pressure, humidity)
```

This program runs in an infinite loop, constantly updating its readings and printing them out to the LED matrix. To stop it, press Ctrl+C.

> **TIP**   All electronics generate waste heat, and the Pi and Sense HAT are no exception. You'll notice that the value read from the Sense HAT's temperature sensor is higher than a sensor placed elsewhere in the room, and rises if the LED matrix is in use, as a result of this.

To use data from the accelerometer, gyroscope, and magnetometer to determine the orientation of the Sense Hat, create a new Python file with the following contents:

```
#!/usr/bin/env python
from sense_hat import SenseHat
sense = SenseHat()
while True:
    orientation = sense.get_orientation()
    print "Pitch %d, roll %d, yaw %d" % (orientation['pitch'],
 orientation['roll'], orientation['yaw'])
```

Save and run the file to see the values printed to the console or terminal. Move the Sense HAT around, and you'll see the values change according to the direction and angle the Pi is facing (see Figure 16-13). Using `sense.get_orientation` takes values from all three positional sensors (the accelerometer, gyroscope, and magnetometer) for the best accuracy; to read from one sensor only, use `sense.get_accelerometer`, `sense.get_gyroscope`, or `sense.get_compass`, respectively. As with the previous example, this program runs in an infinite loop; to quit, press Crtl+C.

FIGURE 16-13: Using the Sense HAT's positional sensors

Further examples, including the use of the joystick to control a simple game, can be found in the /usr/src/sense-hat/examples/python-sense-hat directory. To copy these into a folder in your home directory called sense-hat, type the following commands:

```
mkdir ~/sense-hat
cp /usr/src/sense-hat/examples/python-sense-hat/* ~/sense-hat
sudo chown pi:pi ~/sense-hat/*
```

If your username is not 'pi', be sure to change the username and group in the final chown command to ensure your user has permission to edit the files. You are then free to modify those examples as you see fit, to turn them to a different use or simply to experiment, without fear of losing the originals.

You can find a full reference for the Sense HAT application programming interface (API) at http://pythonhosted.org/sense-hat, and you can find additional resources and examples for both Python and Scratch at http://astro-pi.org and http://raspberrypi.org/resources.

The HAT Standard

The Sense HAT is one of a number of add-on boards for the Raspberry Pi designed around the HAT standard, which stands for *Hardware Attached on Top*. The Raspberry Pi Foundation created the HAT standard to make it easier for developers to produce hardware guaranteed to work with the Raspberry Pi Model A+, Model B+, Raspberry Pi Zero, Raspberry Pi 2, and Raspberry Pi 3.

The standard covers both the physical and electrical design of the add-on board. To qualify as a HAT, the board must attach to the 40-pin GPIO header and include mounting holes that line up with those on the Raspberry Pi Model B+ and newer. It must also be rectangular, measuring 65mm by 56mm (2.56in by 2.2in), to ensure it fits nicely over the top of the Raspberry Pi Model A+ and larger.

The electrical part of the HAT standard requires that the designer include an *electrically erasable programmable read-only memory (EEPROM) module* on the board. This is a small chunk of storage, much like the Pi's microSD card, which contains information about how the board works, how the Pi's GPIO pins are used, and a *device tree* for setting the board up within the operating system.

For users, rather than board designers, the HAT standard means only one thing: a guarantee that the board is compatible with your Raspberry Pi Model B+ or newer. Those with original Raspberry Pi Model A or Model B hardware, though, cannot use HAT modules because they lack the longer 40-pin GPIO header introduced with the Model B+.

More information on the HAT standard is available from `http://github.com/raspberrypi/hats`.

Part V

Appendixes

Appendix A
Python Recipes

THE FOLLOWING RECIPES provide the program code for Example 3 and Example 4 in Chapter 11, "An Introduction to Python", and a sample solution for the combined input-output program suggested in Chapter 14, "The GPIO Port". Each recipe is also available for download from the Raspberry Pi User Guide website at www.wiley.com/go/ raspberrypiuserguide4e. If you're typing the code by hand, look out for the ↵ symbol, which indicates that the line is wrapped because of space constraints in the book. If you see the symbol at the end of a line, don't press Enter until you reach the end of a line that doesn't have a symbol present.

Raspberry Snake (Chapter 11, Example 3)

```python
#!/usr/bin/env python
# Raspberry Snake
# Written by Gareth Halfacree for the Raspberry Pi User Guide
import pygame, sys, time, random
from pygame.locals import *
pygame.init()
fpsClock = pygame.time.Clock()
playSurface = pygame.display.set_mode((640, 480))
pygame.display.set_caption('Raspberry Snake')
redColour = pygame.Color(255, 0, 0)
blackColour = pygame.Color(0, 0, 0)
whiteColour = pygame.Color(255, 255, 255)
greyColour = pygame.Color(150, 150, 150)
snakePosition = [100,100]
snakeSegments = [[100,100], [80,100], [60,100]]
raspberryPosition = [300,300]
```

```python
raspberrySpawned = 1
direction = 'right'
changeDirection = direction
def gameOver():
    gameOverFont = pygame.font.Font('freesansbold.ttf', 72)
    gameOverSurf = gameOverFont.render ↵
    ('Game Over', True, greyColour)
    gameOverRect = gameOverSurf.get_rect()
    gameOverRect.midtop = (320, 10)
    playSurface.blit(gameOverSurf, gameOverRect)
    pygame.display.flip()
    time.sleep(5)
    pygame.quit()
    sys.exit()
while True:
    for event in pygame.event.get():
        if event.type == QUIT:
            pygame.quit()
            sys.exit()
        elif event.type == KEYDOWN:
            if event.key == K_RIGHT or event.key == ord('d'):
                changeDirection = 'right'
            if event.key == K_LEFT or event.key == ord('a'):
                changeDirection = 'left'
            if event.key == K_UP or event.key == ord('w'):
                changeDirection = 'up'
            if event.key == K_DOWN or event.key == ord('s'):
                changeDirection = 'down'
            if event.key == K_ESCAPE:
                pygame.event.post(pygame.event.Event(QUIT))
    if changeDirection == 'right' and not direction == 'left':
        direction = changeDirection
    if changeDirection == 'left' and not direction == 'right':
        direction = changeDirection
    if changeDirection == 'up' and not direction == 'down':
        direction = changeDirection
    if changeDirection == 'down' and not direction == 'up':
        direction = changeDirection
    if direction == 'right':
        snakePosition[0] += 20
    if direction == 'left':
        snakePosition[0] -= 20
    if direction == 'up':
        snakePosition[1] -= 20
```

```python
        if direction == 'down':
            snakePosition[1] += 20
        snakeSegments.insert(0,list(snakePosition))
        if snakePosition[0] == raspberryPosition[0] and ↵
        snakePosition[1] == raspberryPosition[1]:
            raspberrySpawned = 0
        else:
            snakeSegments.pop()
        if raspberrySpawned == 0:
            x = random.randrange(1,32)
            y = random.randrange(1,24)
            raspberryPosition = [x*20,y*20]
            raspberrySpawned = 1
        playSurface.fill(blackColour)
        for position in snakeSegments:
            pygame.draw.rect(playSurface,whiteColour,Rect ↵
            (position[0], position[1], 20, 20))
        pygame.draw.rect(playSurface,redColour,Rect ↵
        (raspberryPosition[0], raspberryPosition[1], 20, 20))
        pygame.display.flip()
        if snakePosition[0] > 620 or snakePosition[0] < 0:
            gameOver()
        if snakePosition[1] > 460 or snakePosition[1] < 0:
            gameOver()
        for snakeBody in snakeSegments[1:]:
            if snakePosition[0] == snakeBody[0] and ↵
            snakePosition[1] == snakeBody[1]:
                gameOver()
        fpsClock.tick(20)
```

IRC User List (Chapter 11, Example 4)

```python
#!/usr/bin/env python
# IRC User List
# Written by Tom Hudson for the Raspberry Pi User Guide
# http://tomhudson.co.uk/
import sys, socket, time
RPL_NAMREPLY  = '353'
RPL_ENDOFNAMES = '366'
irc = {
    'host':         'chat.freenode.net',
    'port':         6667,
```

```
        'channel':          '#raspiuserguide',
        'namesinterval': 5
}
user = {
        'nick':          'botnick',
        'username':      'botuser',
        'hostname':      'localhost',
        'servername': 'localhost',
        'realname':      'Raspberry Pi Names Bot'
}
s = socket.socket(socket.AF_INET, socket.SOCK_STREAM)
print 'Connecting to %(host)s:%(port)s...' % irc
try:
        s.connect((irc['host'], irc['port']))
except socket.error:
        print 'Error connecting to IRC server ↵
        %(host)s:%(port)s' % irc
        sys.exit(1)
s.send('NICK %(nick)s\r\n' % user)
s.send('USER %(username)s %(hostname)s %(servername)s : ↵
%(realname)s\r\n' % user)
s.send('JOIN %(channel)s\r\n' % irc)
s.send('NAMES %(channel)s\r\n' % irc)
read_buffer = ''
names = []
while True:
        read_buffer += s.recv(1024)
        lines = read_buffer.split('\r\n')
        read_buffer = lines.pop()
        for line in lines:
                response = line.rstrip().split(' ', 3)
                response_code = response[1]
                if response_code == RPL_NAMREPLY:
                        names_list = response[3].split(':')[1]
                        names += names_list.split(' ')
                if response_code == RPL_ENDOFNAMES:
                        print '\nUsers in %(channel)s:' % irc
                        for name in names:
                                print name
                        names = []
                        time.sleep(irc['namesinterval'])
                        s.send('NAMES %(channel)s\r\n' % irc)
```

GPIO Input and Output (Chapter 14)

```python
#!/usr/bin/env python
# Raspberry Pi GPIO Input/Output example
# Written by Gareth Halfacree for the Raspberry Pi User Guide
import RPi.GPIO as GPIO
GPIO.setmode(GPIO.BOARD)
GPIO.setup(11, GPIO.OUT)
GPIO.setup(12, GPIO.IN)
GPIO.output(11, False)
while True:
    input_value = GPIO.input(12)
    if input_value == False:
        print "The button has been pressed. Lighting LED."
        GPIO.output(11, True)
        while input_value == False:
            input_value = GPIO.input(12)
        print "The button has been released. Extinguishing LED."
    if input_value == True:
        GPIO.output(11, False)
```

Appendix B

Raspberry Pi Camera Module Quick Reference

THE RASPBERRY PI Camera Module comes with software designed to capture still images and videos, each of which has a variety of options that can control the final output. Options for `raspistill` and `raspivid` are included in this appendix. For more information, see Chapter 15, "The Raspberry Pi Camera Module".

Shared Options

The following options, listed in alphabetical order, are shared between `raspistill` and `raspivid`. For application-specific options, see the individual `raspistill` and `raspivid` entries later in this appendix.

- **-? or --help (Help)**—Displays all options and their uses.

- **-a or --annotate**—Allows for text annotations to be applied to videos or images. Any text provided in quotes following this option will be printed on all images or videos captured, or the following bit fields (used in the form of -a N or --annotate N, where N is one of the following numbers or the sum of two or more numbers if multiple fields are desired) can be used to print other information or change how the text is displayed:

    - 1—Prints the text supplied by the user on the command line.

    - 2—Prints the text supplied by an application calling the utility as a module.

    - 4—Prints the current date.

    - 8—Prints the current time.

    - 16—Prints the camera's shutter settings.

- 32—Prints the camera's CAF settings.

- 64—Prints the camera's gain settings.

- 128—Prints the camera's lens settings.

- 256—Prints the camera's motion settings.

- 512—Prints the current frame number.

- 1024—Uses a black background.

- **-ae or –annotateex**—Controls the appearance of text annotations, in the format: size, text-colour, background-colour, with colours specified in hexadecimal YUV format and sizes from 6 to 160 (default 32) available.

- **-awb or --awb (Automatic White Balance)**—Sets the colour temperature of the captured image or video according to one of a series of preset configurations. If your image or video appears blue or orange, try adjusting this option first. Possible values for this option are off, auto, sun, cloud, shade, tungsten, fluorescent, incandescent, flash, and horizon.

- **-awbg or –awbgains**—Sets the blue and red channel gains which should be applied when the automatic white balance is set to off, specified as a floating-point number.

- **-br or --brightness (Brightness)**—Adjusts the brightness of the captured image or video. Possible values for this option are whole numbers ranging from 0 (minimum brightness) to 100 (maximum brightness).

- **-cfx or --colfx (Colour Effects)**—Allows the user to adjust the YUV colour space for fine-grained control of the final image. Values should be given as U:V, where U controls the chrominance and V the luminance. A value of 128:128 will result in a greyscale image.

- **-co or --contrast (Contrast)**—Adjusts the contrast of the captured image or video. Possible values for this option are whole numbers ranging from −100 (minimum contrast) to 100 (maximum contrast).

- **-d or --demo (Demonstration Mode)**—The -d option runs either raspistill or raspivid in demonstration mode, which displays a preview that cycles through various camera options. In this mode, no image is captured—even if you specify an output file using the --output option.

- **-drc or --drc (Dynamic Range Control)**—Modifies the image by increasing the range available for capturing darker image areas and decreasing the range available for lighter areas, boosting the image visibility in low-light conditions. Possible values are off, low, medium, and high.

- **-ev or --ev (Exposure Value)**—Allows the camera to increase or decrease its exposure value, brightening or darkening the captured image or video. Unlike the brightness and contrast settings, which apply post-capture modifications to the image, this affects the actual capturing of the image or video. Possible values are -10 to 10, with 0 being the default.

- **-ex or --exposure (Exposure Mode)**—Sets the camera's automatic exposure setting, which controls how long the camera spends capturing an individual image or frame and is largely a factor of available light or the speed of the subject: fast-moving objects need a short exposure time in order to remain in focus, while low-light shooting demands a long exposure time. Possible values for this option are: off, auto, night, nightpreview, backlight, spotlight, sports, snow, beach, verylong, fixedfps, antishake, fireworks.

- **-f or --fullscreen (Fullscreen Preview)**—Makes the preview image fill the screen, overriding any other preview option you may have set.

- **-h or --height (Height)**—Specifies the height, or vertical resolution, of the captured image or video. This should be set to the desired height in pixels; for example, a Full HD capture would require a height value of 1080. The minimum value is 64; the maximum depends on whether video or still images are being captured and on the model (5 megapixel or 8 megapixel) of camera in use.

- **-hf or --hflip (Horizontal Flip)**—Flips the captured image or video along its horizontal axis, as though it has been viewed in a mirror.

- **-ifx or --imxfx (Image Effects)**—Enables one of a number of preconfigured special effects on the image or video. Possible values for this option are none, negative, solarise, sketch, denoise, emboss, oilpaint, hatch, gpen, pastel, watercolour, film, blur, saturation, colourswap, washedout, posterise, colourpoint, colourbalance, cartoon. These settings can be seen in action using the Demonstration Mode option.

- **-ISO or --ISO (ISO Sensitivity)**—Sets the camera's sensitivity to light. A lower ISO value provides a clearer image, but requires longer exposures; a higher ISO value can shoot at very low exposure times to capture fast-moving or badly lit subjects, but creates a *noisier* image. Values from 100 to 800 are supported.

- **-k or --keypress (Keypress Capture Mode)**—Captures images or video when the Enter key is pressed, rather than automatically. When capturing still images, one image will be taken on each key press; when capturing video, Enter will toggle between record and pause modes. In both cases, pressing the X key followed by Enter will quit the application and stop the capture process.

- **-md or --mode (Sensor Mode)**—Sets the sensor mode, which controls resolution, aspect ratio, frame rates, field of view (FoV), and binning.

  - 0—Automatically chooses the appropriate mode.

  - 1—Selects 1920x1080 (Full HD) 16:9 mode with 1-30fps framerate, partial FoV, and no binning.

  - 2—Sets a 2592x1944 4:3 mode with 1-15fps framerate, full FoV, and no binning.

  - 3—Sets a 2592x1944 4:3 mode with a 0.1666-1fps framerate, full FoV, and no binning.

  - 4—Sets a 1296x972 4:3 mode with 1-42fps framerate, full FoV, and 2x2 binning.

  - 5—Sets a 1296x730 16:9 mode with 1-49fps framerate, full FoV, and 2x2 binning.

  - 6—Sets a 640x480 4:3 mode with 42.1-60fps framerate, full FoV, and 2x2 plus sklp binning.

  - 7—Sets a 640x480 4:3 mode with 60.1-90fps framerate, full FoV, and 2x2 plus skip binning.

- **-mm or --metering (Metering Mode)**—Sets the light metering mode for image or video capture, which controls the automatic exposure, white balance and ISO sensitivity options. Possible values for this option are `average`, `spot`, `backlit`, `matrix`.

- **-n or --nopreview (No Preview)**—Does not display a preview window while capturing.

- **-o or --output (Output File)**—Sets the name of the file to be saved. The value for this option can be either a filename, in which case the file will be created in the current directory, or an absolute path. If you are using `raspistill` or `raspivid` along with another application that expects image or video data through standard input, you can divert the data through standard output by using a hyphen (-) character as the filename.

- **-op or --opacity (Preview Opacity)**—Controls how transparent the preview window appears. Possible values are any whole number from 0 to 255, where 0 is completely transparent and thus invisible and 255 is completely visible. Using a value around 128 allows you to see the live preview, but also read the text behind the preview.

- **-p or --preview (Preview Window Control)**—Sets the size of the preview window and where it appears. The value should be given as X, Y, W, H—where X and Y are the pixel coordinates where the window's top-left corner should be drawn, and W and H the width and height of the preview window in pixels, respectively.

- **-roi or --roi (Region of Interest)**—Allows part of the camera sensor to be specified as the capture source, rather than the entire sensor—effectively cropping the captured image. This option takes floating-point normalised XY coordinates between 0.0 and 1.0. To use the quarter of the sensor at the upper left, for example, the values 0,0,0.25,0.25 should be used.

- **-rot or --rotation (Rotate Capture)**—Rotates the captured image or video through any arbitrary angle. Values for this option should be given as a whole number of clockwise degrees, where 0 is no rotation and 359 the maximum possible rotation. Values given will be rounded down to the nearest 90 degrees, giving actual rotations of 0, 90, 180, and 270 degrees.

- **-sa or --saturation (Saturation)**—Adjusts the colour saturation of the captured image or video. Possible values for this option are whole numbers ranging from −100 (minimum saturation) to 100 (maximum saturation).

- **-sh or --sharpness (Sharpness)**—Adjusts the sharpness of the captured image or video. Possible values for this option are whole numbers ranging from −100 (minimum sharpness) to 100 (maximum sharpness).

- **-sh or --sharpness (Signal Mode)**—Controls the capture of images or video through a USR1 signal, sent from another process on the system. Toggles capture or recording in the same way as the Keypress Mode option.

- **-ss or --shutter (Shutter Speed)**—Manually controls the speed of the camera's shutter in microseconds, up to a limit of 6000000us (6 seconds).

- **-st or --stats (Statistics Display)**—Displays statistics regarding the capture, including exposure, gains, and white-balance settings, during the capture process.

- **-t or --timeout (Capture Timeout)**—Controls the timeout, in milliseconds, that the preview window will appear. While shared between the tools, the action of the `--timeout` option is different: in `raspistill`, the `--timeout` option will set the time until the picture is captured; in `raspivid`, the option will set the time for which video will be recorded. A value of 0 in `raspistill` will display the preview indefinitely and never capture an image; a value of 0 in `raspivid` continues to record indefinitely. If not specified, the timeout defaults to 5 seconds (i.e., 5000 milliseconds).

- **-v or --verbose (Verbose Messaging)**—Verbose mode tells the capture application to output as much detail as possible about what it is doing to the console or terminal. This is generally used only for debugging errors in the software, as it allows the user to see at what point the capture fails.

- **-vf or --vflip (Vertical Flip)**—Flips the image through the vertical axis. Most commonly used when the camera cannot be positioned the correct way up, with the connecting ribbon cable exiting from the bottom. If the camera is at an angle other than upside down, try using the rotation option to control the final captured image.

- **-vs or --vstab (Video Stabilisation)**—Attempts to correct for the camera's sensor shaking. Commonly used when the Raspberry Pi or its Camera Module is held in the hand or attached to a robot, vehicle, or other moving platform.

- **-w or --width (Width)**—Specifies the width, or horizontal resolution, of the captured image or video. This should be set to the desired width in pixels; for example, a Full HD capture would require a width value of 1920. The minimum value is 64; the maximum depends on whether a still image or a video is being captured.

Raspistill Options

Designed to capture still images, `raspistill` has some specific options that do not apply to `raspivid`. Those options are listed here:

- **-bm or --burst (Burst Capture Mode)**—Captures multiple still images without switching the camera back into preview mode, which prevents dropped frames while capturing images on a short delay.

- **-dt or --datetime (Date Time Mode)**—When capturing multiple images, uses the current date and time in the filename (in YearMonthDayHourMinuteSecond format) instead of an incrementing frame number.

- **-e or --encoding (Encoding Format)**—Sets the format of the output image. This does not affect the file extension of the output file, which must be changed manually using the `--output` option. Possible values for this option are `jpg`, `bmp`, `gif`, and `png`.

- **-fp or –fullpreview (Full Preview Mode)**—Uses the same resolution for the live preview image as set for the capture. This provides a true what-you-see-is-what-you-get representation of the capture, but is limited to 15 frames per second. It also eliminates the sensor switching delay during rapid capture in much the same way as the Burst Mode option; the two do not need to be used together.

- **-fs or –framestart (Starting Frame Number)**—Specifies the number at which to start counting captured frames, used in the output filename. Can be used to continue an interrupted capture sequence without overwriting any existing files.

- **-g or –gl (GL Texture Preview)**—Draws the preview image to a GL texture rather than using the video renderer component.

- **-gc or –glcapture (Save GL Framebuffer)**—Saves the GL framebuffer data rather than the camera image.

- **-gs or –glscene (GL Scene Render)**—Renders the user's choice of GL ES 2.0 scene using the image data from the camera.

- **-gw or –glwin (GL Window)**—Draws a GL ES 2.0 window, specified as single-quote-enclosed coordinates for the upper-left corner followed by width and height (for example, '0,0,1920,1080').

- **-l or –latest (Link to Latest Image)**—Creates a file-system link to the most recently captured image using a user-supplied filename.

- **-q or --quality (JPEG Quality)**—Sets the compression level of the saved JPEG, and has no effect when using any other encoding format. The lower the value, the smaller the final image file; a value of 100 will provide the best possible quality, while a value of 0 will provide the smallest file size. A value of 90 is a good trade-off between size and quality.

- **-r or --raw (Save Bayer Data)**—Saves the output of the camera's Bayer colour filter as metadata in the JPEG image and has no effect when using any other encoding format. This extra data, the output of the camera's sensor without interpolation, can be used in image editing applications to reconstruct a higher quality or more detailed image, but is not normally required.

- **-th or --thumb (Thumbnail Settings)**—Sets the size and quality of the thumbnail saved with JPEG images and has no effect when used with any other encoding format. The value should be given as X:Y:Q, where X is the width, Y the height, and Q the JPEG quality from 0 to 100 of the thumbnail, or give the value none to turn off thumbnails.

- **-tl or --timelapse (Timelapse Mode)**—Puts `raspistill` into timelapse mode, where images will be captured at a set interval. Most useful when using `raspistill` with a script or third-party application by setting the Output file to the standard output with a hyphen (-) character; when used with a filename in the `--output` option, the file will be overwritten every time a new image is captured. The value for this option should be the delay between captures in milliseconds. `raspistill` will still terminate after `--timeout` seconds.

- **-ts or --timestamp (Timestamp Mode)**—When capturing multiple images, uses the current date and time in the filename (in UNIX timestamp format) instead of an incrementing frame number.

- **-x or --exif (EXIF Tag)**—Allows custom Exchangable Image File Format (EXIF) tags to be written to a JPEG image and has no effect when used with any other encoding formats. Tags should be formatted as 'key=value' with one possible example being setting the name of the photographer using `-x 'Author=Gareth Halfacree'`. Or give the setting `--x none` to turn off EXIF tags.

Raspivid Options

Designed to capture moving images, `raspivid` has some specific options that do not apply to `raspistill`. Those options are listed here:

- **-b or --bitrate (Encoding Bitrate)**—Sets the bitrate of the captured video, in bits per second (BPS). The higher the bitrate, the higher the quality of the finished video—but the larger the file size. Unless you have a specific requirement from your video, this should typically be left at the default setting.

- **-c or --circular (Circular Buffer)**—Constantly records video into a memory buffer, writing the most recent chunk (specified by the `-t` or `--timeout` option) to disk when the Enter key is pressed or a USR1 signal is received.

- **-cd or --codec (Codec)**—Chooses between two possible recording codecs: H264 (the default) or MJPEG.

- **-e or --penc (Encoding Preview)**—Uses the preview window to show video frames after they have been passed through the encoder, rather than before. Provides an accurate preview of the final video and is most commonly used when tweaking the Encoding Bitrate.

- **-fl or --flush (Flush Buffers)**—Flushes buffers as a way to reduce latency.

- **-fps or --framerate (Video Framerate)**—Sets the frame rate of the captured video, in frames per second. Higher figures give smoother motion, while lower figures take up less disk space. Recording at a rate above 30 frames per second, which can be turned into slow-motion video with a video editing application, will likely work only at lower resolutions (set with the `--width` and `--height` options).

- **-g or --intra (Intra Refresh Period)**—Sets how often a key frame, also known as an *intra-coded picture* or *I frame*, should be captured. A key frame is an entire image, rather than the changes recorded since the last image. More frequent key frames can result in higher quality video when recording rapidly changing scenes, but will result in larger file sizes.

- **-i or --initial (Initial Mode)**—Controls which mode `raspivid` will be in when it launches: record (default) or pause.

- **-if or --irefresh (Intra Refresh Type)**—Sets the type of key frame that should be used, from a choice of cyclic, adaptive, both, and cyclicrows.

- **-ih or --inline (Inline Headers)**—Inserts inline (SPS, PPS) headers into the video stream.

- **-pf or --profile (Codec Profile)**—Chooses a profile to use when encoding video with the H264 codec, from baseline, main, and high.

- **-pts or –save-pts (Timestamps)**—Saves timestamps to the output video file, which can be used by mkvmerge.

- **-qp or --qp (Quantisation)**—Enables quantisation with a parameter value, which should be set between 10 and 40, with 0 (the default) disabling quantisation.

- **-sg or --segment (Segmented Output)**—Segments the output into multiple files, with the length of each file to be specified in milliseconds.

- **-sn or --start (Segment Start)**—Specifies a segment number at which segmented output should begin, rather than the default of 1.

- **-sp or --split (Split)**—When using a key- or signal-based trigger mode or the timed mode, the split option will begin a fresh file for each time the software is placed into record mode, rather than appending the footage to the end of the existing file.

- **-td or --timed (Timed Mode)**—Continuously switches between recording and pause modes based on times provided in milliseconds in the format record,pause (so to record for 30 seconds then pause for a minute, the option would be -td 30000,60000).

- **-wr or --wrap (Segment Wrap)**—Specifies a segment number after which the software should wrap back to the first segment and begin overwriting existing files.

- **-x or --vectors (Output Motion Vectors)**—Outputs the inline motion vectors to the specified filename.

Appendix C
HDMI Display Modes

YOU CAN USE the values in Table C-1 and Table C-2 with the `hdmi_mode` option in `config.txt` to alter the HDMI video output format. For more information, see Chapter 7, "Advanced Raspberry Pi Configuration".

Table C-1 **HDMI Group 1 (CEA)**

Value	Description
1	VGA (640×480)
2	480p 60 Hz
3	480p 60 Hz (16:9 aspect ratio)
4	720p 60 Hz
5	1080i 60 Hz
6	480i 60 Hz
7	480i 60 Hz (16:9 aspect ratio)
8	240p 60 Hz
9	240p 60 Hz (16:9 aspect ratio)
10	480i 60 Hz (Pixel quadrupling enabled)
11	480i 60 Hz (Pixel quadrupling enabled) (16:9 aspect ratio)
12	240p 60 Hz (Pixel quadrupling enabled)
13	240p 60 Hz (Pixel quadrupling enabled) (16:9 aspect ratio)

continued

Table C-1   continued

Value	Description
14	480p 60 Hz (Pixel doubling enabled)
15	480p 60 Hz (Pixel doubling enabled) (16:9 aspect ratio)
16	1080p 60 Hz
17	576p 50 Hz
18	576p 50 Hz (16:9 aspect ratio)
19	720p 50 Hz
20	1080i 50 Hz
21	576i 50 Hz
22	576i 50 Hz (16:9 aspect ratio)
23	288p 50 Hz
24	288p 50 Hz (16:9 aspect ratio)
25	576i 50 Hz (Pixel quadrupling enabled)
26	576i 50 Hz (Pixel quadrupling enabled) (16:9 aspect ratio)
27	288p 50 Hz (Pixel quadrupling enabled)
28	288p 50 Hz (Pixel quadrupling enabled) (16:9 aspect ratio)
29	576p 50 Hz (Pixel doubling enabled)
30	576p 50 Hz (Pixel doubling enabled) (16:9 aspect ratio)
31	1080p 50 Hz
32	1080p 24 Hz
33	1080p 25 Hz
34	1080p 30 Hz
35	480p 60 Hz (Pixel quadrupling enabled)
36	480p 60 Hz (Pixel quadrupling enabled) (16:9 aspect ratio)
37	576p 50 Hz (Pixel quadrupling enabled)
38	576p 50 Hz (Pixel quadrupling enabled) (16:9 aspect ratio)
39	1080i 50 Hz (Reduced blanking)

Value	Description
40	1080i 100 Hz
41	720p 100 Hz
42	576p 100 Hz
43	576p 100 Hz (16:9 aspect ratio)
44	576i 100 Hz
45	576i 100 Hz (16:9 aspect ratio)
46	1080i 120 Hz
47	720p 120 Hz
48	480p 120 Hz
49	480p 120 Hz (16:9 aspect ratio)
50	480i 120 Hz
51	480i 120 Hz (16:9 aspect ratio)
52	576p 200 Hz
53	576p 200 Hz (16:9 aspect ratio)
54	576i 200 Hz
55	576i 200 Hz (16:9 aspect ratio)
56	480p 240 Hz
57	480p 240 Hz (16:9 aspect ratio)
58	480i 240 Hz
59	480i 240 Hz (16:9 aspect ratio)

Table C-2   **HDMI Group 2 (DMT)**

Value	Description
1	640×350 85 Hz
2	640×400 85 Hz
3	720×400 85 Hz

continued

Table C-2   continued

Value	Description
4	640×480 60 Hz
5	640×480 72 Hz
6	640×480 75 Hz
7	640×480 85 Hz
8	800×600 56 Hz
9	800×600 60 Hz
10	800×600 72 Hz
11	800×600 75 Hz
12	800×600 85 Hz
13	800×600 120 Hz
14	848×480 60 Hz
15	1024×768 43 Hz, incompatible with the Raspberry Pi
16	1024×768 60 Hz
17	1024×768 70 Hz
18	1024×768 75 Hz
19	1024×768 85 Hz
20	1024×768 120 Hz
21	1152×864 75 Hz
22	1280×768 (Reduced blanking)
23	1280×768 60 Hz
24	1280×768 75 Hz
25	1280×768 85 Hz
26	1280×768 120 Hz (Reduced blanking)
27	1280×800 (Reduced blanking)
28	1280×800 60 Hz

Value	Description
29	1280×800 75 Hz
30	1280×800 85 Hz
31	1280×800 120 Hz (Reduced blanking)
32	1280×960 60 Hz
33	1280×960 85 Hz
34	1280×960 120 Hz (Reduced blanking)
35	1280×1024 60 Hz
36	1280×1024 75 Hz
37	1280×1024 85 Hz
38	1280×1024 120 Hz (Reduced blanking)
39	1360×768 60 Hz
40	1360×768 120 Hz (Reduced blanking)
41	1400×1050 (Reduced blanking)
42	1400×1050 60 Hz
43	1400×1050 75 Hz
44	1400×1050 85 Hz
45	1400×1050 120 Hz (Reduced blanking)
46	1440×900 (Reduced blanking)
47	1440×900 60 Hz
48	1440×900 75 Hz
49	1440×900 85 Hz
50	1440×900 120 Hz (Reduced blanking)
51	1600×1200 60 Hz
52	1600×1200 65 Hz
53	1600×1200 70 Hz

continued

Table C-2　continued

Value	Description
54	1600×1200 75 Hz
55	1600×1200 85 Hz
56	1600×1200 120 Hz (Reduced blanking)
57	1680×1050 (Reduced blanking)
58	1680×1050 60 Hz
59	1680×1050 75 Hz
60	1680×1050 85 Hz
61	1680×1050 120 Hz (Reduced blanking)
62	1792×1344 60 Hz
63	1792×1344 75 Hz
64	1792×1344 120 Hz (Reduced blanking)
65	1856×1392 60 Hz
66	1856×1392 75 Hz
67	1856×1392 120 Hz (Reduced blanking)
68	1920×1200 (Reduced blanking)
69	1920×1200 60 Hz
70	1920×1200 75 Hz
71	1920×1200 85 Hz
72	1920×1200 120 Hz (Reduced blanking)
73	1920×1440 60 Hz
74	1920×1440 75 Hz
75	1920×1440 120 Hz (Reduced blanking)
76	2560×1600 (Reduced blanking)
77	2560×1600 60 Hz
78	2560×1600 75 Hz

Value	Description
79	2560×1600 85 Hz
80	2560×1600 120 Hz (Reduced blanking)
81	1366×768 60 Hz
82	1920×1080 (1080p) 60 Hz
83	1600×900 (Reduced blanking)
84	2048×1152 (Reduced blanking)
85	1280×720 (720p) 60 Hz
86	1366×768 (Reduced blanking)

Index